EDGAR CAYCE PREDICTS

Your Role in Creating a New Age

Previously titled
Visions and Prophecies for a New Age

By
Mark Thurston

A.R.E.® PRESS • VIRGINIA BEACH • VIRGINIA

Note to the reader:

Most of the selections from the Edgar Cayce readings appear in boldface type. The number following each reading is the file number assigned to the person or group for whom the reading was given. For example, 317-6 identifies the sixth reading given for the person who was assigned number 317.

All Cayce readings (over 14,000) are available for public inspection at the A.R.E. Library in Virginia Beach, Virginia.

Previously titled *Visions and Prophecies for a New Age*

Printed in the U.S.A.

Contents

Acknowledgments

I wish to thank the many people who assisted me in the creation of this book. To the many friends and colleagues who shared ideas and helped me to shape my own, I extend a note of appreciation. The formulation of ideas and theories rarely happens in a vacuum—and I am blessed with living in a special community of people with whom I share ideals and create through our interactions.

I also thank the people who worked to prepare this manuscript: reading it, suggesting changes, and editing it into its final form. These friends include Cheryl Salerno, Mary Nowak, Elaine Hruska and Ken Skidmore.

And finally, my deepest appreciation goes to my wife Mary and daughter Sarah. Many of the ideas of this book were shaped and refined by Mary's questioning and philosophical mind. Her patience and support were equally valuable ingredients. And Sarah is an inspiration to us both. Coming so recently from realms where God is more clearly known, she reminds me that there is a future for humanity—a future worth believing in and working for.

Introduction

The signs of change are all around us: We live in a world of instability among nations. Our economic system is in chaos, and advances in our standard of living are being eroded by inflation. In many ways the social fabric that has knit us together as a people is now beginning to come apart. There are almost as many divorces as marriages. Crime is continually on the increase—not only among the disadvantaged but among the privileged as well. And there are signs all around us that the earth itself is dying—slowly being killed by humanity's mistreatment of the soil, air, water and wildlife of the planet.

Fortunately these signs of destructive change in the world around us are accompanied by as many hopeful portents. For example, medical science has made tremendous breakthroughs in our capacity to treat otherwise catastrophic illnesses. A worldwide communications network now links the people of the earth in a way unimaginable one hundred years ago. And there is clear evidence of an emerging segment of society which holds a holistic vision of human nature and ways of living. But even these creative, positive signs of change still leave us with the challenges and stresses of living in an environment which is continually and rapidly altering.

The signs of turmoil and change are not just outward ones. Perhaps even more important are those changes going on *within* people. We know these signs very well; unfortunately most are known to us because of the difficulties they create. There has been a tremendous increase in stress-related physical illnesses. To a large measure the problems of high blood pressure, heart disease and cancer can probably be traced to the tensions of living in a world which is changing so quickly.

Almost all of us are more likely than ever before to feel hurried and pushed. It is a natural inner response to a world which seems to demand, "Get things done now before conditions change again and the opportunity is lost." It is frustrating and demoralizing to know that we are not producing things in life with as high a quality as we would if we were not so rushed. A subtle yet profound kind of pessimism has begun to creep its way into the thinking process of so many of us. For some people the sense of hopelessness comes from a feeling of frustration that nothing will ever be done about their disadvantaged states. For others there is a pessimism about the future because it is so difficult to plan reliably for what is coming and build any sense of security.

What does it mean to *live* in these times of change? Do all of these signs of decay make it a cursed period of history? Or is it rather a blessing to have been born in such a time of transition? Perhaps if we can awaken a courageous and creative spirit within, we will see that this truly is an exciting time to be alive.

But even if we adopt the more hopeful view of what is going on around us and within us, we are left to face the challenge of actually *living* in these years of transition. We will have to learn to cope with stresses which are different from those ever faced by human beings. Certainly our ancestors had to deal with adversities—many just as difficult as those we face now. In fact, it should lift our spirits about our own times to observe how past generations have made it through their own challenges. Nevertheless, the fact remains that the problems of dealing with a world which changes as fast as ours does has never before been met by humanity. How will we cope with this sort of adversity?

One eloquent spokesman of our times succinctly described the many challenges we face. Dr. Carl Rogers, a pioneer in modern counseling techniques and humanistic psychology, defined the greatest problem facing humanity today as difficulty in dealing with change. At a conference in San Francisco in 1968, entitled "U.S.A.: 2000," Dr. Rogers had this to say about living in times of change:

"It is not the hydrogen bomb, fearful as that may be. It is not the population explosion, though the consequences of that are awful to contemplate. It is instead a problem which is rarely mentioned or discussed. It is the question of how much change the human being can accept, absorb, and assimilate, and the rate at which he can take it. Can he keep up with the ever-increasing rate of technological change, or is there some point at which the human organism goes to pieces? Can he leave the static ways and static guidelines which have dominated all of his history, and adopt the process ways, the continual changingness, which must be his if he is to survive?"

The primary purpose of this book is to make a creative contribution to meeting the very test which Dr. Rogers has described. The approach is threefold in attempting to provide hope, understanding and creative alternatives. First we need a perspective of *hopefulness*, for without a sense of positive possibilities it is very hard for us to make it through adversity. Without a clear vision of a fulfilling vocation, a student is unlikely to make it through the stresses of higher education. Without a feeling of promise for the fruits of his labors, a gardener or farmer will not find strength to tend the soil and crops. Human beings need the feeling of promise in order to unleash the creative, spiritual energies which make us unique.

And there is much to be hopeful about. Although the final outcome is not insured, there are strong possibilities that this period of rapid change is part of a birth process—that a spiritually renewed earth is about to emerge. Many sources of information, including the Edgar Cayce readings, offer us a promise beyond the troubled times in which we live. They say that the pain and stress we feel is a result of the old ways dying so that a new vision of life can be born and lived.

The second aspect of this book's approach is *understanding*. Much of the stress and trouble created by living in these times of change is because we don't understand what is going on around us. Failing to understand a purpose for what we observe and feel, we easily resort to a state of despair. However, an understanding of what has happened and what is likely to occur soon is a reachable aspiration. The Cayce readings and many other psychics, social scientists and spiritual leaders can provide us with insights to help us grasp the meaning of our times.

And a final element of this book is to propose *purposefully creative* options to contribute to the kind of future world in which we would like to live. With an ideal clearly in mind—with a sense of spiritual purpose—we can make use of the vast creative abilities available to us. We need not passively await the future. A key ingredient of this book is to give you a feeling of being *empowered.* It is to remind you of the many alternatives and methods available to you if you wish to be among the builders of a new age.

As the author, I am keeping in mind an image as I write, because that symbolic image catches the understanding and spirit I hope to sustain about these times of change. It is a metaphor which came to me five years ago as a dream that was a response from my inner self to deep questioning I had about the world in which I found myself. I was discouraged five years ago, having lost the feelings of hope, promise and expectancy which had been mine ten years earlier when I first read about a new age being born. In that initial encounter with the idea of an emergent new world, I had felt a sort of "mission" to be a contributor to its creation. And for many months, perhaps several years, I had carried inside me an enthusiasm and hope about a coming new age which I felt sure was just ahead.

But by 1976 I observed in myself the fact that much of that feeling of promise and expectancy had dissipated. I was certainly still on the spiritual path as an individual, and even trying to help others around me with their growth. But the world in which I lived seemed just as deeply in the old ways and old values as ever before. Despite the outward signs seeming to be so discouraging, I realized how much I missed the enthusiasm and expectancy I once had. I began to pray regularly about my concern and asked that I might understand both what was going on in the world and what had been going on inside me. The dream which came soon thereafter has been a powerful image in my thinking ever since.

In my dream I was aboard a commercial airline flight. Everything seemed to be going quite normally when suddenly there was an announcement over the loudspeaker. The pilot said that we were about to fly higher than a plane had ever flown before. We were asked to be sure our seat belts were pulled tightly.

In the dream there was a tremendous amount of enthusiasm and excitement among all of the passengers (the same sort of excitement I had felt years earlier when I first read of Edgar Cayce's prophecies of a new age). I was pleased to have a window seat so that I could view what was going to happen. But as I looked out of the window for the next several minutes it appeared that nothing changed. We seemed to continue to fly about 5,000 feet above the ground. My fellow passengers began to mumble and complain, "What was he talking about? We aren't flying any higher than before."

Then, one of the passengers said he thought he knew what was going on: We were flying up the side of a mountain, staying about 5,000 feet off the face of the mountain slope. He predicted, "I bet that soon we will reach the top of the mountain, break free of it, and we'll see how far up we have really come." And sure enough, as I looked out of my window, the top of the mountain suddenly appeared and I could see that we were hundreds of thousands of feet in the air. And then, in the dream, the plane disappeared. We were flying by ourselves and there was a tremendous feeling of exhilaration.

At the time I had this dream it profoundly helped me to understand what might be going on in the world. And it has continued to serve as a potent metaphor to help me deal with the ever-present signs that the old world and the old ways of living are still very much with us. To have looked out the window of the plane and to have seen that we were still just 5,000 feet off the ground is much the same experience as watching the evening news or reading the newspaper. The signs so strongly appear to be saying that we have not lifted consciousness in our culture in any significant way. The emergence of a new world order seems like a promise that is not going to be fulfilled.

But the message of the dream is that things *are* changing. Consciousness is being lifted, but in a way that is not always apparent. The time will likely come when we will suddenly see what inner progress and change has been going on. It is at that time when we will need to become full participants in the changes which have happened. In a spiritual sense we will need to demonstrate our capacity to "fly."

EDGAR CAYCE
PREDICTS

Your Role in Creating a New Age

Chapter 1

Experiencing a New Age

Balancing Service and Attunement

Several essential themes run throughout the philosophy of the Cayce readings, major principles which are the foundation of a way of living. Many of them are well-known ancient teachings and have merely been restated or newly interpreted by Cayce. These essential themes include concepts such as the following:

> There is only one fundamental energy or force in the universe.
>
> The spirit is the life, mind is the builder, the physical is the result.
>
> No influence is greater than the soul's free will.

All of these will be seen to be important in our work together *and* as individuals, trying to build a spiritually renewed planetary culture.

However, another principle, perhaps *the* most important one for us to understand in these times, states that our human journey in the earth is best fulfilled by a careful balance between the life of attunement and the life of service. Effective service to others requires the sensitivity developed by an inner life of attunement to God. Even Jesus found it necessary to withdraw occasionally for periods of prayer and meditation. At the same time, extensive efforts to perfect one's own soul through attunement, without an equal commitment to reach out and give to others, will fail to fulfill our purpose in the earth.

It is essential that we understand the need for achieving a balance between these two poles. The importance of working on ourselves cannot be minimized. It is certainly true that the world will be changed, one individual at a time. And that change must *begin* within ourselves. We *do* alter our outer world by transforming first our inner world. But at the same time, we must recognize the responsibilities we have to other members of our human family. We may not be directly guilty of the mess in which another person finds himself or herself. But we do have—in another sense of the word—a "responsibility" *for* and *to* that person. And our lives of service to others cannot wait until we have fully completed the work of attunement which we have started. Giving, caring and serving must begin right now.

The idea of karmic law can be misunderstood and misapplied. Without compassion and sensitivity, the theories of reincarnation and karma will not move us any closer to a new age. Spiritual evolution for this planet cannot move forward if we use the principle of reincarnation to look upon the painful plight of someone else and dismiss that person with the thought, "Oh, he is just meeting his own karma." Technically this may be true. However, it may well be *our* own karmic opportunity in that moment to reach out in love.

At the heart of Cayce's philosophy for building a new age is this ancient Biblical teaching: *We are our brother's keeper.* The human race has a long history of being uncomfortable with this teaching and of finding sophisticated ways to explain it away. As potential co-creators of a new order of values and ideals in our world, we can still stumble over this principle. We might imagine developing an Aquarian age for just our city, or just our nation, or even for just the few who already know about these things. However, this sort of thinking will not work. We are now a *global* culture and the entire human family must eventually move together in consciousness if there is to be any meaningful and lasting transformation.

As students of spiritual and metaphysical teachings, we must be concerned about, and even involved in, solutions for world hunger and social justice. In fact, we may be able to demonstrate new approaches to these problems. The old solutions offered by world leaders do not seem to be working. Our progress with *attunement* may well help us to see creative, new possibilities for how to solve these problems. But we are our brothers' and sisters' keepers, and Cayce's formula for building a new age clearly challenges us to accept this fact. These long passages from the readings are well worth careful study, because they beautifully state an ideal of balancing attunement and service in these times.

With the present conditions, then, that exist—these have all come to that place in the development of the human family where there must be a reckoning, a point upon which all may agree, that out of all this turmoil that has arisen from the social life, racial differences, the outlook upon the relationship of man to the Creative Forces or his God, and his relationships one with another, must come to some *common* basis upon which all *may* agree. You say at once, such a thing is impractical, impossible! What has caused the present conditions, not alone at home but abroad? It is that realization that was asked some thousands of years ago, "Where *is* thy brother? His blood *cries* to me from the ground!" and the other portion of the world has answered, *is* answering, "Am I my brother's keeper?" The world, *as* a world— that makes for the disruption, for the discontent—has lost its ideal. Man may not have the same *idea.* Man—*all* men—may have the *same* IDEAL!. . .

Man's answer to everything has been Power—Power of money, Power of position, Power of wealth, Power of this, that or the other. This has *never* been *God's* way, will never be God's way. Rather little by little, line upon line, here a little, there a little, each thinking rather of the other fellow, as that that has kept the world in the various ways of being intact—where there were ten, even, many a city, many a nation, has been kept from destruction. Though we may look upon, or feel that that which was given to Abram—as he viewed the cities of the plain and pled for the saving of same—was an allegorical story, a beautiful tale to be told children—that it might bring fear into the hearts of those that would have their *own* way—may it not come into the hearts of those now, today, wilt *thou,* thine self, make of thine *own* heart an understanding that thou must answer for thine own brother, for thine own neighbor! and who is thine neighbor? He that lives next door, or he that lives on the other side of the world? He, rather, that is in *need* of understanding! He who has faltered; he who has fallen even by the way. *He* is thine neighbor, and thou must answer for him!   3976-8

It is also understood, comprehended by some, that a new order of conditions is to arise; that there must be many a purging in high places as well as low; that there must be the greater consideration of each individual, each soul being his brother's keeper.

There will then come about those circumstances in the political, the economic and the whole relationships where there will be a leveling—or a greater comprehension of this need.

For as the time or the period draws near for these changes that come with the new order, it behooves all of those who have an ideal—as individuals, as well as groups or societies or organizations, to be practicing, applying same in their experience—and their relationships one to another.

For unless these are up and doing, then there must indeed be a new order in *their* relationships and their activities.   3976-18

The Cayce Readings on a New Age

In our times we are experiencing the *limits* of physical consciousness. Like an embryonic chick which is straining against the confines of the egg's shell, our culture is pressing against the boundaries of the old world ways. To transcend those limits will be a birth into something new for humanity.

In these days of testing and confusing changes, we find ourselves to be "time bound." Our lives are too full of things which have to be done right away. We are frustrated that we cannot often give the care and attention to what we know will produce the quality results of which we are capable. Our society is also experiencing at a mass level the condition of being "energy bound." We are dependent upon imported petroleum and we feel hemmed in by this situation.

But in confronting the limits of physical consciousness, we may find that the most significant boundary is our experience of feeling "power bound." Frequently in our society we see the frustration of people feeling powerless to do anything to solve chronic problems—whether inner city crime, inflation, the rising incidence of divorce or other difficulties facing us.

At a deep level, the essential problem of our times is that we are living in a *new* world with *old* world rules. In a sense a new age is already here. Technology has already made us one world. Because of nuclear weapons, global warfare is unthinkable. Because of international trade in the raw materials needed for industry, worldwide cooperation is a necessity. And because of communications breakthroughs (such as satellite relay stations), we can no longer claim ignorance of what is happening for any failure on our part to help our troubled brothers and sisters in other parts of the world. Thus we may say that a new age has already arrived.

However, the world is still being run with the same procedures and ideals as in the previous hundreds of years. Feelings of national (or even regional) pride and sovereignty are stronger than feelings of global family. And things will not work this way. We cannot play a new game with old rules. The new game is already upon us and we don't have a choice about it. Humanity's decision does rest with the rules we choose to follow—the ideals and intentions we decide to have toward each other. Much of the stress we call living in times of change is created by this tension between a new age which is already here and rules for living and relating which do not meet these new needs.

The Edgar Cayce readings offer profound insights into what is going on in our times. More than 40 years ago Cayce was able to see from his psychic state the major challenges and trends in the creation of a new world order. Despite the importance of these prophetic readings, they are actually very few in number. In perhaps only a half dozen readings (out of 14,256 we have on record) did Cayce directly address the topic of a new age. There are, of course, more readings given on geological earth changes which might accompany the changing times, and these will be examined in the next chapter. But in just a very few readings does Cayce speak directly about the possibility of humanity co-creating with God a spiritually renewed "new age."

The most detailed and specific of those readings was given in 1939 to a 41-year-old woman. In a series of questions and answers the reading makes very important points that we will want to keep in mind throughout our study of adjusting to a new age. The question-and-answer exchange begins in this way:

Q-1. Three hundred years ago Jacob Boehme decreed Atlantis would rise again at this crisis time when we cross from this Piscean era into the Aquarian. Is Atlantis rising now? Will it cause a sudden convolution and about what year?

A-1. In 1998 we may find a great deal of the activities as have been wrought by the gradual changes that are coming about.

These are at the periods when the cycle of the solar activity, or the years as related to the sun's passage through the various spheres of activity become paramount or catamount [tantamount?] to the change between the Piscean and the Aquarian age. This is a gradual, not a cataclysmic activity in the experience of the earth in this period. 1602-3

We should take note of the phrase "gradual...activity," because many people have thought that Cayce predicted a cataclysmic and rapid switch from an old age to a new age. The reading picks up later on the same topic.

Q-12. What will the Aquarian age mean to mankind as regards physical, mental and spiritual development? Is the Aquarian age described as the "Age of the Lily" and why?
A-12. Think ye this might be answered in a word? These are as growths. What meant that awareness as just indicated? In the Piscean age, in the center of same, we had the entrance of Emmanuel or God among men, see? What did that mean? The same will be meant by the full consciousness of the ability to communicate with or to be aware of the relationships to the Creative Forces and the uses of same in material environs. This awareness during the era or age in the age of Atlantis and Lemuria or Mu brought what? Destruction to man, and his beginning of the needs of the journey up through that of selfishness. 1602-3

This response best answers our own wonderings about what it would be like to live in a new age such as Cayce envisions. Although it does not describe the life style, it defines the kind of consciousness we would have: a full awareness of our ability to communicate with God and with our own higher selves, *and* the ability to use these higher vibrational expressions of energy in our material lives. We can well imagine the commonplace use of ESP, psychic and spiritual healing, meditation and the like. However, we are left with a warning in this answer by Cayce. In prehistoric times humanity had similar access to creative energies and misused them to cause destructions. Continuing the answer to question 12, the reading goes on to say:

Then, as to what will these be— *only* those who accept same will even become aware of what's going on about them! How few

realize the vibratory forces as create influences from even one individual to another, when they are even in the same vibratory force or influence! And yet ye ask what will the Aquarian age bring in mind, in body, in experience?   1602-3

Apparently in these times of change there are likely to be many confused people. Cayce seems to be predicting that only those individuals who are willing to think in terms of the reality of the psychic and spiritual realms will be aware of and understand what is going on in the world around them. Our responsibilities would be great in times of mass confusion and disorientation. Having at least some understanding of the purposes of what is unfolding, we would need to share this in a form that would make sense of these times for others.

Q-13. Is the Aquarian age described as the "Age of the Lily" and why?
A-13. The purity. Only the purity as it represents will be able to comprehend or understand that awareness that is before those who seek the way.
Q-14. Can a date be given to indicate the beginning of the Aquarian age?
A-14. This has already been indicated as the period when it should pass, but that is when it begins to affect. It laps over from one to another, as is the natural sources, as he holds to that which has been, which is. As has been indicated, we will begin to understand fully in '98.
Q-15. Are there any thoughts along these lines, beyond these, that can be given at this time?
A-15. Holy, holy is His name!   1602-3

These final three questions and answers beautifully summarize the Cayce vision of a new age. First, it must be a time of greater purity. To be builders of a new world order, we will have to cleanse our bodies as well as our emotional and thinking processes. Most crucially, our purposes will need to be pure. And then, what is required of us is patience. The new age will not suddenly drop on us in 1998. In fact the prophecy is that "we will *begin* to fully understand" what is going on by 1998. We should expect that times of change will extend well into the 21st century. What will particularly characterize the period *up to* 1998 is the confusion and lack of understanding about these changing times. What is needed from us is not just lectures, books and other "words" to explain in an intellectual way what the changes are about; we must also express *in the midst* of stressful times qualities such as faith and hope. This is how we can personally catch our own vision of a new age *and* help to lift others into this perspective.

Then, as ye show forth the fruits of the spirit. What are these? Faith, hope, patience, long-suffering, kindness, gentleness, brotherly love—these be those over which so many stumble; yet they are the very voices, yea the very morning sun's light in which the entity has caught that vision of the *new age*, the new understanding, the new seeking for the relationships of a Creative Force to the sons of men.   1436-1

Finally, the Cayce readings once gave to a woman an affirmation that she could use to better cope with changes in life. We can imagine that there is an archetypal, universal quality to these words—that in our own prayer life or meditation time, these words can quicken within each of us, as well, a spirit of peace.

Q-2. Any advice regarding the world changes beginning June 25th, as they might affect my husband and me; also as to the attitude for us to hold?
A-2. . . .The attitude of all should be:
"Thy will be done, O God! And let me find myself content with that I cannot change, and to change that which I may that will be in closer keeping with Thee."   1100-37

When Will a New Age Come?

The question of timing is in all our minds. How long will it be until we see signs of a new consciousness directing human affairs? Will it be in 1998 or 2000? Or is it still hundreds of years off? What seems obvious is that the old systems and the old consciousness will not keep on working indefinitely—or even for much longer. Some type of major change must be just ahead, and there are three basic scenarios for how a new age could emerge out of the present state of our world.

The first hypothesis is a grim one. It suggests that things will have to get much worse before people will be willing to work together to build something better. This theory presupposes a sort of Dark Ages that would precede renewal. Books like *1984* and

10

Brave New World could be included in this first category of scenarios, with its frightful images of modern technological ideals carried to their absurd and freedom-destroying ultimate.

A second theory is that a spiritually refocused new age society will emerge relatively soon—at least by the early years of the 21st century. There are two versions of this hypothesis. One is anti-technology and supposes that by the year 2000 the world will clearly see how a consumer-based culture doesn't work. It predicts that we will turn to a more contemplative alternative which features the individual in harmony with nature and a suspension of scientific development until the spiritual development in humans can catch up.

There is another version of that theory: that a new age is coming very soon, but this version is protechnology. It suggests that science is going to discover what religion has been asking us to accept on faith. Through science we will find evidence for life after death, for psychic healing and for the values of meditation. There will be a wedding of science and religion which will move us into a new world order. This version predicts that the scientific-technological establishment will still be running the world in the 21st century, but it will be with new, spiritual values which research has proven.

A third theory of when a new age will come suggests that it is still hundreds of years away. In this scenario the transition is very gradual. Each generation will make a little more progress. It rests on the assumption that a new age can come only as a reflection of changes in human thinking and ideals, and it points out that humans are slow to change. According to this third hypothesis, the seeds are being planted right now—particularly in this period from 1958-1998—but it will take many generations for these new values to flower in humanity as a whole.

The Cayce readings do not seem to support directly any particular theory about the timing for a new age. Various people claim to have found in the Cayce material passages to support each of the three basic hypotheses. However, it is probable that the majority of those who have studied the readings personally feel that the antitechnology version of the second theory is most likely—a new age will be here by the year 2000.

However, the majority interpretation does not always prove to be the one that is true. We should not be too quick to dismiss the idea that a new age may be hundreds of years away—at least in the sense of a new age in which *all* humanity is participating. Individuals or groups could enter a new type of consciousness and life style even *now,* and for them it will be as if a new age is here. But more broadly speaking, humanity must eventually travel together in spiritual evolution, and it is a crucial question as to when the planetary family as a *whole* will experience new age renewal. Will that be in 1998 or 2098 or maybe even later?

This question cannot be answered. We must decide for ourselves what we understand the Cayce readings to predict. We must develop for ourselves a perspective of how we build toward a new world. Are we "sprinters" racing toward the year 2000; or are we "long-distance runners" who believe that in this lifetime we may not see the fruits of all we are trying to accomplish? If we look back historically at some of the great transition times for humanity, we can see an example of each kind of change.

Consider the 60-year period from 1940 to 2000. Will it be more like the years 30 to 90 A.D. or the years 1490 to 1550? The first choice is the period of Christ's ministry and the formation of an infant church. The second period was the time of a flowering Renaissance. To look at the *secular* history of the world from 30-90 A.D., it appears that nothing of great importance happened. The Romans merely consolidated their hold on all of the known Western world. Seen from this point of view these 60 years were *not* particularly times of great transformation and change. However, we can look back on those years from another perspective and see that they really were the beginning of a new age. A relatively small group of people went through a quantum jump in consciousness evolution. However, it took hundreds of years for that experience to be recognized and accepted by the mainstream culture in which they lived.

Is this what is happening in our own time? Perhaps once again a relatively small group of people are going through a different but equally important quantum jump in consciousness evolution. This time it may be hundreds of thousands of people, whereas in the 1st century it was only thousands. But the pattern may be the same: It may take many years for society as a whole to be affected.

However, this is not the only pattern for changing times. It may be that our lives more closely parallel the lives of those who lived in the years 1490 to 1550. In those years, there were dramatic transformations that in many ways are reminiscent of our times. As Columbus went to America, we are going to the moon. As in the Reformation, we are finding ways to combine the best of Eastern and Western religions. At the end of that 60-year period, an entirely new social system was in place in Europe. The Middle Ages were over and the Renaissance was in full swing. Perhaps there will be an equally dramatic shift for us between 1940 and 2000.

We are left to decide which of these two historical times of change is the better model for what we feel is happening in the world now. We should be keen observers of inner and outer change. Of course, it can be argued that since the soul is eternal, then timing is not that important. Whether a new age comes in 20 years or 200 does not make that much difference in the cosmic scheme of things. Nevertheless, the building of a new world requires choice and action. The personal strategy which we follow as individuals in making our contribution may be largely affected by what we expect, by the type of changing times in which we believe we live.

Chapter

Prophecies of Cayce: Dealing with the Problems

It has all happened so quickly, so unexpectedly. It began only three weeks ago, but since then the changes have been so great that the world we used to know is only a memory. Looking back, we should have seen that there were signs that all this was coming. Just the frequency with which the earth was rumbling should have alerted us.

Those warning signs which nearly all of us dismissed began about two months ago. There were strong earthquakes in the Mediterranean Sea area. There were some minor eruptions of Mt. Etna. But even when Mt. Pelée, which had been quiet for so long, began to show signs of awakening once again, few people realized that this was much more than merely a coincidental set of earth changes happening. Who would have expected that those signs were an overture to the cataclysms which have followed?

Three weeks ago, on a sunny October morning, in the middle of rush hour traffic, the land began to shake in California. Not the small tremors that these people had come to expect and live with. Instead it was an earthquake of unprecedented intensity and duration. The loss of life and property was so severe that it will be difficult ever to make a count. Portions of what had been dry land that morning are now under several feet of ocean water.

But things did not stop with California. In the past three

weeks there have come reports from around the world of severe earth changes. Devastating earthquakes and tidal waves in Japan; tremors of record intensity in Turkey and the southwestern portion of the Soviet Union. There have even been strong earthquakes in northern Europe, although as yet there has been no loss of life there.

The nation and the world have not yet begun to deal with the effects of what has already happened. In the months to come those of us who have not been directly affected will quickly come to realize how interconnected the world is. The unavailability of food and industrial goods will soon be painfully noticeable. And everywhere there is the rarely spoken fear— what if all we have seen so far is just the beginning?

This scenario is from the imagination of one who has read the prophecies of earth changes found in the Edgar Cayce readings. Probably every person who has studied this material has created his or her own story of what it would be like to live in a world whose geography was rapidly and violently changing. For most of us, it is a sobering and anxiety-producing exercise.

In many ways the relatively few readings which Cayce gave on earth changes have done more to popularize his name than any other part of his work. There is without doubt a sensational quality to the idea of California going into the sea or a once dormant volcano reawakening with a fury. It is the kind of sensational material that sells magazine articles and books. It often seems a shame that so many people know of Edgar Cayce in terms of his visions of a possible earth catastrophe, rather than for his quiet, humble work of helping individuals with physical healing.

Because of the dramatic quality of these few readings on earth changes, we can well expect that they have been frequently misquoted and misinterpreted. Perhaps it is fear that causes a person to (even unconsciously) alter slightly the wording in one of Cayce's prophecies. Or perhaps there are those who are so frustrated with the way our world is run that they take pleasure in quoting and often misinterpreting Cayce readings which suggest widespread destruction. Whatever the causes, the fact remains that the earth change prophecies are among the most misunderstood readings that Cayce gave.

Before looking more closely at what those readings *do* say and alternative ways of interpreting them, let us get a measurement of how well you already know what *is* and what *is not* in the readings. Here are seven true/false questions. Which ones are accurate statements from the Cayce prophecies? See how many you can answer correctly.

1. By the year 1920 Cayce readings were being given which mentioned earth changes. (Note: Cayce began giving readings around the turn of the century.)
2. America should expect more earth changes than any other country in the world.
3. There will be a three-month warning period, or safety period, before severe earthquakes hit California. That warning is either Mt. Vesuvius or Mt. Pelée erupting.
4. Cayce once predicted that in the year 1936 there would be a shifting of the earth's poles or the earth's rotational axis.
5. Cayce identified certain regions in America as being safety lands, Ohio among them.
6. The period from 1958 to 1998 is identified as the time span for the *beginning* of the earth changes. We would expect, in the time frame of the Cayce readings, that earth changes would also extend into the 21st century.
7. According to Cayce, we might expect the destruction of New York City around the same time (i.e., plus or minus 10 years) as that of Los Angeles and San Francisco.

So misunderstood and misquoted have the earth changes readings been that even the most experienced student of this material rarely gets all seven of these questions correct. Instead of simply giving the answers at this point in the text, let us examine more closely the readings themselves and in the process of this chapter and the next one we will discover the correct response to each of the seven items.

Problems with a Study of the Earth Changes Readings

The question we want answered by a study of the Cayce earth changes readings is something like this: "What did he *actually* predict is going to happen in terms of geological and geographic changes?" However, there are two more fundamental issues which need to be addressed first and they are really more problematical than our primary inquiry. These two fundamental questions require more of us than just studying and reporting on readily available written materials; they require us to think for ourselves.

The first problem is, "Why should we even bother to be concerned with these prophecies? Either they are inaccurate and we would be wasting our time; or they are accurate and the severity of destruction which is predicted seems to be far beyond the coping powers of humanity."

There is probably a fault in this kind of "no-win" thinking. In fact, geologists say that in the history of our planet Earth there have been periods of widespread geological change; for example, a shifting of the poles has occurred a number of times in the past. Some of these scientifically verifiable periods of cataclysmic earth changes have happened with advanced forms of life already developed. And obviously life survived! Surely the resourcefulness of humanity would continue to find ways to cope and rebuild even if all of the earth changes Cayce warned of do come to pass.

A deeper reason for our concern about these prophecies is that perhaps we can do something about them. Technologically we might build structures in earthquake zones which are less likely to collapse, for example, and things like this might be very important to do. But at a more profound level it might well be that the attitudes and actions of humanity as a whole create the conditions which either foster or prevent geological catastrophes from happening. Even if this is only a possibility, it is probably reason enough for us to be concerned with these predictions which Cayce made and our responses to them.

The second question is probably more difficult to answer. (It was hinted at in the previous problem.) It asks quite bluntly, "What if Edgar Cayce were wrong? In fact, what evidence is there to suggest that Edgar Cayce had even the slightest skill in making accurate predictions about earthquakes?" There is no argument about the fact that the Cayce readings were fallible. Hugh Lynn Cayce and Edgar Evans Cayce have written a book documenting some of the cases in which their father was wrong. Entitled *The Outer Limits of Edgar Cayce's Power,* it has sold fewer copies than almost any other book on his psychic work, perhaps because people generally do not want to hear about a psychic's errors.

Yet we cannot avoid this issue in a study of the earth changes prophecies. We must each consider what it is about this man's work that gives us reason to consider seriously the happenings of which his readings warn. In fact, there are probably only two reasons for us to treat the earth changes readings with curiosity and respect.

First, there is the almost undeniable evidence that Cayce was a gifted psychic. His accuracy in diagnosing physical ailments was astounding. There is a remarkable frequency of dramatic health improvements in people who followed the individualized recommendations which they had received in their readings. The sheer volume of accurate physical readings is a persuasive reason for us to consider seriously statements he made in readings which were outside the scope of health care.

Persuasive to make us want to consider them, yes. But positive research findings about his medical clairvoyant powers do *not* prove his ability with past life readings, dream interpretation or prophecies of earth changes. To a large measure, does not each of the areas in which Cayce gave readings need to stand on its own for testing? For example, just because your general practitioner gave you good advice for healing a sprained ankle, does this mean you automatically would go to him for brain surgery? Of course not, because different physicians have particular areas of specialty. There might be some excellent brain surgeons who also have a general practice, but we cannot assume that is always the case.

The problem is a difficult one in evaluating Cayce's work. First, we are faced with the fact that many areas his readings touched upon other than health care are hard to verify. Some types of readings are especially difficult, such as reincarnation readings in which a person might be told of specific past lives. How are we to evaluate the accuracy of such readings (more than 2,000 in number)? We might ask some of those people who received such readings whether or not they were "helpful." The term "helpful" is rather vague and will likely be understood in different ways by the people whom we interview. Nevertheless, it gives us at least one criterion which we might consider in evaluating the accuracy of Edgar Cayce's "past life psychic powers."

But even if every person were to respond that this purported past life information was helpful (e.g., it allowed them to understand their present situation better and to make creative, hopeful choices for the future), it still does not prove reincarnation nor Cayce's accuracy in reading past lives. At most, it suggests that he was good at becoming sensitive to the current personality of various individuals and identifying the key issues which faced them in relationships, self-image, vocation, etc. The past life scenarios of his readings *may* have been only convenient metaphors—much in the way that our dreams provide stories—to communicate perceived patterns of the personality.

So, at best we can claim that Cayce was in some instances gifted psychically in becoming aware of the mental and emotional make-up of people, whom he often had never met personally. The reincarnation theory itself probably cannot be proved through Cayce's readings. A more modest appraisal of his psychic gift in this area is all that we can realistically expect.

And what of other types of readings he gave? Do any of them provide evidence for the range within which Cayce's psychic gift is dependable? Hundreds of dreams were interpreted through the readings, but in most cases it is difficult, if not impossible, to know if he was correct. Perhaps the closest we can come to validation here is to say that many people have tried to repeat the approach Cayce used to decipher a dream and have found those techniques to be helpful with their own dreams.

A considerable amount of clairvoyant information relating to prehistory is also available for us to evaluate. Frequently, the readings spoke of Atlantis and Lemuria. Yet what evidence is there for the existence of these places? How can we judge the accuracy of these readings? Fortunately, specific hypotheses, if proved, could go far to validate this area of the material (e.g., a hall of Atlantean records buried near the Sphinx, an ancient "City of the Hills and Plains" in Iran). Nevertheless, such discoveries have not yet been made. The nearest to this sort of dramatic validation of the ancient history readings has come from Qumran along the Dead Sea. A rather nonspecific reference in one reading recommended searching in this general area in order to find the remains of an Essene community.

And so, with what conclusion are we left? Recall that our problem stated, "What evidence is there to suggest that Cayce had even the slightest skill in making accurate predictions about earthquakes?" Our initial response might be that he was so accurate as a psychic in every other area, why not in this one, too? However, that argument is unsound. There are simply too many areas of the readings in which we cannot easily prove, one way or the other, the degree of reliability.

That approach is even more untenable when we consider the one area of readings which was perhaps the closest to the earth changes prophecies: those readings given on where to drill for oil. Like the earth changes readings, these psychic surveys attempted to look deep beneath the earth's crust to perceive unseen geological facts. The problem is that these readings appear to have been generally *wrong*. Admittedly, the readings were accurate up to a point, correctly predicting what type of rock would be found at various levels as the well was being drilled. However, Cayce and his group never did hit oil!

Furthermore, the case in favor of the accuracy of the earth changes prophecies begins to look even worse. There are clear instances in which specific ones were *wrong*. First, let us have a look at this potentially damaging evidence; and then we will see if there are ways of countering these problems.

Cayce Prophecies Which Proved Wrong

Most of the prophecies do not have specific dates associated with them. For this reason, it is usually difficult to judge whether or not they are correct. If a psychic says, "Someday Los Angeles will be destroyed by an earthquake," it can never be proved wrong. If that psychic says that between 1958 and 1998 we can expect to see Los Angeles destroyed, then at least we will be able to evaluate the information by 1998. There were cases, however, in which Cayce gave very specific dates for major changes to happen. Unfortunately, in every one of those instances it appears that his prediction failed to materialize.

Most difficult for us to understand are the prophecies concerning the year 1936. For a number of years before 1936, Cayce foresaw that year as a great turning point in the physical changes to befall the planet. He made a number of very specific references about what to look for in that year: a shifting of the poles which determine the rotational axis of the earth, an earthquake in San Francisco more severe than the one in 1906, and perhaps even a reappearance of the Christ. Note the dates on which each of the following passages from these readings were given.

. . .the catastrophes of outside forces to the earth in '36, which will come from the shifting of the equilibrium of the earth itself in space. . . 3976-10, February 8, 1932

Q-10. What will be the type and extent of the upheavals in '36?

A-10. The wars, the upheavals in the interior of the earth, and the shifting of same by the differentiation in the axis as respecting the positions from the Polaris center [the North Star]. 5748-6, July 1, 1932

Q-14. Will the earth upheavals during 1936 affect San Francisco as it did in 1906?

A-14. This'll be a baby beside what it'll be in '36! 270-30, February 13, 1933

And those that seek in the latter portion of the year of our Lord (as ye have counted in and among men) '36, He will appear!. . .

Q-1. What are the world changes to come this year physically?

A-1. The earth will be broken up in many places. The early portion will see a change in the physical aspect of the west coast of America. . .There will be new lands seen off the Caribbean Sea, and *dry* land will appear. 3976-15, January 19, 1934

In addition to these obvious errors (at least in timing), there are other, smaller or more debatable mistakes in the Cayce prophecies. In one case he was willing to pinpoint the dates October 15-20, 1926, and predict "Violent wind storms—two earthquakes, one occurring in California, another in Japan—tidal waves following. . ." (195-32, August 27, 1926). There is no evidence to suggest that anything of a significant magnitude took place. Furthermore, the prediction was made for a period of time less than two months in the future!

In another instance, regarding the rising once again of the hypothetical, lost continent of Atlantis, Cayce referred to dates: "And Poseidia will be among the first portions of Atlantis to rise again. Expect it in sixty-eight and sixty-nine ('68 and '69); not so far away!" (958-3, June 28, 1940) There is currently no clear evidence to suggest that this prophecy was fulfilled. Some investigators feel that they have found evidence of the ruins of an underwater civilization near Bimini. This claim is still arguable; and the fact remains that Cayce predicted the *rising* of land in 1968 and 1969—something which seems fairly certain *not* to have happened.

Admittedly, all of these instances in which Cayce prophecies appear to be wrong may be interpreted and analyzed from a variety of perspectives. The reader who wants to make a full investigation of this topic is encouraged to study other points of view, such as can be found in *Earth Changes Update* by Hugh Lynn Cayce (also published by A.R.E. Press).

Alternatives for Understanding Mistaken Prophecies

There are at least four ways in which we can approach the problem created by the mistaken readings just cited. It would be far easier for us if only we had a few *successful* earth changes predictions to which to point. Unfortunately, we do not. The remaining prophecies await the coming few years. Cayce's outside time limit for at least the beginning of these changes was 1998. In the meantime we must conclude something about the obvious errors which already exist. Of course, the simplest answer would be merely to say that all of the prophecies are probably wrong. But perhaps we should explore some more creative solutions before jumping to that conclusion.

Let us consider the nature of time. Many theorists who speculate about higher dimensional reality feel that time, as we understand it, is probably a quality of only this three-dimensional, physical world. That is not to suggest that "there is no such thing as time outside the earth plane," as some say. We need to retain something *like* time if we are to speak of developing or unfolding consciousness. Without a measurement like time it is difficult to imagine the evolution of the soul. Nevertheless, from our physical perspective we may have a very limited notion of time. Perhaps, for example, time is multidimensional. Instead of being like a line, as we usually think of it, it may be like a surface, allowing for parallel and yet different time lines to exist simultaneously as possibilities. We certainly know that space is not just one-dimensional (there is more to space than just our position along a single line). Why not time as well?

At this point we are involved in interesting, yet fanciful speculation. However, it does suggest an alternative way to view Cayce's earth changes mistakes. Might it be that when a psychic like Cayce moves his awareness beyond physical consciousness, he finds himself in a place where time means something different? Perhaps Cayce was in a place of multidimensional time, where likely events in physical space appeared accurately to his perception, and yet their location in three-dimensional time was clouded or ambiguous. This would suggest that even the events which were predicted and did not happen may yet come to pass.

This still leaves us with the problem of why Cayce allowed himself to get locked in to specific dates on some predictions. On the one hand, we must admire his willingness to do this. Nothing is more frustrating than trying to evaluate a source of information which refuses to be specific. On the other hand, if Cayce was so perceptive from the heightened awareness in which he gave readings, why was there no admission in those prophecies of how variable the dates might be? Perhaps this is just a shortcoming or limitation in his psychic gift.

However, other approaches have also been proposed in order to explain the apparent errors regarding 1926, 1936 and 1968-69. It has been postulated that many of these prophecies are *symbolic* in nature. In other words, could it be that in 1926 California and Japan *did* experience jolting changes—if not geological, then perhaps economic, social or political? Could it be that 1936 was a year in which the poles did shift—not the literal rotation of the earth, but the spiritual, economic or political equilibrium of the world? And, with this kind of reasoning we might wonder if certain elements of Atlantean *consciousness* rose to the surface in 1968-69. These were particularly turbulent years of social unrest in Western society and a case might be made that Atlanteans, who were determined not to let the world go down the way it did before, chose that point in time to push their opinions.

This is an attractive theory to some, but it leaves us with two problems. First, how could we even begin to prove it? Where would we start in an effort to collect evidence that Cayce was speaking symbolically? But even more troublesome is the question of whether or not we would then expect to find *all* the Cayce prophecies to be symbolic (not to mention the question of whether or not reincarnation and health readings are also symbolic). The symbolism theory may be correct, but it should have little to attract us to it. It tempts us to the "heads I win, tails you lose" approach which characterizes cults. The Cayce readings can never be taken seriously by our society at large if those studying this material are so self-serving with their evaluations. It is a dangerous game to be proud of the prophecies which physically come true and to claim a "symbolic fulfillment" for those which by physical standards were wrong. Admittedly, the symbolism theory could be correct; but in an honest examination of Cayce's work and predictions we cannot afford to follow that approach.

We are left, then, with at least one other approach—perhaps the most insightful and promising one. This point of view suggests that "something happened" between many of Cayce's predictions and the date on which they were to have taken place. For example, most of the predictions about 1936 were made in the period from 1932-1934. Could it be that between 1934 and 1936 changes took place which altered the previewed course of events? This approach presupposes a notion of prophecy which is probably very sound: that the future is not fixed and predictions can only be statements of likelihood or probabilities. The course of events is like a train rushing down the tracks, with repetitive forks in the tracks which present alternatives. Yet at each fork the switch has been set in one position or another; and we might predict that, unless some intervening action is taken, it is most likely that the train will follow a foreseeable path.

The Cayce readings themselves present this picture of prophecy. There is repeated reference to the way in which the actions and attitudes of humanity will shape the course of the future. We will examine this in greater depth in a later chapter. It concerns the effect that we can have on building a new age and building the way in which the transitions can materialize.

The exact mechanism by which we could have such an effect is still somewhat of a mystery. Later we will speculate on how the thoughts and actions of even a relatively small percentage of humanity could alter the decision-making process of world leaders to enhance the prospects for peace. We will also look at a way in which the thoughts of humanity may influence even the forces of nature. For the moment, perhaps the basic principles from the readings are sufficient: The universe is an interrelated whole. Part of this connected universe is the unseen realm of thought energy.

What we experience as physical reality is primarily a result of what has been collectively built by humanity at the level of thought or consciousness.

Operating under the assumption of these principles, how could the readings have occasionally been wrong? If Cayce's psychic gift allowed him to see clearly into this causative realm of thought energy, how could he have been mistaken about 1926, 1936 and 1968-69? One theory to explain the errors is that new thoughts are continually being created. If sufficient numbers of people change their consciousnesses *after* a prophecy has been given, then they might redirect the flow of events which materialize in the physical world. This is certainly the Biblical notion of prophecy. The Old Testament spokesman of God always had the same message: Change your ways *or else* a destruction or calamity will befall you. In the story of the prophet Jonah, the people *did* alter their ways and the catastrophe did not occur.

It is to the credit of the Cayce readings that in at least one case they detected the changing course of events. We have seen the rather dramatic way in which Cayce's detailed prophecies concerning 1936 proved to be wrong. However, in January of 1936 at least one reading showed that Cayce had a new view of what was to take place that year. He specifically stated that the tremendous earthquake previously forecast for San Francisco would not happen that year. Unfortunately, he provided no explanation as to *why* the prophecy had changed. And it is furthermore unfortunate (from the perspective of those who want the Cayce readings to be proven correct) that even in January of 1936 he still foresaw some major changes which never came to pass.

Q-20. What is the primary cause of earthquakes? Will San Francisco suffer from such a catastrophe this year? If so, give date, time and information for the guidance of this body, who has personal property, records and a wife, all of which it wishes safety.

A-20. We do not find that this particular district (San Francisco) in the present year will suffer the great *material* damages that *have* been experienced heretofore. While portions of the country will be affected, we find these will be farther *east* than San Francisco—or those *south*, where there has *not* been heretofore the greater activity. **270-35, January 21, 1936**

The point here, nevertheless, is that the readings include a dynamic or changeable vision of prophecy. Whereas in 1933 Cayce predicted an earthquake in San Francisco of unprecedented proportions, by January of 1936 he correctly saw that this was not going to happen. We are left to wonder if he simply had blurred psychic vision in 1933 which got clearer as the target date approached, or if some changes in the consciousness of people began to steer world events in a new direction. The latter of these two alternatives is much more challenging and exciting. It makes us *participants* in these times of transition.

The notion of participating in the building process of a new age is a crucial idea. If we must sit back and wait for things to happen to us, then these times of change become all the more frightening. But with a sense of our own creative powers, the difficulties can be met with hope.

We have a responsibility for how history will unfold. This is true not only for questions on international warfare, population and the distribution of food resources, but even for the geological and geographical changes which may or may not come to pass. It is vital that we accept this sense of responsibility. And for this very reason, one of the four alternatives seems clearly to be the best in our effort to explain how Edgar Cayce could have been incorrect on some prophecies.

Recall that four options have been proposed:

(1) Edgar Cayce simply had no skill at predicting geophysical changes. Not only were 1926, 1936 and 1968-69 wrong, but we should expect that all the earth changes readings will prove to be wrong.

(2) Timing is difficult for a psychic to judge. Cayce predicted things which may still come to pass; he just had his years wrong.

(3) The prophecies which *appear* to have been incorrect have actually come true, but in a *symbolic* way. Sometimes Cayce predicted things which were to come true literally; other times they were prophecies which would come to pass in a symbolic fashion. We can see only in *retrospect* which of the two possible varieties a particular reading fits.

(4) Cayce's prophecies occasionally failed because of changes in the consciousness of a sufficient number of people between the time of the prediction and the target date. The consciousness changes effected a new direction in the course of physical events.

Why is the last of the options the superior one? In fact, how does it really differ from the third one? At first glance both seem to be self-serving to the followers of Edgar Cayce; both seem to provide a convenient excuse for Cayce's fallibility. Whether we claim "symbolic fulfillment" or assert that the changed thoughts of people got in the way of the prediction's fulfillment, doesn't it look the same? Are not both of these two alternatives dangerous games that leave students of the Cayce material open to attack as cultists?

Perhaps not. There is a subtle but important distinction between the third and fourth options. The third option is a game that permits us to maintain the idea of Cayce as an infallible seer. It suggests that the fault is never his; it is rather in our misperception of how he gave prophecies. It is a method to maintain hero worship.

However, the fourth option is different in a fundamental way. It says that the creative potential of human consciousness is more powerful than the psychic power of the prophet. It shifts the focus *away* from anxieties about proving Cayce's psychic gift, and it moves the attention toward the responsibilities we all have in shaping the future. The fourth alternative is superior because it does not fall into mere skepticism like the first option nor resort to vague speculation like the second choice. It also does not leave itself open to charges of hero worship or cultism like the third alternative. Instead it puts the ultimate responsibility on us. It is actually the beginning of a much needed redefinition of "psychic." It says that the "psychic" is not the only one who can "tune in" to likely future events; the psychic realm is the level on which all of us are operating as we actively *create* the future together.

The Case in Favor of the Cayce Prophecies

We have no solid evidence for Cayce's skill at predicting earth changes. We have no single earthquake, volcanic eruption or tidal wave to which we can point and say that here is evidence that this man's predictions of what may occur before 1998 are really worth our study. In fact, we have clear cases of errors, and we have gone to great lengths to explore what will be the best strategy for dealing with the problems they create for us. Is it worth our while to push on and to look more closely at the details of what Cayce predicted? Our dilemma on this matter could be restated by way of an analogy.

Imagine that you went to a psychic and asked her for three predictions about events of the coming twelve months. Suppose you were a sports fan and wanted to know who would win baseball's World Series, football's Super Bowl and hockey's Stanley Cup. Her predictions were that the winners of these three events would be the Chicago Cubs, Los Angeles Rams and Boston Bruins. After several months the World Series has now just been completed and you find that Chicago did not win. What is your attitude toward the remaining two predictions?

Your inclination might be to dismiss what is left of the prophecies. If she was wrong about the World Series, what reason is there to expect that her predictions about the other two events will be any better? However, what would you do if you came across some other evidence and facts that put the remaining predictions in a new light?

Suppose you discover that this same psychic also made a series of predictions about several dozen political elections which occurred just three weeks after the World Series. All of those election predictions proved to be correct, even several which were unexpected outcomes. The fact that this psychic has proven herself to be reliable (although admittedly in an area other than sports predictions) probably gives you new hope that she still may prove to be right on the two sports events yet to happen.

Furthermore, suppose that you come across several *other* psychics who have *independently* made predictions about the Super Bowl and the Stanley Cup. They also think that the Los Angeles Rams and Boston Bruins will be the respective winners. This new evidence will probably strengthen your interest in the prophecies you originally received from this woman and will help you retain some expectation that she may eventually prove to be correct with a majority of her sports predictions.

In this analogy, the sports prophecies clearly correspond to the earth changes readings. For whatever reason, some of the critical ones made by Edgar Cayce have shown themselves to be wrong. However, we have another category of readings which is very evidential of his gift. Especially in the category of the physical, health care readings, we have documented evidence of Cayce's psychic powers. Just as the hypothetical psychic's election accuracy forced us to reconsider our skepticism about her World Series prediction, we cannot easily dismiss the remaining Cayce readings on earth changes. And furthermore, when we find other, independent sources of information which also predict cataclysmic changes before the year 2000, there is an even stronger case to consider a careful study of the details in the Cayce predictions.

Among those additional sources of information is a mysterious man named Nostradamus who lived 400 years ago and yet made many prophecies which now seem to have uncanny accuracy. Writing in poetic verse, often clouded with symbolism and astrological references, Nostradamus is claimed by many to have foreseen several of the great world events since his day. Some of these prophecies have been interpreted to say that a great cataclysm will befall the earth near the end of this century.*

Nostradamus and Cayce are not alone as psychics in predicting the likelihood of earth changes in our generation. There have been literally dozens of psychics in the years since Cayce's death who say similar things, often giving greater details and more specific dates than did Cayce. In many instances those specific earth changes predictions have already proved to be incorrect. It is also hard to say to what degree the post-Cayce psychics were primarily mimicking Cayce, whose influence on the profession of prognostication can hardly be overestimated. No, the case for the study of the Cayce earth changes readings is not significantly strengthened by psychics who followed him and who have basically reiterated his ideas on the topic. What we need are more sources of information that are likely to be independent of Cayce, and preferably *before* his own work.

The best such material comes from other cultural traditions. One source is the ancient societies of Central America. For the Mayans, Aztecs and Toltecs, their culture-hero and god-like figure Quetzalcoatl was a source of prophecies about changing times. His name roughly translates as "spirit of light," and he was revered as an ancient teacher of the people in the areas of mathematics, agriculture, theology and the arts.

Legend has it that Quetzalcoatl returned (that is, reincarnated) in a year now calculated to be about 947 A.D. In this second life with his people he foretold many important events and cycles of change to be experienced in the coming 1,144 years. His prophecies stated that within the ongoing fifth age there would be 13 cycles, each comprised of 52 years. During these 676 years

*See the book *Predictions,* by Joe Fisher with Peter Commins, New York, Van Nostrand Reinhold Co., 1980.

there would be decreasing consciousness and free will. Then would come 9 cycles, once again of 52 years each, which would be characterized by darkness or hell.

If we use the year 843 A.D. as the starting point of all these cycles (that is, Quetzalcoatl's reincarnation would have come after two of these 52-year cycles had already been accomplished), some very interesting correspondence can be found to recorded history. Then 676 years into the period (that is, the full 13 cycles of diminishing consciousness and free will), Cortez arrived in America in 1519 with his armies. And after a brief struggle he conquered and enslaved the people of this region.

The year 1935 marks the beginning of the final 52-year cycle of darkness and hell. It is interesting to note that this date marks well the time when Hitler began moves to start World War II. The year 1987—that is, 1935 plus 52—will be the final one in this last cycle of darkness. Then will come the "great purification," reminiscent of Cayce's vision of global changes between 1958 and 1998. Writing in *Alternatives* magazine, Nathan Koenig, Louis Acker and Michael Cornett had this to say about Quetzalcoatl's final two prophecies about the coming 20 years:

"The keepers of the calendars have said that we shall not realize the outcome of the nine cycles of darkness until 1987. Then Texcatlipoca, the Aztec Satan, or Lord of Death and Evil, will remove his mask, and the nine cycles will end with a supreme cleansing and purification.

"Quetzalcoatl prophesied. . .that 'in the future we have to expect a day when the equipoise of nature will be lost, when the ocean tides shall obey no more.'   Cities and mountains would collapse, leveled by great earthquakes. Explosions would also create great destruction, and fires would   'leap forth on the forests and grassy meadows, wrapping all things there in a winding sheet of flame, and melting the very elements with fervent heat.' "

According to the second prophecy, the intensity of suffering accompanying this purification would depend upon mankind's choices. However, despite the intensity, a new age of cooperation, peace and plenty would be born. Quetzalcoatl promised to return "in the time of the great-great grandchildren of the white conquerors," initiating a new set of cycles, "a golden age of spiritual rebirth, planetary harmony, and for many the awakened consciousness of the Divine Life."

The Hopi Indians of North America provide another ancient

tradition of times of change which is remarkably parallel to the one given by Edgar Cayce. The prophecies of the Hopis are said to have come from Massau'u, their spiritual teacher for the age. Ancient Hopi prophecies were handed down on stone tablets accompanied by an oral tradition of interpretation which was passed on by the elders of the community.

Certain of these prophecies concern events near the end of this current age in the Hopi framework of history. Some seem to have been already fulfilled, including the coming of automobiles, telephones and space travel. Koenig, Acker and Cornett also wrote of this: "The legends that surrounded this central symbol included 'horseless chariots' that would roll along 'black snakes' across the land, 'cobwebs' through which people would speak over great distances, 'roads and man-made houses' in the sky, and interplanetary travel including the landing of a man on the moon."

With these signs and others seemingly fulfilled, the Hopis then feel that they can expect the next phase predicted for the years 1980 to 2000. It includes the "Great Day of Purification" to usher in the next age. Certain cataclysms like war, famine and earthquakes are predicted. However, their severity is something to be determined by humanity. The Hopi vision includes the option for these catastrophes to be lessened, if humankind will work together in the proper spirit.

Conclusions

There are strong reasons to look more deeply into the Cayce prophecies. Although at first glance we see glaring errors in earth changes predictions, perhaps there are solid reasons not to be deterred by these mistakes. Edgar Cayce was not alone in his predictions. Psychics and seers of other times and cultures had come before him to make these prophecies, although we have no reason to suspect that the waking Cayce ever knew of them. The correspondences among these independent sources are compelling. It is not enough evidence to claim any sort of "proof," because who can ever prove the future? But it does suggest that we should explore this man's vision of the future in great detail. The sheer volume of his accurate readings in other fields, such as health care, is persuasive. Additionally, it is exciting and hopeful to see his emphasis on our participatory role in helping to create the future—a future which can only be hinted at by prophets. We begin our careful review of Cayce's predictions in the next chapter.

Chapter 3

Predictions for
the Coming Years

The majority of the Cayce prophecies have not yet proved to be right *or* wrong. The predictions yet to be fulfilled fall into two primary categories: geophysical earth changes and political/economic prophecies which are found in the "world affairs readings." Let us begin our detailed study with the earth changes material.

Probably no other portion of the Edgar Cayce material has been more misquoted and misunderstood than his statements about land mass changes which might accompany the beginning of a new age on earth. When compared to the immense volume of readings he gave, these predictions of earthquakes, volcanoes and tidal waves are almost insignificant in number. And yet, no other readings have had such an impact on the thinking of people who are familiar with his work.

One reason that these particular readings are so easily misunderstood is that they are studied improperly and, to make matters worse, are frequently quoted out of context. Rarely does one hear of or see a report of the Cayce prophecies which presents a *chronological* unfoldment of what he said on this topic. We need to review the timing sequence in which he *gave* the readings. In the few instances where timing has been considered, it has been a matter of reporting on prophecies in the order in which we can expect to see them materialize. For example, most writers on this topic would present predictions about the year 1936 before predictions about the years 1958-1998. However, what if Cayce *gave* some of his prophecies about 1936 *after he gave* the ones for 1958-1998. If we are really to experience prophecy as an unfolding, dynamic phenomenon, then the best study would be to recreate for ourselves what it would have been like to be with Edgar Cayce between 1926 and 1944 and to hear these predictions being made and sometimes changing over the years. This is the approach that we will use in this chapter.

The problem of the context in which statements were made by Cayce is also crucial. Many of the misunderstandings about this material can largely be traced to the misleading publication of readings fragments. By far the biggest error has been to reprint the *answer* Cayce gave to a question without showing what the *question* had been (or even to note that it was in response to some question). We shall soon see what an important factor this can be.

Our attempt to recreate the earth changes readings begins with the year 1926. Before this date we find no reference to major geological changes for the immediate future. In other words, Cayce had been giving readings for more than 20 years before this topic even came up.

In 1926 a man in his early 40s asked Cayce for readings on the topic of long-range weather forecasting. At the end of the second reading, after the questions had been dealt with, Cayce offered some additional information. In it he specified the dates October 15th and 20th (some two months into the future) when certain astrological conditions would tend to trigger major changes on earth. He mentioned geological, climatic and political disturbances. Here is the exact wording of Cayce's first earth changes prophecy. Following it there is a question-and-answer exchange from a reading given five days later in which clarification is sought.

As for the weather conditions, and the effect same will produce on various portions of the earth's sphere, and this in its relation to the conditions in man's affairs: As has been oft given, Jupiter and Uranus influence in the affairs of the world appear the strongest on or about October 15th to 20th—when there may be expected in the minds, the actions—not only of individuals, but in various quarters of the globe, destructive conditions as well as building. In the affairs of man, many conditions will arise that will be very,

very strange to the world at present—in religion, in politics, in the moral conditions, and in the attempt to curb or to change such, see? For there will be set in motion [that indicating] when prohibition will be lost in America, see? Violent wind storms—two earthquakes, one occurring in California, another occurring in Japan—tidal waves following, one to the southern portion of the isles near Japan.   195-32, August 27, 1926

Q-6. In reading given on August 27th regarding weather, where in California will earthquake predicted October 15th-20th be the worst? Will there be a tidal wave at that point, or where in California?

A-6. Tidal wave being, as is given, in the far East, the earthquake being in lower California, see?
                    195-33, September 1, 1926

What do the records show about the accuracy of these predictions? They are not very supportive, as we have already seen in the last chapter. This 1926 prophecy must be viewed as essentially one which failed to materialize—or at least the earth changes portions of it. There was no significant earthquake or tidal wave in Japan on those dates. There was a moderate quake in California on October 22, 1926 (two days beyond the predicted dates). However, it was hardly of the magnitude which we might have expected, considering the fact that Cayce had gone out of his way to even bring up this topic. Earthquakes of equal intensity were happening about every two months in California. There were quakes of about equal strength to the October 22 one on July 25, 1926, and January 1, 1927.

After the 1926 readings, *six years pass* before we again find someone asking Cayce about earth changes. In 1932 a 30-year-old man questioned him carefully about the details of what might happen if severe geological changes were to take place. There are important passages about timing in this series of readings. On the one hand, Cayce suggested a sign to watch for which would signal the beginning of the change period: the breaking up of lands in the South Pacific and activity in the Mediterranean Sea area (especially around Mt. Etna). However, there is some question about whether or not this still holds true as a reliable signal. This is because Cayce went on to indicate that this should be well under way by 1936. We are left to wonder if events have just been delayed and the warning signs still hold true.

In this second series of earth changes readings, more details are given concerning exact locations. The eastern seaboard of America (particularly New York and Connecticut) is identified, as well as Alabama.

Q-12. How soon will the changes in the earth's activity begin to be apparent?

A-12. When there is the first breaking up of some conditions in the South Sea (that's South Pacific, to be sure), and those as apparent in the sinking or rising of that that's almost opposite same, or in the Mediterranean, and the Aetna [Etna?] area, then we may know it has begun.

Q-13. How long before this will begin?

A-13. The indications are that some of these have already begun, yet others would say these are only temporary. We would say they have begun. '36 will see the greater changes apparent, to be sure.

Q-14. Will there be any physical changes in the earth's surface in North America? If so, what sections will be affected, and how?

A-14. All over the country we will find many physical changes of a minor or greater degree. The greater change, as we will find, in America, will be the North Atlantic Seaboard. Watch New York! Connecticut, and the like.　　　　　　　311-8, April 9, 1932

Q-29. Are there to be physical changes in the earth's surface in Alabama?

A-29. Not for some period yet.

Q-30. When will the changes begin?

A-30. Thirty-six to thirty-eight.

Q-31. What part of the State will be affected?

A-31. The northwestern part, and the extreme southwestern part.　　　　　　　311-9, August 6, 1932

Q-14. Are the physical changes in Alabama predicted for 1936-38 to be gradual or sudden changes?

A-14. Gradual.

Q-16. When will the physical changes start in Norfolk and vicinity?

A-16. This would be nearer to '58 than to '38 or '36, as we find.
　　　　　　　311-10, November 19, 1932

In the next important series of predictions, Cayce became even more specific. These readings were given to a man in his late 40s who lived in San Francisco; they covered a period from early 1933 to 1936. There is a paradoxical quality to these particular passages: Cayce began in 1933 sounding quite sure that in 1936 there would be a major destruction of San Francisco. By mid-1934 he was less inclined to specify dates and even suggested that what would come to pass depended upon people's attitudes (something we will look at more closely in a later chapter). By 1936 he had backed away from his San Francisco prediction for that year, although still seeming to predict major quakes which never did actually occur.

Q.14. Will the earth upheavals during 1936 affect San Francisco as it did in 1906?
A-14. This'll be a baby beside what it'll be in '36!
270-30, February 13, 1933

Q-20. Are details of the earth's eruptions in 1936 so fixed that you can give me an outline of the Pacific Coast area to be affected, along with precautionary measures to be exercised during and after this catastrophe?
A-20. All of these are, as is ever on or in such an activity, dependent upon individuals or groups who are in or keep an attitude respecting the needs, the desires, the necessary requirements in such a field of activity. That some are *due* and *will* occur is *written,* as it were, but—as we find—as to specific date or time in the present this may not be given.
270-32, June 12, 1934

Q-20. What is the primary cause of earthquakes? Will San Francisco suffer from such a catastrophe this year? If so, give date, time and information for the guidance of this body, who has personal property, records and a wife, all of which it wishes safety.
A-20. We do not find that this particular district (San Francisco) in the present year will suffer the great *material* damages that *have* been experienced heretofore. While portions of the country will be affected, we find these will be farther *east* than San Francisco—or those *south,* where there has *not* been heretofore the greater activity.
The causes of these, of course, are the movements about the

earth; that is, internally—and the cosmic activity or influence of other planetary forces and stars and their relationships produce or bring about the activities of the elementals of the earth; that is, the Earth, the Air, the Fire, the Water—and those combinations make for the replacements in the various activities.

If there are the greater activities in the Vesuvius, or Pelée, then the southern coast of California—and the areas between Salt Lake and the southern portions of Nevada—may expect, within the three months following same, an inundation by the earthquakes.

But these, as we find, are to be more in the southern than in the northern hemisphere.   270-35, January 21, 1936

The final two paragraphs of the last quoted passage above are especially interesting. Here we find the famous prediction of a warning sign before the great California quakes: the eruption of Mt. Vesuvius or Mt. Pelée. But look carefully at several often missed details. First of all, the answer here was in response to a specific question about a possible catastrophe that year (that is, 1936). Would a warning sign to be watched for in 1936 still be applicable to 1982 or 1990 or any other year? A strong case can be made that it *is* still a reliable signal because Cayce was presumably viewing with his clairvoyance the intricate interconnections of happenings beneath the earth's crust. Geological relationships which have been hundreds of thousands of years in the making probably do not disappear in just a few decades.

However, this Vesuvius/Pelée warning sign for California is still frequently misinterpreted. The reading clearly warns that *within* three months the inundations by earthquakes will have occurred. It does *not* say, as many have misquoted, that once Mt. Vesuvius or Mt. Pelée erupts in a major way, then California residents have a three-month safety or grace period in which to sell their houses and get out!

The final sentence of reading 270-35, A-20, raises another interesting point. Earlier predictions indicated that the earth changes would be a world phenomenon—not just something confined to America. It then mentioned great upheavals in the southern hemisphere. This is a significant line because of the way in which some people have misunderstood the prophecies. Because many more specific references to catastrophic changes point to America than to other countries, some people believe that

Cayce predicted America would be hardest hit. Others have gone so far as to believe that Cayce implicitly suggested that America is especially deserving of punishment; therefore, if she receives a disproportionate share of the global earth changes, it would be only just.

However, that last sentence from reading 270-35 puts this argument to rest. In fact, there is a more plausible and very simplistic reason that the majority of Cayce's predictions were for changes occurring in America. The people receiving the readings were most often Americans and were naturally most concerned about their own part of the world. People from Alabama worried about what would happen to Alabama; people from San Francisco, about their own home town. Cayce generally met people at the level of their own concerns, so naturally we have a majority of predictions about earthquakes and flooding in America. But this frequency should not give us a distorted view of Cayce's vision of the global quality of these changes.

In fact, the most international of the prophecies was given in 1934—in one of the world affairs readings. The first paragraph is an inspirational prologue in which Cayce asserted the spiritual significance of the predicted changes. It seemed to suggest strongly that in 1936 the Christ might be expected to reappear.

As to the material changes that are to be as an omen, as a sign to those that this is shortly to come to pass—as has been given of old, the sun will be darkened and the earth shall be broken up in divers places—and *then* shall be *proclaimed*—through the spiritual interception in the hearts and minds and souls of those that have sought His way—that *His* star has appeared, and will point the way for those that enter into the holy of holies in themselves. For, God the Father, God the teacher, God the director, in the minds and hearts of men, must ever be *in* those that come to know Him as first and foremost in the seeking of those souls; for He is first the *God* to the individual and as He is exemplified, as He is manifested in the heart and in the acts of the body, of the individual, He becomes manifested before men. And those that seek in the latter portion of the year of our Lord (as ye have counted in and among men) '36, He will appear!

3976-15, January 19, 1934

Then follows a long passage of specific prophecies. This is perhaps the most often-quoted portion among all the predictions.

It seems very clear in this case that Cayce was *not* speaking of what might happen in 1936. A forty-year range of time between 1958 and 1998 was identified for the *beginning* of the changes he listed. This point has often been missed in articles and books about Cayce's prophecies. The readings do not say that all of the changes will be accomplished by 1998. Rather that the forty-year span ending in 1998 is a period of the beginning of major global upheavals. We might well expect them to continue into the 21st century.

As to the changes physical again: The earth will be broken up in the western portion of America. The greater portion of Japan must go into the sea. The upper portion of Europe will be changed as in the twinkling of an eye. Land will appear off the east coast of America. There will be the upheavals in the Arctic and in the Antarctic that will make for the eruption of volcanoes in the Torrid areas, and there will be the shifting then of the poles—so that where there has been those of a frigid or the semi-tropical will become the more tropical, and moss and fern will grow. And these will begin in those periods in '58 to '98, when these will be proclaimed as the periods when His light will be seen again in the clouds. As to times, as to seasons, as to places, *alone* is it given to those who have named the name—and who bear the mark of those of His calling and His election in their bodies. To them it shall be given.   3976-15, January 19, 1934

Unfortunately for those who desire to have credence in Cayce's ability to predict geological changes, he continued in the same reading and gave another series of *mistaken* prophecies. The passage quoted below is disconcerting for two reasons. First, it is unsettling to see how wrong Cayce could be in trying to predict what would happen within that very year. The date of the reading is January 19, 1934, and the first question of the reading concerns what is to be expected for 1934. It is obvious in retrospect that virtually none of his statements came true. Perhaps something happened during 1934 that profoundly altered the whole scenario. There was a reference to "one risen to power in central Europe," which some people have speculated to mean Hitler. Clearly Hitler did not come "to naught" that year, so perhaps the other earth changes predictions were also tied to some cosmic plan that changed during 1934. We can only guess at what might have created this apparent mistake.

However, what is equally disconcerting about the following passage is the way in which it is often quoted out of context. If one quotes only the answer and not the accompanying question, then it can seem to be a statement about the period of time from 1934 until 1998. But this is not an honest report of what the reading said. We can *speculate* that predictions for 1934 which did not come true may be off only in timing and are yet to be fulfilled. However, a responsible reporting of Cayce's work will make us want to admit to this assumption. This final, relevant paragraph of reading 3976-15 is as follows:

Q-1. What are the world changes to come this year physically?
A-1. The earth will be broken up in many places. The early portion will see a change in the physical aspect of the west coast of America. There will be open waters appear in the northern portions of Greenland. There will be new lands seen off the Caribbean Sea, and *dry* land will appear. There will be the falling away in India of much of the material suffering that has been brought on a troubled people. There will be the reduction of one risen to power in central Europe to naught. The young king son will soon reign. In America in the political forces we see a restabilization of the powers of the peoples in their own hands, a breaking up of the rings, the cliques in many places. South America shall be shaken from the uppermost portion to the end, and in the Antarctic off of Tierra Del Fuego *land,* and a strait with rushing waters. **3976-15, January 19, 1934**

In 1936 a unique contribution was made to the earth changes predictions; it came through a dream of Edgar Cayce. On a train returning to Virginia Beach from Detroit, Cayce dreamed about being born again in the future. This dream came at an important point in his life: He was deeply discouraged about his own work, having lost the Cayce Hospital in the Depression and having just spent a night in jail in Detroit on the charge of practicing medicine without a license.

"I had been born again in 2100 A.D. in Nebraska. The sea apparently covered all of the western part of the country, as the city where I lived was on the coast. The family name was a strange one. At an early age as a child I declared myself to be Edgar Cayce who had lived 200 years before.

"Scientists, men with long beards, little hair, and thick glasses, were called in to observe me. They decided to visit the places where I said I had been born, lived and worked, in Kentucky, Alabama, New York, Michigan, and Virginia. Taking me with them the group of scientists visited these places in a long, cigar-shaped, metal flying ship which moved at high speed.

"Water covered part of Alabama. Norfolk, Virginia, had become an immense seaport. New York had been destroyed either by war or an earthquake and was being rebuilt. Industries were scattered over the countryside. Most of the houses were of glass.

"Many records of my work as Edgar Cayce were discovered and collected. The group returned to Nebraska taking the records with them to study." 294-185, June 30, 1936

A reading was taken to interpret the dream. In essence it said this dream had come to encourage him about his work ("in which there may be help, strength, for periods when doubt or fear may have arisen"). However, the reading goes on to suggest that there may also be a more literal and precognitive interpretation as well.

This then is the interpretation. As has been given, "Fear not." Keep the faith; for those that be with thee are greater than those that would hinder. Though the very heavens fall, though the earth shall be changed, though the heavens shall pass, the promises in Him are sure and will stand—as in that day—as the proof of thy activity in the lives and hearts of those of thy fellow man. . .

That is the interpretation. That the periods from the material angle as visioned are to come to pass matters not to the soul, but do thy duty *today*! *Tomorrow* will care for itself.

These changes in the earth will come to pass, for the time and times and half times are at an end, and there begin those periods for the readjustments. For how hath He given? "The righteous shall inherit the earth."

Hast thou, my brethren, a heritage in the earth? 294-185

How are we to understand a prophecy of the Pacific Ocean reaching as far inland as Nebraska by the year 2100? As improbable as this may sound, it is difficult to rule out anything if the poles of the planet are to shift, as Cayce also predicted. Unimaginable changes could occur under such conditions. At present, many geologists are willing to go along with Cayce's predictions, such as California's and Japan's vulnerability to severe earthquakes. These regions are well known to be earthquake-prone. However, it would require very unexpected changes in the geological patterns of North America for the Rocky Mountains to sink far enough to make Nebraska a west coast state! Nevertheless, if Cayce is right, the event that could trigger such changes is scheduled for the year 2000 or 2001.

Q-9. What great change or the beginning of what change, if any, is to take place in the earth in the year 2000 to 2001 A.D.?
A-9. When there is a shifting of the poles. Or a new cycle begins.
826-8, August 11, 1936

A final thought about Cayce's dream concerns the nature of dreaming itself. It is a well-recorded observation among dream interpretation theorists that dreams often overstate a point to get across a message—they amplify the message. For example, if you need to drink a *little more* water each day, you may instead dream of swimming in an *ocean* of water. If you are soon to receive a small but unexpected check in the mail, you may dream pre-cognitively of striking a silver mine. We might then wonder if Cayce's dream is an example of amplification. Might the message be, "The geography of our nation is going to be altered in the coming 164 years"? Perhaps the dream is overstating the point in order to convey the dramatic quality of the changes which *will* occur. We can only speculate, but it seems to be worthwhile to examine all possible meanings of this unusual prediction for the year 2100.

Two final readings are especially significant; both were given in the later years of Cayce's work. The first, given in 1939 and mentioned in the first chapter, contains an important phrase concerning the intensity of the changes. For the most part, the picture we have gotten from the readings up to this date has been one of impending cataclysm. In contrast to this view, at least this one reading presented the picture of a world that will *gradually* alter. Certainly this is a much more hopeful perspective for anyone who wishes to maintain a continuity between the old world and the emerging new one. Rather than an apocalyptic transition from the Piscean age to the Aquarian age, prospects of a more gradual change exist—even if it is dramatic in scope.

Q-1. Three hundred years ago Jacob Boehme decreed Atlantis would rise again at this crisis time when we cross from this Piscean era into the Aquarian. Is Atlantis rising now? Will it cause a sudden convolution and about what year?

A-1. In 1998 we may find a great deal of the activities as have been wrought by the gradual changes that are coming about. These are at the periods when the cycle of the solar activity, or the years as related to the sun's passage through the various spheres of activity become paramount. . .to the change between the Piscean and the Aquarian age. This is a gradual, not a cataclysmic activity in the experience of the earth in this period.

1602-3, September 22, 1939

The last important earth changes reference came in 1941 to a woman in her mid-60s. Very detailed descriptions were presented of the future map of America. Again Cayce's timing seems to be off, because there were phrases (such as, "in the next few years") to suggest that many of these changes would have happened by now. However, some interesting points were made concerning timing. For example, the destruction of New York City was indicated for a later generation, with the severe earthquakes of California foreseen as coming sooner.

As to conditions in the geography of the world, of the country—changes here are gradually coming about.

No wonder, then, that the entity feels the need, the necessity for change of central location. For, many portions of the east coast will be disturbed, as well as many portions of the west coast, as well as the central portion of the U.S.

In the next few years lands will appear in the Atlantic as well as in the Pacific. And what is the coast line now of many a land will be the bed of the ocean. Even many of the battlefields of the present will be ocean, will be the seas, the bays, the lands over which the *new* order will carry on their trade as one with another.

Portions of the now east coast of New York, or New York City itself, will in the main disappear. This will be another generation, though, here; while the southern portions of Carolina, Georgia—these will disappear. This will be much sooner.

The waters of the lakes will empty into the Gulf, rather than the waterway over which such discussions have been recently made. It would be well if the waterway were prepared, but not for that purpose for which it is at present being considered.

Then the area where the entity is now located [Virginia Beach for reading] will be among the safety lands, as will be portions of what is now Ohio, Indiana and Illinois, and much of the southern portion of Canada and the eastern portion of Canada; while the western land—much of that is to be disturbed—in this land—as, of course, much in other lands. . .

Q-2. I have for many months felt that I should move away from New York City.

A-2. This is well, as indicated. There is too much unrest; there will continue to be the character of vibrations that to the body will be disturbing, and eventually those destructive forces there— though these will be in the next generation.

Q-3. Will Los Angeles be safe?

A-3. Los Angeles, San Francisco, most all of these will be among those that will be destroyed before New York even.

Q-4. Should California or Virginia Beach be considered at all, or where is the right place that God has already provided for me to live?

A-4. As indicated, these choices should be made rather in self. Virginia Beach or the area is much safer as a definite place. But the work of the entity should embrace most all of the areas from the east to the west coast, in its persuading—not as a preacher, nor as one bringing a message of doom, but as a loving warning to all groups, clubs, woman's clubs, writer's clubs, art groups, those of every form of club, that there needs be—in their activities— definite work towards the knowledge of the power of the Son of God's activity in the affairs of men.

Q-19. Is Virginia Beach to be safe?

A-19. It is the center—and the only seaport and center—of the White Brotherhood.   1152-11, August 13, 1941

The notion of "safety lands" found in this reading is a provocative one. Did Cayce say that only the areas specifically mentioned in this reading were safe from earth changes? If so, shouldn't anyone who seriously believes these readings move to one of those locations?

But surely that is not what he meant. First of all, it is inconceivable that any area in our country would be unaffected if the predicted changes do happen. Even if that effect is not geological, it will surely be felt in terms of food, energy or, most importantly, the emotional ties we have with others.

There is *no* place to go to sit out the changes. Our nation has grown to the point where we are one, interdependent people. The very resources with which we live our lives have come to us through a complex exchange in relationships among people across this country. If one aspect of the whole is interrupted—by earthquake or whatever—it will be felt through the nation.

The same principle now exists in the world as a whole. We are a world community. The old philosophy of isolationism is no longer an alternative for any country. When something which disturbs the balance occurs in even remote parts of the globe, it is usually felt within days throughout the world. Perhaps one of the hidden blessings of the oil import crisis of the '70s and '80s for Europe and North America is the chance to realize how much of a world community we have become.

And so, where does this principle of an interrelated world leave us in terms of so-called "safety lands"? It makes us look carefully at our definition of "safety." What could Cayce himself have meant by that word? On the one hand, he may have been trying to identify actual areas of the continent where there would be little or no flooding or shaking. And yet one wonders how any spot could be entirely "safe" in this sense of the word. Even Cayce's home, Virginia Beach, seems very vulnerable, even though it was mentioned several times as a safety place. If the prophecies prove to be right—if, for example, land rises off the east coast of America—logic suggests that these upheavals would at least splash a little sea water up over the narrow sand dune that stands between Virginia Beach and the Atlantic Ocean.

However, it may well be that the readings were sensitive to geological realities that would make some of the central states of America and parts of southeastern Canada safe from earth changes. Perhaps Virginia Beach will be geologically rising so as not to be inundated.

Nevertheless, we should look at other meanings to the phrase "safety lands." It would be inconsistent with other Cayce readings to think that a soul is safe just because physical harm is unlikely. The entire thrust of the philosophy of the readings is that real security is an inward thing. We are truly safe when we are right with God, when we are living in accordance with the spiritual ideal we have set. For example, in 1942 one person asked in a reading if he was safe in his home town in New York—safe from bombing or enemy attack. Cayce's answer: "Why should he not? if he lives right!" (257-239, January 15, 1942)

What is needed is another hypothesis concerning the meaning

of Cayce's "safety lands" concept. Not a theory which contradicts the possible literal interpretation, but instead a complementary one which suggests multiple levels of meaning of that concept. A promising approach is that cities, regions or even states can create, by the attitudes and actions of their people, a kind of group consciousness and aura which gives a location a particular vibration. That vibration, if it is one of spiritual attunement, can afford to its people a sort of protection. This protection may be from outside threats or even disturbances of the earth—but more importantly it affords a protection for the individual from those parts of himself or herself which would lead to fear and doubt in times of testing.

This notion of group vibration for a location is found in at least one reading which says: "Each state, country, or town makes its own vibrations by or through the activities of those that comprise same; hence creates for itself a realm in which the activities of each city, town, state. . .may be in the realm of those forces where the activities bring the associations through relativity of influence in the material plane." (262-66, July 11, 1934)

Perhaps in the 1941 reading, 1152-11, Cayce was identifying those areas of the country which especially had large numbers of people who were creating a vibration or aura of attunement. However, that was in 1941. It is hoped that since that time many more areas of America and of the world have developed to the status of safety lands. Even though some of these places may some day be physically shaken—even though every one of them will feel the effects in *some* way if the earth changes take place— they may, nevertheless, be places of special opportunity and of psychological and spiritual safety in times of change. What is exciting is that we do not have to move to one of those existing "safe" locations. We can each work to build that status for the community in which we already live.

World Affairs Prophecies

An important and interesting appendix to the earth changes readings are those given by Cayce on the political, spiritual and economic futures of nations. The so-called "world affairs readings" most often focused on questions of Cayce's own day— the Depression and the developing tensions which led to World War II. However, occasional statements were made that attempted to look beyond the War and predicted the course which nations would take well into the 21st century.

The essential ingredient in these predictions is the need which Cayce saw for a "leveling" in the world. In calling for equality he was not associating himself with any particular political system. Rather his political philosophy, as well as his vision of the direction in which the world must head, was toward the oneness of humanity. That "leveling," as the readings called it, is a process that pertains to both judgment as well as resources. All persons must be seen as equals in the way they are measured or judged. All persons must have an equal opportunity to share in the resources which sustain life. This means not only food, shelter, clothing and energy; but also the resources of knowledge, appreciation and love which sustain the mind and soul. A reading given just before the outbreak of World War II stated:

It is also understood, comprehended by some, that a new order of conditions is to arise; that there must be many a purging in high places as well as low; that there must be the greater consideration of each individual, each soul being his brother's keeper.

There will then come those circumstances in the political, the economic and the whole relationships where there will be a leveling—or a greater comprehension of this need.

For as the time or the period draws near for those changes that come with the new order, it behooves all of those who have an ideal—as individuals, as well as groups or societies or organizations, to be practicing, applying same in their experience—and their relationships as one to another.

For unless these are up and doing, then there must indeed be a new order in *their* relationships and their activities. . .

And there *cannot* be one measuring stick for the laborer in the field and the man behind the counter, and another for the man behind the money changers! *All* are equal—not only under the material law but under the *spiritual.*

And *His* laws, *His* will, will not come to naught!

Though there may come those periods when there will be great stress, as brother rises against brother, as group or sect or race rises against race—yet the leveling must come.

And *only* those who have set their ideal in Him and practiced it in their dealings with their fellow man may expect to survive the wrath of the Lord.   3976-18, June 20, 1938

This is certainly a lofty ideal and one that may take decades or longer to work out. In one passage the readings made clear that all this task of leveling was not a call for communism, even in the pure sense of the word. This was expressed as, "Not that all would be had in common as in the communistic idea, save as to keep that balance, to keep that oneness. . ." (3976-19, June 24, 1938) On the other hand, the readings seem to have been even more strongly against the notion of survival of the fittest (or of the greatest and most powerful) which has characterized pure capitalism. It will not do for us to sit back and say that those people of the world who are exploited are simply not motivated enough. Nor will it do to slip into a distorted notion of karmic responsibility and claim that the disadvantaged of the world are merely meeting their own karma. Cayce's vision of the world affairs of the future was that peace can come only when the ideal of "I am my brother's keeper" has been adopted. How will that come about? What changes will we have to see in specific nations if that purpose and ideal is ever to be achieved? The theory of the readings was that the problem lies in a particular tendency of all nations to "set some standard of some activity of man as its idea." (3976-29, June 22, 1944) In other words, nations have different concepts about how human life should be evaluated, different ideas about what constitutes the good life, about what constitutes justice, what scope of authority a government should have over individuals. And the efforts of nations to impose their own standards on other nations create international tensions and wars. For each major nation Cayce saw a work or a change to be done.

In the case of Russia, Cayce foresaw a tremendous transition possible. He warned that there would never be peace in that country until there was freedom of speech. He predicted a reawakened religious spirit in Russia, which if developed would be the hope of the world; and he clearly predicted a major role in world leadership for this nation as well.

Q-5. [Comment on] the Russian situation.
A-5. As we have indicated, here a new understanding has and will come to a troubled people. Here, because of the yoke of oppression, because of the self-indulgences, has arisen another extreme. Only when there is freedom of speech, the right to

worship according to the dictates of the conscience—until these
come about, still turmoils will be within.

3976-19, June 24, 1938

*Q-6. What should be the attitude of so-called capitalist
nations toward Russia?*

A-6. On Russia's religious development will come the greater
hope of the world. Then that one, or group, that is the closer in its
relationships may fare the better in the gradual changes and final
settlement of conditions as to the rule of the world.

3976-10, February 8, 1932

**In Russia there comes the hope of the world, not as that
sometimes termed of the Communistic, of the Bolshevistic; no.
But freedom, freedom! that each man will live for his fellow man!
The principle has been born. It will take years for it to be
crystalized, but out of Russia comes again the hope of the world.
Guided by what? That friendship with the nation that hath even
set on its present monetary unit "In God We Trust."**

3976-29, June 22, 1944

The third excerpt is especially interesting. What could Cayce
have meant by "The principle has been born"? Could it be that in
1944 when this reading was given that a group of souls had just
incarnated into Russia with a purpose to turn that nation around—
to make it a champion for peace and permit a religious rebirth
within its borders? If so, it would take years for this possibility to be
crystalized. If those souls were born in 1940 or thereabouts, it is
unlikely that they would be in a position to exert much influence on
the decision-making process of the government until they were at
least 50 years old, since that nation is currently characterized by
aged leadership. So it would be 1990 or later before such an effect
might materialize. This is, of course, only one interpretation of this
Cayce passage. And even if it is what he meant, we are left to
wonder if those souls have remembered the purpose for which
they came or perhaps they have become caught up in the ideals
and purposes of the old system.

In the case of America, Cayce had some strong words of
warning, but words of promise as well. Again the notion of a
leveling came up. There is a warning that unless creative, loving
steps are taken to insure greater equality within this nation, there

will come a revolution. In Cayce's predictions this revolution will be one of physical, armed struggle, because this is the means that some people will resort to when they feel helpless to effect change in any other way. There was not an endorsement of such methods in the readings—only a warning that they may be just ahead for us.

The readings on America emphasize freedom. The ideal of freedom is one to be admired, but the readings seem to have questioned just how honestly America lives that ideal. There was an accusation that our nation was being run in such a fashion that the hearts and minds of many people were bound. Is this still the case?

What is the spirit of America? Most individuals proudly boast "freedom." Freedom of what? When ye bind men's hearts and minds through various ways and manners, does it give them freedom of speech? Freedom of worship? Freedom from want?
3976-29, June 2, 1944

Pursuing this concept of freedom further, another reading identified the great fear of Americans: servitude in any form. We are afraid of losing our freedom, and yet we may have distorted what that very word means. We have made the quality of obedience a sign of weakness and in so doing have undermined the spirituality of our people. Our actions cannot fulfill the challenge and opportunity of spiritual leadership in the world if we have a self-serving definition of freedom. True freedom comes from the desire and ability to be obedient—not to another nation—but to God. That nation that would be greatest—and most free—must be servants to all.

Unless this is done, turmoils and strifes will arise. And that which has made and does make the people of America afraid, is the fear of servitude in *any manner!*
All, though, must learn that those who *are* to be the greater, those who would make the greater contributions to activity in every sphere and phase of influence, are to be the servants of all; not those who would be lords over others.
3976-19, June 24, 1938

This is a hard principle for our nation, or for any nation, to understand and to live. Misunderstanding it, we slip into what Cayce called the great sin of America: pride. It is this quality which could stand between America and its spiritual destiny to provide leadership for the world. It is pride, not just on the part of the government, but in the people as individuals, that needs to be overcome. Our tendency to boast separates us from other nations and people of this world.

Once Cayce was asked very directly about America's spiritual destiny. His answer first suggested that every nation has a specific spiritual destiny—that each one is led by forces from the heavens. More specifically, America can fulfill her destiny only by adopting greater brotherhood and love of others. Otherwise the leadership of the world will once again move westward. And from other readings we can ascertain that that westward movement would be to the Orient. The key will be what *individuals* do with the spiritual knowledge they have. It is not so much the choices of government officials or the legislative bills passed by Congress that determine whether or not we will fulfill our national challenge. It is what each of us does as individuals which will collectively create our future.

Q-3. Is America fulfilling her destiny?
A-3. . . .each and every nation, is led—even as in heaven. . .If there is not the acceptance in America of the closer brotherhood of man, the love of the neighbor as self, civilization must wend its way westward. . .

Is it filling its destiny?. . .What have ye done with the knowledge that ye have respecting the relationships of thy Creator to thy fellow man?. . .   3976-15, January 19, 1934

Perhaps the beneficiary of a movement of civilization westward would be China. This mysterious nation has only in the past few years made efforts to become part of the world community once again. Its resources and people are vast. Its spiritual heritage is matched by no other major nation except India. It is exciting to imagine what good could be done by these people if their national ideal and purpose became unity and spirituality. It was just such a vision that Cayce put forth in the world affairs prophecies. However, no time frame accompanies this prediction beyond the caution that "it is far off as man counts time. . ."

[China] will be one day the cradle of Christianity, as applied in the lives of men. Yea, it is far off as man counts time, but only a day in the heart of God—for tomorrow China will awake.
                                  3976-29, June 22, 1944

Are we then to expect that someday there will be a Baptist Church of Shanghai or a Methodist Church of Peking? Not necessarily. The key phrase in the prediction is "Christianity, *as applied* in the lives of men." Perhaps it is in this country that the way of living with each other which Jesus proposed will find a willing climate. Whether or not the Chinese accept Jesus is secondary *to this prophecy.* Here is a nation, in Cayce's estimation, which may be especially ripe for the application of Christ's teachings. In doing so, they would truly assume the spiritual leadership of civilization on this planet. But, as the prophecy says, this may be many years away. We have our own work to do now toward that same ideal.

Finally, it should be noted that amongst all the world affairs predictions of revolution, turmoil, changes of government and so forth is a word of profound encouragement. It is so easy for us to be discouraged by current events and to dwell upon the great confusion which has been created among the nations. However, Cayce may have been able to look at the world from a broader perspective. In that remarkable state from which he gave readings, he may have been able to see the unfoldment of history in terms of ages and not just the decades and centuries which we see. And from this vantage point, he said that there is hope. In his own time Cayce stated that he could see a tremendous seeking in our world. Remarkable numbers of people were desiring oneness with God and an understanding of God's purposes. The seeking was greater than it had been for *ages!* And we can well imagine that this is increasing each year, giving us good reason to be hopeful.

Interpreting the Earth Changes Predictions

How are we to understand these predictions about earth changes and geopolitical changes? How do we cope with the measure of uncertainty and anxiety they are likely to instill in almost anyone who reads them? The best answer probably lies in a careful look at what the prophecies really are.

The *essence* of Cayce's prophecies was not earthquakes or tidal waves or volcanic eruptions, not cities destroyed or the changing coastlines of the earth's continents. Instead it was the vision that a new world is being born. It is a world that is so different than what has been experienced for a long time on this planet that some kind of a transitional experience is required. The old patterns of living, the old ways of thinking, are so contrary to what the new must be that it is no small step for humankind. There needs to be some rite of passage.

However, options exist in transitional scenarios: There are several ways to get from where we have been to where we need to be. All that a psychic or prophet can do is to *read the momentum of the present day*. All that Cayce could do was to say, in effect, that there were trends and likelihoods on the pathway which humanity would choose in the transition. And in 1932, 1936 and 1941 Cayce kept seeing the same probability. The inertia of our choices seemed to be taking us on a pathway leading to tremendous earth changes.

But the question remains, "Have we stayed on that course since Cayce stopped giving readings?" We can only look at our world and guess. The signs do not look very promising. Humanity continues to pollute the earth and to detonate atomic weapons underground. Surely these are the kinds of things which alienate us from the earth—from the mother aspect of God. A symbolic way of viewing earth changes, if they literally do happen, is that the earth will shake us to our senses. We will be forced into a new humility and a respect for the forces of nature. We will have to re-examine what we have been doing to the earth and, by consequence, what we have been doing to each other.

However, all of that is only one pathway. Remember the vision. Remember what the prophecy really is: a spiritual rebirth on this planet. A global family. An era of peace and cooperation. And there are many paths to get there. Some of those ways are more catastrophic than earth changes would ever be, such as nuclear war which would finally force us to build a world of peace. Others are more "graceful" (that is, full of God's grace). Not that they would be without their pain, because certain things must be surrendered, and there is always discomfort and pain in letting go of old possessions and self-images.

The choice is still with us to select a transitional scenario full of grace. Our primary concern about times of change should be to find such a pathway. We should not be as concerned about whether people believe the Cayce prophecies of earth changes as we are with how people can begin to live with a new age consciousness. If sufficient numbers of us will live *now* the vision of what the world and humanity are to become, then it is quite likely that our collective rite of passage can be survived by most all of humanity.

What are the alternatives to such a hopeful and promising view? One is skepticism and doubt, which asserts that the world is going down the drain. People who hold this attitude are becoming the survivalists. Whereas the 1970s were characterized as the "Me Decade" and the "Era of Self-Improvement," the 1980s are being called the "Survivalist Decade" and the "Era of Impending Apocalypse."

Another alternative is to hold fast to the prospects of earthquakes and other natural cataclysms. This is probably one step better than the pessimistic survivalist outlook. It usually retains the hopefulness that after it is all over, *then* we will see a spiritual, new age begin. But this approach is terribly naive and sometimes blatantly lazy. We must be deeply honest with ourselves. What possible reason is there to believe that earth changes will *cause* a new age to begin? What excuse do we have to sit back and wait for Cayce's earthquake predictions to come true, expecting a new world order to magically emerge when all the shaking is over? There is no reason. There is no excuse.

If earth changes happen, they will not of themselves create a new age. What they *will* do is to upset the old order. What they *will* do is to force the survivors to look for a different way of living on this planet Earth. In fact, all that the earth changes can do is to create an *opportune moment in history.*

If the earth and humanity go the way of earthquakes to make the transition, the question remains, "Will we be ready to seize that opportune moment and create within it?" If our answer is "Yes," then the work begins now. Only those who are prepared today to start living a new age consciousness—even if it is in small modules—will really be willing and able to do it when the big moment arrives. As one Cayce reading suggested, those who say they would contribute money if they were millionaires and do not give a little of what they do have, would not really give even if they had a million dollars. Likewise, we are kidding ourselves if we say that we would try living with a new faith and a new cooperative spirit, if only earthquakes would shake up things and rid us of the old world. We probably would not do it after the earth changes either.

Not only can we use the prospect of earth changes as an excuse to keep us from changing our lives right now, but we can also become fascinated with the idea of them. There is something incredibly awesome about the power of nature in an earthquake or

54

volcano. There is a spectator in us, conditioned by television to expect to see more and more incredible views, yet with the detachment and safety provided by the television in our living rooms. Many people want to see the earth changes happen. They are fascinated by the idea of it all. It is not that these people are cruel. They have merely forgotten. They are numbed by disaster movies. They forget that real lives are involved, including their own.

Others of us do not so much want these things to happen but have become psychologically hooked on the idea. Our very thinking process may not say, "*If* the earth changes happen. . ." it says, "*When* they happen. . ." And with the mind's creative power, such thinking probably makes the occurrence more likely. We all know how self-fulfilling prophecy works.

A story from the life of Edgar Cayce and those around him illustrates this point. Before America had entered World War II, Cayce told a group of people in a reading that they could have an impact on the course of events. He said that America would not be invaded if all in the group gathered in the room that day would begin to pray and live their lives in a spiritually attuned way. That was certainly a powerful promise, but one which apparently was not fulfilled. Within two years Pearl Harbor was attacked.

Yet, what is most interesting about this story is the report of one person who was present that day and recalls the discussion among the group when the reading ended. Instead of talking among themselves about when and how they should pray and live, the group members wondered aloud, "Where do you think the attack will come?"

We can look back upon that group and wish that each had looked more to the promise than just the warning. But aren't we now faced with a similar opportunity? There are still many transitional paths to a new age. Perhaps the likely path which Cayce foresaw our world heading toward has now been delayed. It seems apparent that few, if any, of the major earth changes he predicted have happened—and we are well beyond the halfway point in the 1958-1998 time period. But if a delay has occurred, it is a blessing. Each year more and more of humanity is coming to understand the spiritual laws by which life operates and is coming to realize the creative options we have in moving in to a new world order. In the remaining chapters of this book we will explore just how we might build cooperatively and harmoniously the kind of spiritually reborn planet which Cayce and others have foreseen.

Chapter 4

Understanding the Inner Earth Changes

When earthquakes, volcanoes or tidal waves appear in our dreams, they are usually appropriate symbols of inner upheavals. In times of personal stress, these kinds of images are likely to emerge from the unconscious. Although the prophecies in the Cayce readings concern outward, physical changes, we can well expect inner earthquakes when the old ways of perceiving life break up so that new forms may surface. It may well be that for many of us the inner earth changes will be more difficult to deal with than any outer, geographic changes which may occur.

In fact, for most of us, the inner changes have already begun. The geological transitions which Cayce foresaw may have been delayed, but the more personal kind of testing is already upon us. The inner changes are not always traumatic or catastrophic. Sometimes they are more subtle in their expression, but potent in their impact.

One characteristic of the inner earth changes with which many people are struggling is a sense of frustration, in not feeling purposefulness in their lives. Ironically it is *not* always the person who is ignorant of esoteric teachings who experiences this phenomenon. We might expect that people who have no understanding of spiritual evolution and the special meaning of these times would be good candidates for such feelings. However, they are joined from time to time by many of us who have read about and understood for years that in these times there will be a necessary breaking up of the old ways. But simply having that knowledge does not make us immune from experiencing the effects. Even though a part of our minds is objective about these changing events and are "on top of things," still another part of our minds is very much involved in the old world. This is the part that must go through the dying process, and feelings of fatigue and lack of direction as this takes place are natural. We need not feel guilty for those days when we are caught up in our own inner earth changes.

Not only do many of us feel a lack of energy as old patterns are dying, but also a lack of enthusiasm frequently exists. We may go through periods when the desire is just not there to do what we have long thought was good for us. This may surface as a dry spell with our meditation life, it may be a period of having no interest in our dreams, or it may be a general lack of caring and enthusiasm for healing a problem relationship.

For other people a nagging sort of anxiety sets in when the inner earth changes begin. They start to worry that they never again will feel a sense of purposefulness in life which they once had. This can often be due to the frustrations of no longer being able to make reliable plans for the future. In a society that is changing as fast as ours, what can we depend on? Not interest rates, not prices. Not our political leaders nor our physical environment. Next week there may be an earthquake in our back yards or we may discover that our community's water supply is polluted with industrial waste. We can fall into worrying, "What will come next?" We can become numbed by all the changes. We can become frustrated to see the many people, institutions and conditions which were once so stable now appear so unreliable. In the midst of this, who can really plan for the future? And without a future to work toward, how can one have a sense of purposefulness in life?

Many people follow that line of reasoning. Recently a series of public opinion polls in America revealed a startling new situation. A majority of people no longer feel that the lives of their children will be better than their own have been. This reveals a dramatic change in the attitudes and spirit of America. It suggests that the inner earth changes are undermining the morale of this nation. People in great numbers are anxious, pessimistic and unenthusiastic about their own lives and the future.

However, this is not the only line of reasoning available to us as we observe our society shifting so rapidly that it is hard to find any steady points of reference. Periods of confusion, fatigue and anxiety are natural. Most likely all of us will experience this to some degree as we pass through inner changes. But such feelings need not become a way of life or a permanent state of consciousness. In this chapter we will be exploring some of the alternatives.

And so, we have identified one broad category of how people are experiencing the inner earth changes. A second area should also be noted because it probably plays an equally significant role in the struggles we all face. In order to understand it, we must see that we are each being tested in these times by the Creative Forces of the universe. In this case, the "testing" is not so much an exam that we might fail and then be expelled from school. Instead, it is a kind of testing which comes for our own benefit—to strengthen us. It is a testing which will force us to make changes in ourselves—so that we are more likely to be able psychologically and spiritually to cope with life in a new age.

This may seem an unusual notion to many people. You may wonder, "How could anyone have trouble coping with life in a new age? If everything is to be cooperation, love and peace, then that sounds like a pretty nice and easy world to live in!" However, such thinking about a new age is probably too simplistic. In fact, some of us would find it occasionally difficult to live in a world that was all cooperation. Perhaps there are some things about life that we value above cooperation. Others of us might find it hard to live in a world which holds peace as an ideal. Perhaps some issues or desires within us simply have a higher priority than being at peace with others.

This is why we are being "tested" now. For each of us there already is—or soon will come—a test. In some part of our lives we are especially being made to feel uncomfortable, to feel pinched. It may be in a particular kind of interpersonal relationship. For some it may lie in finances. For others, it will be a desire pattern of body or mind which needs to be curtailed. But whatever it is, there is one thing we have in common during this testing: the pressure is on what we have most directly placed between ourselves and God. The test is a challenge to *change our relationship to* God by changing a desire pattern, a worry, an attachment to a person or whatever.

In many cases the requirement of the test is merely to *move* something, *not* necessarily *remove,* it from our lives. For example, if our test is in terms of preoccupation about money, then the challenge is to assign money a lower priority in our lives and put

God first. Having moved through the test, we might still use money in our daily affairs, but its importance in our lives would have changed. In another case, the test might be in a relationship with a person to whom we are overly attached. Perhaps what is required is a change of priorities, not necessarily removing that person totally from our presence. *The test is to discover how to put God first in our lives.* If we can do that, then we are much more likely to be psychologically and spiritually comfortable with new age values. However, the work that is required of us in order to pass through such a test—the alterations we have to make—will indeed feel like upheavals and earth changes inside of us.

The Dynamic Quality of God

In order to cope with and understand the inner earth changes which we are experiencing, we need a clearer notion of how God works in the material plane. So many spiritual teachers and writers of sacred literature have spoken of the timeless, eternal, unchanging quality of God. They might counsel us in these times when outer conditions change so rapidly to put our trust in the one thing that never changes: God's perfect spirit and love for us. Undoubtedly great comfort may be found in experiencing firsthand this characteristic of the Divine. However, if our knowledge of God never grows beyond that experience, it implies that the world of change around us has nothing to do with God. Simply understanding God to be the steady point of reference in the midst of transition and evolution misses the profoundness of what God is all about.

The nature of God is paradoxical. God can be seen as a polar tension from the point in consciousness where we are. Certainly God is a steady, reliable consciousness of love that never wavers. However, God is *also* the god of unfoldment and of evolution. God is creativity and hence the change which accompanies any creation. To depict this in a diagram we have:

God as static, timeless, unchanging ⟵ ⟶ **God as evolution, creation, change**

Dealing with this paradox is a crucial challenge for our times. As with most polarities or paradoxes, we might be tempted to embrace one side of the truth and exclude the other side. A good example of this is in religious fundamentalism (not just in Christianity). Fundamentalists have a strict notion of God's nature; it is basically a static one. Admittedly, God may cause some changes now and then (as, for example, the destruction of people or cities in Old Testament days when the laws were not being followed, or the havoc predicted in The Revelation which would precede the Second Coming). But basically, God is to be worshipped because of the unchanging reality of His existence and His laws. For example, Judaic or Christian fundamentalists would say that the Ten Commandments are just as true for today as they were the day they were given. This, plus many other examples, may in fact be true. But that is not where the problem lies. That is not the reason that religious fundamentalism fails to be the best response to the paradoxical nature of God. The problem comes if change, evolution and upheaval are automatically viewed as the work of a demon's force. The shortcoming of religious fundamentalism is to place outside of God's domain one entire aspect of the polarity which propels life.

Nevertheless, it is interesting to note one significant strong point of the fundamentalists' approach: It fosters a sense of community among people. The formation of community (in the broadest meaning of the word and not just a rural commune) usually requires some steady point of reference around which the people can gather. Religious fundamentalism asserts the static, timeless nature of God as such a point of reliability. Numerous examples exist in our society of the powerful feeling of community which has been able to coalesce around this belief. It is ironic that many new age thinkers list "spiritual community" among their dreams for new age life styles, and yet simultaneously find themselves easily being critical of the very people who are doing the best job of demonstrating it.

In the same light, inherent problems exist whenever we exclusively adopt the opposite end of the scale and claim that God is *only* the God of creation and evolution. There are times when many so-called new age thinkers seem to succumb to this temptation. But what happens if we say that God changes? What happens if we say that each generation must discover its own spiritual realities? Such a theory which eliminates continuity easily falls into the mire of relativism. Suddenly we have no point of reference. Everyone is doing his or her own thing. We may muddle the distinction between genuinely creative acts and self-indulgent habits. Claiming that *everything* is always changing leaves us with no awareness of where we are going—simply because there is nothing against which we can measure ourselves. And our ideal of new age spiritual community becomes impossible. How can we make any sort of bond or covenant with each other when the only thing we worship is changingness?

No, the answer lies at neither end of the polarity. Like all polarities the answer is the middle way—the midpoint of the continuum. Like all paradoxes, the answer lies with neither of the two seeming truths but rather with a third truth that can include both of the others. Simply put, God is a god of change, creativity and evolution. When we feel the tests and pressures of times of change, we are feeling God at work in our lives. But *everything* which is of God is not changing. There are also constant, reliable points of reference within the divine nature. It is a balancing trick for us: to be guided by the unchanging truths of spiritual law and at the same time to embrace and accept the divine nudges to evolve and to grow into something more than we have been.

An analogy will be very helpful at this point because it so clearly illustrates the difficulties which we face in maintaining that balancing act. This analogy was proposed in its essence by Lama Anagarika Govinda in his book *Creative Meditation and Multi-Dimensional Experience.*

Imagine that your self-awareness is two-dimensional. Suppose, for example, that it is just the surface area of a square. You have length and width—but not height, because you are just a surface. But suppose you are entering times of change. You are to experience things which will test you, challenge you and try to push you to grow into a higher dimensional being. Just as the current times in which we live may be trying to force us into a higher dimensional awareness to characterize a new age, so in our analogy we, as squares, are being pushed to become three-dimensional *cubes.*

(a)
initial
state
as a
two-dimensional
square

(b)
forces at work on
us in times of change

(c)
possible
new state

What do we experience when we are in this transitional point between the old and the new? We are aware of being stretched and pushed, and it comes quite naturally for us to be afraid. But afraid of what? Primarily the fear is of our own destruction. The square worries that in becoming a three-dimensional cube its original "squareness" will be destroyed. We worry that in these times of change — inner and outer— our old identities will be destroyed. The fear has good cause only if we allow ourselves to be shaped exclusively by forces of change in the old dimensions we already inhabit. The square need fear only in the case in which it exclusively allows forces of length and width to work on it. In that instance it might well be "destroyed" and changed into a triangle or a circle! In our case, we need fear only if it is exclusively the forces of the old world that we are letting shape us. However, that is not what is going on. The forces of the times of change do not generally come from the old world itself. The old world would be content to keep going on the way it has been. The forces of change come from the next dimension, trying to stretch us into a higher awareness of life. In this case the fear of self-destruction is based on a misunderstanding.

The analogy demonstrates beautifully why fear is unfounded. If change is one which truly leads to a higher-dimension kind of life, then the original state is *not destroyed* in the process but rather *built upon*. The square is not eliminated as the cube is created. Look at the cube in the illustration and see that the original square is still there. But what has happened to the square? *Its relative importance has been redefined.* Before, it was the "whole show," and now it has become only a part of a greater whole. This is what we can expect as the inner earth changes do their work on us. Our current identity is not to be destroyed, but instead put into a new perspective. We are being tested to become more than what we are now. The old will be given a new place. Many of our current likes and dislikes, many of our current habit patterns of living, must be seen in a new perspective. Their relative importance in our lives must be redefined.

A final point in this analogy should also be made, because it illustrates one of the dangers of these times of inner earth changes. Notice that numerous arrows in the illustration indicate forces trying to stretch and push the square into a cube. However, not all the arrows are directly vertical—not all are perpendicular to the surface of the square. Depending on which of the forces are allowed to shape the square into a higher-dimensional creation, different shapes can be the result. For example:

The cube is obviously the more stable of these three-dimensional objects. In our analogy it is like the higher-dimensional mind which has been directed by the Christ ideal. The other three-dimensional objects have been shaped by forces and influences that are slanted and not exactly consistent with that ideal of love and cooperation.

In other words, there may come opportunities for us to be stretched into higher-dimensional awareness but in ways which are not really in keeping with our best spiritual evolution. Not everything of a higher dimension is necessarily closer to attunement with God. (This is a mistake sometimes made by spiritualists, who feel that anything coming from a deceased person in the next higher dimension is necessarily accurate and spiritually wise.) *If* we move into a higher-dimensional awareness of ourselves along the path of the Christ ideal, then our experience of God will be fuller and richer. But there is also the option to move to higher-dimensional awareness and have a more complex and profound experience of fear or confusion. So-called "bad trips" on hallucinogenic drugs are good examples of this.

And so, during these times of inner earth changes, what should we beware of? What are those influences that might stretch us into a higher-dimensional awareness but take us no closer to God nor to our own spiritual purposes? Mind-altering drugs have already been mentioned as one example. Another is the use of psychic perception—a latent talent which we all have—in a way that only serves selfish ends. It is very likely that in the coming decades there will be a more general understanding in our society of the mind's power to effect physical change. But toward what end, what purpose? When we are feeling pinched or tested by inner changes, the temptation may be to use mental, psychic powers selfishly to avoid the changes we need to make. In doing so, we might well create for ourselves an identity that was of a higher dimension but not "upright"—not shaped to experience best what a new age will be all about.

A Model for Understanding Inner Changes

One way to characterize the nature of inner earth changes is the notion of a "gestalt," from a type of perceptual psychology formulated in Germany (gestalt psychology). Many people who work with their dreams are familiar with a technique from gestalt *therapy* (a psychotherapeutic technique based on gestalt psychology). It involves the role-playing of specific symbols in one's dreams.

However, the problem which gestalt psychology addresses is largely one of perception. Consciousness itself is largely a perceptual matter. My awareness is determined mainly by what I "see," both in an outward physical way and in my subjective impressions of the inner world. Gestalt psychology questions the mechanism within us which makes certain objects or patterns in an overall field of view *stand out,* whereas other objects or patterns remain as *background.* The classic example is the visual paradox which most of us have encountered:

What do you see? A white goblet or two darkened faces? Probably you see both, but not at the same time. In any specific moment of perception, certain items stand out as foreground and others recede as background. The "gestalt" under which we operate in our perceptions is merely a control system that selects certain things to perceive while others are generally ignored. If your gestalt defined white space to be insignificant in the drawing above, then you would see the two faces. However, another gestalt would also have been possible for you.

Gestalts become ways of thinking or states of consciousness. Suppose as a teenager you were frequently lonely and never had dates, even though you wished you could. With the consciousness you had at that age, what kind of gestalt controlled your perceptions of life around you? For example, walking through a shopping center on a Saturday afternoon, what did you see? What emerged as foreground perceptions most likely were members of the opposite sex about your own age. Most else was not of interest to you and was little noticed. But suppose you are now 40 years old, married with three children, and it is the last weekend before Christmas. You are in a shopping center trying to get last-minute shopping done. What do you notice? What is your current consciousness, your present gestalt selecting as foreground perceptions? Perhaps bargain-priced toys in store windows. Perhaps the clothes that other children you pass are wearing. You are a different person than you were as a teenager. Your consciousness has changed and, therefore, so have your patterns of perception.

This principle of a gestalt very naturally leads us to a related concept which will give us a key to inner earth changes. That concept is the *paradigm.* Simply stated, a paradigm is a set of assumptions which creates a mind set for perceiving the outer world or oneself. It is essentially much like a gestalt, although the word *paradigm* is more frequently used. Gestalt is found most often in the more narrow circles of perceptual psychology; whereas, the notion of paradigm is widely used in many disciplines.

Usually a paradigm refers to an agreed-upon set of assumptions which a group of scholars or even a whole society has adopted. However, this "agreement" is often done in an automatic or unconscious way. Within a given academic discipline, new students learn the old paradigm from their teachers and then years later pass it on to more new students. For example, there is a paradigm within the domain of Egyptology. Those assumptions include a time frame which does not permit much in the way of civilization to have occurred in Egypt before 3,000 B.C. With that mind set each new archaeological discovery is viewed and categorized within the agreed-upon assumptions. The paradigm of modern Egyptology is made up of perhaps several dozen key assumptions. Rarely are those assumptions questioned. Anyone trained in this field professionally "joins the club" by ascribing to the mind set of his colleagues.

Some latitude may be permitted within a group which shares a paradigm. There is occasionally room for creativity. *But* that creativity is to be directed toward the discovery of further assumptions which can be *added on to* the existing paradigm. However, within some groups, such as religious orders with their assumptions about God and the proper way to live, there may be no room at all for truly creative thinkers. In some disciplines or groups there is a rigid paradigm which does not lend itself to additions. The assumptions have been set; there is no room for more. The only "creative" work to be done within such groups is to discover new ways to match up the assumptions, to find new correlations. In other words, groups or fields of study with rigid paradigms are only interested in finding new ways to "prove" what they have already assumed is true.

In fact, all this business of paradigms can become rather confusing. There are so many different varieties of paradigms, how does one know which are relevant to one's personal journey toward understanding? The problem is complex because our modern world is comprised of so many different fields of study. It was far easier in earlier times. There might have been only the religious and the political paradigms of the day. With only two— which rarely got in each other's way—life was more straight-forward. The local priest would tell you about the religious assumptions that created your mind set about God and life hereafter. The king or his local representative would tell you about the political assumptions—who were the good guys and who were the bad guys, and whose orders to follow. Areas of study like agriculture and science had to fall in line with religious and political paradigms of the day. People such as Galileo discovered this when they tried to assert new assumptions for science which contradicted the established norms.

But in our day things are a bit more hazy. It is hard to tell what the perceptual mind set is for areas like religion and politics. And the set of assumptions for certain scientific disciplines, such as physics, has been changing quite rapidly. Nevertheless, there seems to be a common ground to the mind sets of the various groups, disciplines and organizations of the *mainstream* culture. A point of overlap and a point of agreement exist upon a few basic assumptions which the *majority of people* in Western culture hold in common. We will call this the "old world paradigm" to contrast it to a "new world paradigm" which would characterize a new age.

Before attempting to identify the specific items of the "old world paradigm," we should make it clear that not every person in our country or Western culture ascribes to these assumptions. There are people who are already living fully under the "new world paradigms" of different assumptions, creating a markedly different mind set toward life. Others of us shift back and forth. We have days or moments in which our consciousnesses move and we suddenly see life and ourselves through the eyeglasses of the new assumptions. But then we find ourselves slipping back into the familiar, old world view.

What, then, does this "old world" view of life look like? What are its assumptions which create a very particular kind of consciousness and behavior among people? The list might well include the following beliefs:

(1) Humans are not really part of nature. Even though we may have descended from ape-like ancestors, we are now apart from the natural world. It is not necessary to try to be one with the planet Earth because it is basically dead. We do things *to* the earth and nature—*not in cooperation* with them.

(2) Supply is limited. There is only so much energy and so much food. The universe is running down. Entropy controls not just the cosmos but our own little microcosms as well. There is simply not enough for everybody.

(3) People are generally selfish or evil. The essence of the human spirit is to get what you want. People cooperate only when it is likely to lead to some reward.

(4) Bigger is better. Quantity determines value. The more people who buy a book or see a movie, the better it is. The more money a person or a company makes, the more successful they are.

(5) You only live once. There is no such thing as reincarnation.

There might be something to life after death, but not in the sense of ever coming back here to planet Earth.

(6) Things are real only if they can be measured. Things like thought energy, ESP, healing vibrations, astral bodies and the like are all mere delusions.

(7) There is only one truth and once we think we have it, it is our obligation to make sure others adopt it and the world is run by it.

These seven assumptions create a mind set for perceiving the outer world and ourselves. They create an interlocking matrix. They may be added to but they are very resistant to any one of them being removed. However, it is just this paradigm that is under siege in today's world. It is not locked in a bank vault somewhere to keep it safe, but is within human minds, within the human consciousness. And the old world paradigm is being challenged by an emergent new set of assumptions—directly contradicting not just one or two of the seven, but all of them.

Because the old world paradigm is within us, we feel the strains of it being challenged. Our own minds are the battleground. This is what we mean by inner earth changes. The foundations of the old world view of life are being shaken and we feel it.

Alternatives for Handling Paradigm Shifts

History shows us that occasionally the assumptions by which humans view life can shift dramatically. The change from the Middle Ages to the Renaissance is a good example. During this transition period which spanned more than 100 years, some of the cornerstones of medieval thought were shaken. A world which was universally understood to be flat was discovered to be spherical. The earth, believed to be at the center of the solar system, was found to be only one of many planets traveling around the sun. The Protestant Reformation transformed Christianity. There was a clear paradigm shift in Western culture.

Since the beginning of the Renaissance, there have certainly been major changes in our world and in human assumptions about reality. Breakthroughs in science and in the technology of warfare have particularly altered our life styles and thoughts about the world in which we live. However, the transition in human awareness which could be upon us in the coming generation is potentially the fullest example of a paradigm shift since the 16th century. Once again, there is a possibility that nearly all the assumptions held by the vast majority of a society will be challenged and replaced.

It is not easy to live in days of a paradigm shift. The ancient Chinese curse, "May you live in times of change," seems very apt. One reason that it is so difficult to live under such conditions is the variety of ways in which people respond to the change in assumptions and perceptions. Because responses are so varied, it is hard to know where people stand. It is frustrating to feel the lack of common understanding and belief which normally characterizes civilization. In 1550 you might not have known if a new aquaintance was a "flat earth man" or a "round earth man." Or you might have worried whether your neighbor was joining the new Reformation movement or remaining loyal to the traditional Church. In our times we wonder how the person sitting next to us on the airplane will react if we talk about reincarnation. Or we hope that our relatives will understand if we quit a job paying a *quantity* of dollars to take something which provides a high *quality* of experience. The sense of community among people is easily threatened in times of paradigm shift. And added to this is the *personal* stresses we feel—these inner earth changes—as the old ways in us begin to die. What it produces is an exciting, troublesome, anxious age.

And so, how are we to respond to times like these? How can people confront changing assumptions? Basically there are three alternatives: Try to hold on to the old paradigm; jump to a new paradigm even though it may not be the optimal, new one trying to emerge; or join with that best new set of assumptions which is being born. Let us take a close look at these in turn.

Holding On to the Old Paradigm

Seen from a detached observation point, this sort of thinking reminds us of the saying, "Let's go down with the ship." It looks as though some people are so determined to stay with what is familiar that they will create their own destruction. However, it may not look that way to them. For those who persist with the old mind set, the adversity may be seen as merely a challenge testing their loyalty to the truth. We admire this quality in many of our cultural heroes. George Washington at Valley Forge did not say, "Well, it looks like the paradigm is shifting and I'd better become a loyal British subject again." The heroes and heroines of Old Testament

Judaism did not give in to beliefs and values of one culture after another that challenged them. And so the people of our times who want to retain the seven assumptions previously listed may be able to make a strong case for their persistence. Those seven assumptions—that paradigm—has been a world view which has served us well in the past. Look at the progress of humanity in the past two centuries, they argue. Their case is that there is no reason to believe that the same world view cannot continue to produce results.

However, the problem with this approach has so often been an unwillingness to look at facts. The old world mind set operates with a gestalt that makes anomalies (events or conditions which contradict one of the assumptions) seem as background. In fact, there may *not* be a *conspiracy* on the part of this group to hold on to the old values at all costs. It may simply be that they do not see what others see. For those of us who have experienced contradictions of one or more of the old assumptions, it is very frustrating to have old-paradigm thinkers refuse to see or admit to what we know to be true. However, it may not be lying or conspiracy or deceit on the part of the people trying to hold on to the old assumptions. Perhaps they really cannot see something because for them it is only a part of the background. For them it is as if the anomalies do not exist.

Let us look at some modern examples of this process. There are many instances in which a group of people seems to refuse to look at the evidence. In the following examples, that group, in fact, constitutes the vast majority of our society. First, consider psychic ability. Although a majority of people may say that they believe there is something to ESP, this is not the case among decision makers, scholars, scientists and others in positions of intellectual authority. For this influential group, it is as if the strong scientific evidence for ESP does not exist. Generally they either refuse to admit that the reports of parapsychologists are true or they refuse to make the effort to look into these matters. Naturally it is frustrating for those who are backers of parapsychology or who feel that an understanding of ESP might help change people's attitudes about the human family.

However, we might wonder *why* so many intelligent individuals in our society so resistantly hang on to the old world assumption which claims that there can be nothing to telepathy or psychokinesis. But consider how threatening such a shift in assumption would be to some of the leading thinkers of our world. For example, most all of the previous findings of psychological research would become circumspect, because possibly telepathy (conscious or unconscious) might have influenced the experimental subjects to do or say what the experimenter hoped. Or consider what would happen to research methods in physics or chemistry if one had to be continually accounting for the possible effects of psychokinesis. Here is a phenomenon which, if true, is so elusive that it cannot easily be controlled and measured.

Or let us look at what is happening to the ecology of planet Earth. To some people there is clear evidence that we have polluted the oceans and air, perhaps to a point beyond repair. Furthermore, it seems increasingly clear that humans are very much a part of an ecological whole—we cannot affect nature and not expect to get something of equal quality back in return. And yet that sort of assumption runs contrary to the mind set which has created a heavily industrial world. It threatens a life style based largely on plastic and mass-produced, interchangeable goods. The leaders of such industries, *and* the people who have become dependent upon them, are inclined not to see the anomaly. Their gestalt places in perceptual background the disturbing new evidence of what we are doing to our planet. They tenaciously hold on to the old paradigm.

Or, as a final example, consider the debate in Western culture over reincarnation. However, perhaps one should say "lack of debate," because those in positions of responsibility and authority are generally unwilling to have meaningful discussions on the matter. How do they deal with the anomaly created when early Church historians find that a number of second and third century branches of Christianity incorporated reincarnation into their theology? By and large this threat to the old paradigm is handled by refusing to look at the evidence. With a perfunctory dismissal of this evidence, all discussion on the matter is shut off and a key assumption in the old world paradigm is maintained.

But this is only one method by which people try to hold on to the old set of assumptions when the world is changing. Refusing to consider the evidence which might require a shift in mind set is the most simplistic response. A more subtle technique is to try to patch up the old system in a manner that looks like an open-minded willingness to change but in essence is not that at all. The procedure for this approach is quite well known. First, consider the assumption which seems to be disproven by an anomaly. Do not consider that perhaps this shaken assumption is a sign that *all* the major assumptions should be seriously questioned. No, instead maintain one's strong emotional ties to the existent world view. Try to arrive at a rewritten assumption for the one under attack. Perhaps one can add a footnote to the original assumption which will account for this disturbing new evidence. Or, at worse, the whole assumption will have to be rewritten, but it is hoped in a form *(no matter how awkward)* which will let one hang on to all the rest of the old paradigms.

For example, what do we do when statistics show the rising incidence of cancer in our society? Do we question the entire package of assumptions—the stress created by "big is better" thinking, the sense of animosity created by a competitive economic system, the horrendous things we do to nature to extract the resources we demand? Here is a blatant anomaly that announces that something is not right with our paradigm of living. But rather than look for a new set of assumptions, a strong tendency exits to try to hang on to the old world view and merely make some patchwork. So what happens? Medical science selects a few scapegoats; it finds several dozen things which are carcinogenic. Then it announces that you can still be safe and healthy within the old paradigm if you just pay attention to the new footnotes which say, "Do not let yourself come in contact with any of these known cancer-causing substances."

By the way of analogy we can see that conditions are like a man with a leaking roof on his old house. He springs a leak in March and patches it up. But another one occurs in April and two in May. He keeps up this patchwork process, never considering that the time has come for a new roof. He can conceivably keep this up, but the day will come when his entire roof will be an awkward-looking array that is totally patchwork. The sum of his time and dollar expense in all that patchwork will be greater than having only once gotten a new roof.

Sometimes the patchwork looks ludicrous. Like the emperor with no clothes, the situation almost begs for someone to demand courageously "How could that be?" But the stakes are high. If people are determined to hang on to the old mind set, then the old assumptions with its new footnotes will do just fine, no matter how awkward it looks. In fact such people would even proudly point to such a transformation as proof of their open-mindedness and willingness to change with the times.

Let's look at some examples of this technique for handling changing times. First, there is an interesting historical instance related to the old theory that the sun and planets travel around the earth. That was a major assumption in the medieval paradigm. However, there were anomalies which should have alerted people of that day to the fact that their view of reality was inadequate. For example, anyone who watched the planet Mars night after night would observe a strange phenomenon. It would seem to move gradually across the background of the fixed stars. Over the course of weeks and months, it would seem to be traveling through the various constellations of the sky. This progression was very much expected because people were sure that Mars was circling the earth.

But occasionally it would do a curious thing—it would reverse its course and for several weeks seem to move backward. An astrologer would call this a planet "going retrograde." Yet how could this be? This observation, which could readily be made by anyone, seemed to cast doubts upon the assumption that the planets, the sun, and the moon were all revolving around the earth. For hundreds of years after this retrograde motion was noticed, people were not willing to part with the assumptions of their paradigm. It was difficult to ignore the evidence of an anomaly; therefore, the next best technique was employed. They patched up the old assumption and the theory was changed. According to the revised notion, the earth was still the center of the solar system, but some of the planets did not traverse a circular, or even eliptical orbit around the earth. No, planets like Mars traveled with a periodic loop-de-loop in their paths! In the next illustration we see first the pathway Mars would appear to take as one watched it over the weeks move against the background of the fixed stars. Then there is a diagram showing the "patched-up" assumption, which one ascribed to if one were not willing to create a new paradigm.

The idea of such an orbital pathway of a planet was ludicrous. But what else could the people of that day do? Their world view and mind set were too precious for them ever to consider seriously new

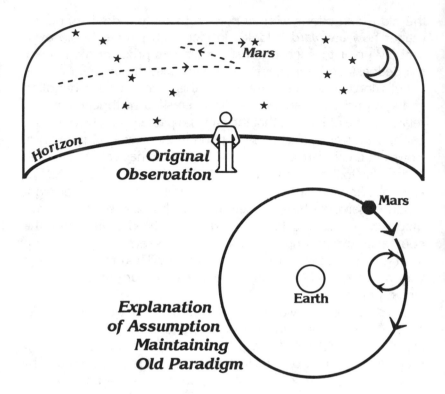

Original
Observation

Horizon

Mars

Mars

Earth

Explanation
of Assumption
Maintaining
Old Paradigm

assumptions. It was not until the Renaissance that a sensible idea of the solar system was generally accepted and the retrograde motion of the planets was easily explained. The relative difference in speed between the earth's movement around the sun and that of another planet would create the occasional appearance of backward movement.

We can laugh at the people of 600 years ago in their naiveté and stubbornness. But isn't it possible that 600 years from now our ancestors will view some of our patched-up assumptions as equally amusing? To what degree do we now try to modify old assumptions to avoid having to develop an entirely different world view? Or, in what ways do we take something which is of the new world and distort it so that it looks like part of the old world?

For example, how do traditional Christian theologians deal with reincarnation? On the one hand, this is an *ancient* assumption. But it is probably an assumption of the emerging *new* paradigm as well. Perhaps this time around the mind set which includes reincarnation will give it a different interpretation than it has ever had before. And how is the theory of reincarnation treated now in Western society during the times of change? As has already been mentioned, the theory is often ignored. Many contemporary theologians will simply not admit to evidence that 1700 years ago Christianity and reincarnation were compatible. But even more curious is the way it is treated by those who *will* look at some of the clues. There is, for example, an interesting passage in the ninth chapter of John in which Jesus is questioned about why a particular man was *born* blind—because *he* sinned or because his parents sinned? Admittedly Jesus did *not* respond, "Oh, it was his karma from a past life." Nevertheless, isn't the question a curious one? Isn't it a sort of anomaly to those who would believe that Jesus and His followers never thought in terms of reincarnation? And what is the contemporary thinking on this passage?

In one case a theological commentator on the book of John was clearly baffled in trying to deal with these verses. To people who do not see life from the assumption of reincarnation (or at least the pre-existence of the soul before birth), this question on the part of a disciple must seem very odd. Perhaps as odd as the retrograde motion of Mars looked to people of the Middle Ages. And in one commentary the patched-up assumption (that is, hanging on to the belief that the soul did not exist before conception) looks almost as ludicrous as the loop-de-loop orbit of Mars.

The solution which is offered says basically this: The person who questioned Jesus felt that if the blindness was not caused by the parents' sin, then either the blind man must have sinned while in the womb(!) *or* God knew the man was going to sin once he was an adult so He went ahead and punished him in advance. We can only conclude that this interpreter has an interesting concept of embryonic life and an even more novel idea of God's faith in us.

Another example of how modern people try to patch up the old paradigm concerns the application of certain new age techniques. It is both amazing and disconcerting to see how clever the old mind set can be in diffusing the power of certain new paradigm approaches. Take, for instance, meditation. This ancient procedure for making personal attunement to the God within is re-emerging. Like reincarnation, it is a key assumption in the new mind set being born. And yet the old paradigm tries to grab on to it for its own. For instance, sales managers teach meditation to their salesmen—not because they hope to enlighten these people—but because they hope it will give them more energy and willpower to make more sales. Some athletes have taken up meditation, not to experience the harmony of the spirit with the body but to provide greater concentration to sharpen their competitive instincts. This is not to say that every business person or athlete who meditates has distorted its true purpose. Rather, we should observe how frequently and how easily any of us can take something which is of the *new* and make it serve us toward the *old* purposes.

Finally, let us consider a third way in which we may try to hold on to the old paradigm in times of change. The first approach was to refuse to look at the evidence for a new set of assumptions; the second approach was to try to patch up the old paradigm. The last option is to surrender or sacrifice a part of ourselves, which then allows the old ways to continue. This is often a sad and damaging path to follow. Sometimes it trades a diminished state of consciousness for the security of holding on to what is familiar. Other times it exchanges conditions which hurt us physically for the psychological comfort of not having to face the new.

All around us are examples of how we do this—in our personal lives and as a society. We sacrifice our dream recall because we sense that it will push us toward changing. We are afraid to let go of a troubled and dying interpersonal relationship. We would often rather surrender some of our self-respect than to let go of that emotional attachment. Or we frequently suppress an inner knowing that it is time to part ways and to move on to the new people life has for us.

As a society we do this with the way we allow the world to be run. It is more comfortable to let the old paradigm stay in charge. It is easier to go ahead and drink tap water which is contaminated with toxins or breathe polluted air. In this case we sacrifice our own health because the old paradigm is familiar, and it just seems like too much work to come up with a whole new set of rules and assumptions.

However, this technique is no more effective in the long run than are the others. Surrendering a precious part of ourselves is far different from self-sacrifice for a high ideal. This approach which merely tries to maintain the old, the comfortable and the familiar will not work. When the world is changing the way ours is now, such methods can only temporarily slow the movement. Those who would hang on to the old assumptions may still be in the majority—but the evolution of consciousness on this planet does not depend on majority vote. If it did, then things would never really move forward. Human fears and desires would keep us stuck. Paradigm shifts on the order of the Renaissance or in our own times happen *in spite of* the majority.

Many of those who insist on being a part of this first category— the ones who try various methods to maintain the old set of assumptions—will find the coming decades to be especially troublesome. They are likely to feel acutely the inner earth changes. The temporizing, patching-up, denying techniques will not work for long. They will have to face, like all of us, the new world being born around them, and more importantly being born *within* them.

Jumping to a Different Paradigm

There is a second direction in which some people go when confronted with changing times and inner earth changes. This category of individuals senses that the old way of seeing things must go and some new mind set is needed. Unfortunately, these individuals choose a set of assumptions which is not at all the one which is trying to be born for the world as a whole. These people currently perceive that the old world is dying, but they mistake what is emerging. Usually the error takes place out of *fear* or *impatience.*

The different set of assumptions which they adopt is not really a productive one. It does not ease in a permanent way the sense of inner earth change. Its failure lies in the fact that their different paradigm is still at odds with the one trying to be born within humanity as a whole. And so they still feel the stress. The jump was half correct; it did not effectively ease the tensions.

There are numerous variations on this approach. One of them is represented by the survivalists. Such people accurately see that the support systems of the old world cannot continue to sustain society. They notice the signs of a possible economic collapse, an ecological disaster, a series of natural catastrophes, or whatever else can be imagined. Indeed there does exist the *threat* of some or all of the events which they expect. But as they view the world of old assumptions failing, what do they offer as a replacement? It is the ideal of "every man for himself." It is the assumption that people are essentially fearful and selfish. They assume that a small part can survive comfortably even if the greater whole is suffering.

But the mind set created by these kinds of assumptions is just as contrary to a new age paradigm as are the assumptions of the old world. Survivalists, being only half correct, will not find the real sense of security which they need—the *inner* security which comes from being in the flow with God's plan.

Another variation of this approach concerns the desire for an authoritarian leader. When times are changing and an old paradigm is dying, there easily arises a desire for someone— anyone—who claims to have the answers. Sometimes we turn to a person who promises to patch up the old paradigm and return to the way life used to be. Other times we accept the authority of someone who advocates a different set of assumptions. All we are asked to do by such a leader is to buy in to the teaching and accept his or her authority. It may be a political figure: There are always such instances when the old system doesn't seem to be working anymore. Or it may be a religious figure: It isn't hard to find one when people are confused and looking for quick answers. But no matter what kind of leader emerges, one thing is common to all: They offer a different view—a different paradigm—and they ask belief of their followers based only on their personal authority.

However, this variation will work no better than that of the survivalists. Once again, it is a half-truth. Yes, a new set of assumptions is needed, but the ones proposed are not in keeping with the spirit of the times. Even if the authoritarian, charismatic leader proposes a paradigm of reincarnation, ESP, meditation and holistic health, it is still not what is needed. The paradigm being born—which will usher in a new age—includes the opportunity for each person to find answers within self. It permits us to think for ourselves—even challenging us and requiring us to do so. A world view based on an authority figure, be it political, religious or whatever, is not what our times are about.

Another unproductive variation is rushing to the opposite paradigm when the old ways are dying. Again it is a matter of seeing that new assumptions are required but of being ineffective in choosing a different world view. It is a human tendency to conclude that the exact opposite of something found to be false must necessarily be the desired truth. In our own times some people may adopt a different paradigm based primarily on the polar opposite of the previous assumptions. Seeing what the industrial state has done to the environment they offer a mind set which rejects any kind of centralized manufacturing. Seeing what organized medicine has done to the health care consciousness of the nation, they suggest a world with no medical profession. This sort of process is extended to cover almost all aspects of our present culture.

Such drastic swings from one end of the scale to the other rarely produce a productive new condition. It doesn't work in our personal lives. A relationship with someone to whom we were over-attached may change and we may shift to the other extreme, becoming resentful or hateful. But we do not find a resolution or peace of mind in the new state. America went through such a dramatic shift after Viet Nam and Watergate. The once proud self-image of a nation which could do no wrong changed to the self-image of a flawed and weakened people. In both these examples, we see that the initial impulse to create a new set of assumptions was correct. Emotionally binding attachments to another person may need to be changed if the relationship is not productive. The arrogance of any nation needs to be altered if it blinds a people from seeing that sometimes it can be wrong. However, simply moving to *any* different mind set or paradigm will not do. The shift must be done carefully.

Joining the Emergent Paradigm

There is a third direction in which people can go when confronted with changing times and inner earth changes. This category of people includes those who sense that the old ways are dying *and* who know how to recognize the new which is being born. They are people who are generally patient and not driven by fears. They trust that there is a plan to what is going on in the world—that there is a spirit of the times which is in keeping with God's plan. They know themselves to be co-creators with God in the transformation to a new world view, but they humbly recognize that their work is to *respond* to the divine initiative which will be revealed to them.

What are the characteristics of such a person? In fact, such an individual is within each of us. All of us have the potential to be among those who make this kind of response to inner earth changes. All of us have the capability of being *receptive* in these times—a first characteristic of this sort of person. This is not mere passivity, because the builders of a new world need to be active and involved. Rather it is a matter of listening *before* acting. By way of an analogy, it is like taking the time to become aware of the position and direction of a current. Once that perception is made, one can then actively swim in the current and be carried along by it.

It is a matter of being able to sense the true spirit of these times. Such listening must reach beneath the surface of current events in the outer world. The true spirit of these times is not inflation, nor social unrest, not even earth changes. Those sorts of events may be symptoms of what is going on, but they are not the real spirit of what is being born. The nightly television news is more likely to document the dying of the old world than the birth of the new. The real listener—the real co-creator of a new age—senses the elements of a new paradigm which are emerging. He or she then *acts in response* to what has been noticed. That person is able to give expression and form to the new assumptions about life.

This sort of person—who is within us all—is also able to put aside fears. He or she is able courageously to accept that moment of void which we encounter when we have let go of the old and yet the new is not yet fully within our grasp. We might wonder what it is that most scares people about times of change and paradigm shifts. Do we fear that the future might be worse than the past has been? Or rather, are we more afraid of the void—of that moment of uncertainty and vulnerability—when the old assumptions have faded but we are not yet clear about the new? What we need is the confidence of a trapeze artist who has let go of one swing and momentarily hangs helplessly out in space before grabbing on to the next swing: He knows his own momentum will carry him forward to meet the swing he trusts will be there.

People confront the difficulties posed by that void in discussions about vocation and in their choices about close personal relationships. Many individuals stick with an old job even though they cannot imagine having any other job that would be more distasteful to them. But they are afraid to quit—oftentimes not so much worried that they would remain unemployed as because they cannot stand the thought of being in that uncertain, vulnerable void for any amount of time. Other people experience this with interpersonal relations. They stick with old and now counterproductive relations because they are afraid of the period of transition. They have not yet built up a sense of personal identity and strength which is needed to survive the void. A young man or woman will frequently stay with someone who he or she knows is not the right person because of fear. The fear is not that they will never find someone else. Sometimes they even imagine that most any new relationship would be better than what the current one has turned into. Rather they fear that lonely, helpless period of being in between the old way of seeing things and the new. It takes courage to move on to a new vocation, a new friend, or a whole new set of assumptions for living—and the capability to overcome the fear is within each of us.

Another characteristic of the person who embraces the new paradigm is an alchemical type of skill. The alchemists of ancient times attempted to turn lead into gold. Or, some would say, they tried to transform the base or earthly aspects of human consciousness into enlightenment. A version of this process is one of the skills of the new age pioneer. Remarkable occurrences become possible when there is a shift in paradigms. Some things which had been viewed as weaknesses by the old set of assumptions can be seen as strengths by the new. In the definition of many qualities an incredible transformation takes place.

Certainly *not everything* which was held in low esteem by the old paradigm will suddenly be much admired in the new one. It is the skill of the co-creators of a new world to recognize and work with those qualities which are good candidates for the alchemical change. Let us consider some examples of what they might be.

One candidate is *sensitivity.* In the old world it is often considered a weakness to be sensitive. In the competitive worlds of our vocations, the sensitive person is likely to get ulcers. Sensitivity generally runs counter to the assumption that there are limited resources and one had better be tough to struggle hard for his own share. But in a new paradigm, sensitivity may be transformed from weakness to strength. A requirement for leadership may become sensitivity to others. The best healers may be those who have developed a form of psychic sensitivity.

Another candidate is *interdependence.* This is a good illustration of the process at work on a global scale. In the old paradigm, it is weakness for one nation to be dependent on another nation. For example, we say that America is weak because it requires the oil of the Persian Gulf countries. We say that Belgium is a weak nation because it is dependent upon France, Germany and America for military protection. And by old world assumptions these instances and many more are true. However, with a new age paradigm the assumptions have changed. Now we can see that we are one people on planet Earth. What benefits the people of one nation, in turn, benefits those throughout the world. Our interdependence becomes a strength. It is alchemically transformed into a stimulus for cooperation. A characteristic which was once held in low esteem can become something which is newly admired and appreciated. Such is the work of the builders of a new world—to recognize and nurture the qualities of life which can go through such a dramatic switch.

Finally, the people who follow this direction in times of inner earth changes will treat with respect the elements of the old paradigm. It is not with anger or hatred that they allow the old world view to run its course and die. Instead it is with love that they take the elements of the old ways and find new places for them. To understand this point and to realize how crucial a principle it is, we must recall our original notion of paradigms and gestalts. Remember that when we moved to a new gestalt (for example, seeing the two faces instead of the goblet), the elements of the scene did not change. Instead it was our way of ordering them which was altered. We created new priorities, putting the background into the foreground. Or when we stretched a square into the higher-dimensional life of being a cube, we did not destroy the square. We merely changed the relative importance and priority of its position.

The same must hold true if we are to move properly from a world which is run by the old paradigm to a world run by the new. Many of the elements of living will remain. The challenge is to arrange, order and relate them to each other based on a new set of rules. We will still have families, businesses, governments, schools and agriculture in a new age. The shift in paradigms does not mean eliminating business just because it may have been poorly operated under the old set of assumptions. Nor does it mean throwing out the idea of governments just because wars and hatreds were created when governments operated under the old rules of the game.

The meaning of paradigm shift must be clearly understood if we are to have hope in building a new kind of world. This is far more challenging than just watching the old one die. The current transformation is not so much one in which the individual elements of the scene change; it is rather the emergence of a new gestalt that sees those elements in entirely new relationships. And with this new perception of the previous conditions, institutions and needs of the human family, a different and more productive way of living can also be born.

Living Creatively with Inner Earth Changes

The inner levels at which individual people experience and deal with these changing times are far more significant than outer, geological changes which could happen. Perhaps we can even go so far as to speculate that in the collective way in which we deal with the *inner* earth changes, the *outer* forms will be created for us to experience physically.

In the last chapter we explored the aspect of God which is evolution and change, and we examined the three broad categories of response to shifts in gestalt or paradigm. Of the three alternatives from which people can choose in times of inner change, one was proposed as the best to follow. In this chapter we will venture in that direction a bit further and try to answer the question, "How can I begin to prepare myself right now to become one of those people who will co-create a new world?" In other words, what do we *do* if we feel willing to make a paradigm shift to living our lives by new assumptions? What if we are willing to stop hanging on to the old mind sets and stop trying merely to patch up the old assumptions that don't work so well any more? What if we feel capable of resisting the temptation to jump to just *any* different paradigm out of fear or impatience?

There are, in fact, tasks we can do to prepare ourselves for the work of building a new world. Nothing is more important than clarifying our ideals and purposes. An entire chapter is devoted to this crucial process. Perhaps second in importance is purifying and attuning our physical bodies. The birth of a new age will

happen at this physical dimension. And how are we to be participants—even helpers—in its birth unless we have the bodily
structure with which to be involved? The stresses of changing
times hit the body hard. Through nutrition and exercise we must
diligently work to do the best we can with our own physical bodies.
This is *not* to say that *only* young people with bodies in the prime
of health and vitality can be the real co-creators of a new age.
Instead, the principle is this: Each of us can fulfill the potential of
what we personally have to contribute only if we have taken the
best care of the physical forms we will need to express that
contribution. And these extraordinary times require of us
extraordinary diligence in making sure that our physical systems
are kept in balance and harmony.

Beyond these two most significant tasks are also smaller tasks,
exercises and disciplines which we can perform from time to time.
These will aid us in being better prepared to meet the challenges
and difficulties of the inner changes.

Exercises in Consciousness

We can exercise and strengthen the "muscles" of our mental
and spiritual bodies, just as calisthenics or weight lifting will
strengthen physical muscles. By using our wills to do or think
something which is out of the routine, we prepare ourselves for the
coming new ways of living.

One good exercise is to introduce change voluntarily into our
lives. This might mean altering a routine or a habit. Try driving to
work by a different route. Wear your wallet in the opposite side
pocket for a week. Change the habit patterns for a few days of what
you do in the evenings after supper. Obviously these sorts of
changes will not create a new age, but they are excellent awareness
exercises. They prepare our minds for dealing with novelty. In little
ways they can even raise consciousness, because sometimes a
routine dulls our awareness.

Another way of voluntarily introducing change is to try living
without something for a week or more. Go without television for
seven days and see what effect it has on your consciousness. Try
living without the telephone for even a day and see what impact
that has on you. This is not to say that televisions and telephones
will not be around in 20 years. Instead this is an exercise to
strengthen a muscle of consciousness. People lift 100-pound

barbells so that later they can lift 100-pound storage boxes. The exercise in itself may seem artificial if viewed only in its form; therefore, we must look to the inner process and purpose to understand its value. As times of change deepen, we may have to go without familiar conveniences. If we have experienced in advance—even if only occasionally—that we can make such sacrifices and survive well, then we are much more likely to make it successfully through any period of testing.

Another strategy to exercise our consciousness is derived from some recent speculation in parapsychology. One branch of psychical research investigates evidence for the survival of bodily death. Recent speculation revolves around the question of what consciousness would be like in the afterdeath state. Some thinkers argue that the sense of one's personal identity is just as clear and strong after death as it was before death. They claim that our mental sense of self-identity is not really created very strongly from having a body. Others argue that our personal identity would scatter at death, becoming diffuse and unlike anything we experience now. Taking a more or less middle position, Dr. Charles Tart suggests that for certain categories of people, there is probably a much greater likelihood of surviving the transition of death with one's identity intact. He describes one such category as "people who have already 'survived' (maintained personal identity during) a number of drastic changes in their lives, such as having experienced many altered states of consciousness, marked changes in environment, etc. They would have, as it were, 'practiced' for the shock of death, and so be less likely to be completely 'fragmented' by it." (*Journal of the American Society for Psychical Research,* October, 1980, p. 419)

In other words it may be that people who have "practiced" experiencing levels of consciousness somewhat like the afterdeath state will be better off. Death would not be as confusing an experience. Through meditation, dream study (especially lucid dreams) and other experiences of altered consciousness, they might begin to build for themselves, in advance of death, a feeling of familiarity with that dimension of consciousness.

If this principle is true, perhaps it also pertains to transitions other than just physical death. Perhaps it would be relevant to the transition from the old paradigm in our world to the new one. It may be that the people who can best make the switch with a continuity of identity and a minimum of confusion will be those who venture out in advance. This suggests that we try exercises to experience beforehand the post-change conditions. We can only guess at what those conditions might be, but Edgar Cayce and others have made predictions concerning what assumptions will constitute a new age paradigm. As we make it a point to try living some of those principles right now, then our passage through these times may be smoother. Much of the second half of this book will concern new age life styles and how we might begin to live them now.

A third type of exercise is a type of self-observation. Recall that one important way in which we feel inner earth changes is experiencing pain at the point at which we have placed something between us and God. For some people the awareness of what that something is can come by simple self-observation. For others there need to be preliminary exercises to reveal that process. In other words, we are often so caught up in living our own lives that it is difficult to see things objectively—to "step back and watch self go by," as the Cayce readings put it.

The exercise of setting ideals can be a helpful procedure. (This will be covered in detail in a later chapter.) It works by challenging us to get clearly into focus just where we want to go in conscious- ness. As that place in awareness comes into focus, even momentarily, it frequently makes clear which items in our current way of living stand in the way.

The variety of situations which individuals have placed between themselves and God is enormous. However, some recurrent patterns and themes are shared among many people of our society. One example is an attachment to money which permits a certain standard of living. In fact this attachment is probably a preoccupation with something deeper, which can be seen if carefully analyzed. It may be a worry about physical security with a belief that money will create peace of mind. It may be a fear of powerlessness, which preoccupies the mind of a person. In that instance, money could be seen as a symbol of power. But in either case, the individual will most likely have put concerns about personal finances ahead of concerns about relating to God.

Other recurrent patterns of this process involve relationships and distractions. In the first instance, it is usually not other people themselves whom we have made more important than God—

although it may look that way. It is rather our emotional reactions to a person which have become most important in our lives. The emotion could be jealousy, resentment, worry, fear or any of a wide variety of other possibilities. Rarely is it love; not because we rarely ever love someone else, but because those genuine love relations usually bring us closer to God instead of acting as a barrier.

The example of distractions is another frequent pattern. It would be well for most of us to examine closely our lives and see how we may use distractions to avoid putting energy into drawing nearer to God. The effect of most distractions is to put our lives on "hold." They are ways of tuning out most of the world and retreating to an awareness that does not challenge us at the growth points of our souls. And certainly our society offers many opportunities for this. Some of the ways are overt, such as drugs—whether we mean tranquilizers, alcohol, cocaine, marijuana or whatever. It isn't hard to see that these sorts of things can put barriers between us and God by *disengaging us* from the evolutionary life stream. But let us be clear that abstinence from various drugs does not necessarily mean that we do not partake of the other various consciousness-dulling distractions which society offers.

In the book *Brave New World,* Aldous Huxley presents a rather dim view of what the future might hold. Perhaps no book other than George Orwell's *1984* has had such a sobering effect on those of us who are taking a serious look at where the future may be leading us. Huxley's fantasy includes a world which uses a hypothetical drug, soma, to dull the wits of people at the end of the work day.

What is the "soma" of our times? We might observe some scarey parallels between the effects of soma in *Brave New World* and television in our world. Both allow people to unplug their minds from what is actually before them. Both can easily become avoidance mechanisms. We might consider the degree to which television watching has become for each of us a daily life procedure which has begun to interfere with our relationship with God. It is not so much the *content* of what we watch—although that can be significant for various reasons, too. The point here is that the *process* of disengaging our minds from the realities of our personal lives is a distraction which for some people stands directly in the way of spiritual growth.

Another kind of distraction for some people is sports. It is not so often participatory sports in which our bodies are exercised and aided in health, although it is conceivable that our preoccupation with this could become a spiritual problem, too. Instead, it is spectator sports, in which people are "drugged" into believing that the "games" being enacted before them are somehow more important than anything else in their lives.

Somehow men are particularly vulnerable to this kind of psychology. Ask someone who has succumbed to this type of distraction and he will say that his wife, children, home and job are much more important to him than his favorite football team. But watch his emotions and his behavior. Sometimes you might not be sure what his priorities really are.

Food is a distraction that some of us have placed between ourselves and God. Of course, our bodies need healthful food to be nourished and attuned so that we can even go in search of God. Not that food and God are contrary, but some individuals have placed a desire for food before a desire for God. Sometimes it is a particular food or a particular additive like sugar. We may even get a certain physical response within our bodies to that foodstuff, and we can be "addicted" to that feeling. Or we may be attached to certain times of the day for food. Perhaps this is an extreme instance, but we might wonder, "What would I do if I began to have a very deep, intense experience during a meditation period before lunch? Suppose I began to feel hungry in the midst of all this? Would I cut my meditation short to keep my regular mealtime or would I be able to say 'no' to this habitual desire of my body?" This hypothetical question might help us decide whether food is a balanced and necessary part of our day, or if it has become a life-avoiding distraction.

No matter what you have placed between yourself and God, it is to your advantage to discover it. In times of inner change, it will be a point at which pressure is put on your life to grow and change. If you can complete exercises of self-observation and find that place on your own, then you can begin to work on it right away. Making some changes in your life *before* you are *forced* to do it could help these times of testing go a lot more smoothly.

A final exercise can also be used to strengthen the "muscles" of our mental and spiritual bodies. It involves practicing the process of shifting gestalts. It teaches us to see unnoticed sides of life. In many ways it is a game, but it very subtly can prepare us in little ways for changing times. This exercise can bring to the surface the abilities we all have to see that which is usually unseen—to make a foreground of that which is habitually background.

The arena for this exercise is our everyday lives. Make it a daily five-minute experiment to exercise your "gestalt-shifting muscles" of awareness. Try it even for just a week. During those daily five minutes, attempt to notice the items in your surroundings to which you usually pay no attention. Perhaps it is what people are wearing. Maybe it is the appearance of nature, or the objects and colors in your environment.

One version of this exercise is to pay attention to the shapes of *spaces* between objects rather than the shapes of objects themselves. For example, you walk through a wooded area and look up; what do you see? Most people's gestalt leads them to see the shape of leaves and branches. However, with an act of will we can change that mental selection mechanism and see the shape of spaces *between* the leaves and branches. The shape of the patches of blue sky can become foreground.

Another version of this exercise is with music. Usually we hear the melody even though there are numerous background instruments. These harmonies and rhythm sounds are there, but our perceptual set does not allow us to notice them. Often the assumption of our music-listening paradigm is that the melody is what the music is all about. But what if your brother was playing the background harmony on the violin in a large orchestra? Wouldn't your assumption change and wouldn't you experience a gestalt shift as you carefully listened to hear that violin? This sort of playful exercise can be fun and challenging. It can also be instructive. It teaches us not to be too quick in assuming there is only one way to perceive life. It helps us to appreciate the relativity of human consciousness and prepares us to experience more significant paradigm shifts during these periods of inner earth changes.

We Can Make the Difference

An essential feature of the Cayce prophecies is that we can make the difference as humanity collectively creates its future. The purpose for our careful study of inner earth changes is that if we will meet these changes in a creative way, they would help to build a more balanced, harmonious form through which the outer earth changes may occur. In the Biblical terminology of the Cayce readings, "the little leaven can leaven the whole lump." In his own down-to-earth way, Cayce is suggesting a powerful principle: A few spiritually attuned souls can lift the consciousness of humanity.

This philosophy has been called the principle of "critical mass." We are likely to have heard this term in a much more gruesome setting: the explosion of an atomic bomb. To build an atomic bomb, physicists know that it requires a *threshold amount* of certain radioactive substances, such as one form of uranium. If we have less than that threshold amount—be it 1 pound, 3 pounds or whatever is the significant level for that particular substance—no explosion can happen. But once we reach the threshold point or the critical mass, something suddenly starts to happen. In the graph of this below, the broken line represents our common thinking which says, "The effect I get *out* is in direct proportion to the amount I put *in*." Many processes of life follow this kind of relationship. However, in contrast, the solid line represents a process controlled by the principle of critical mass. Other processes of life follow this kind of relationship.

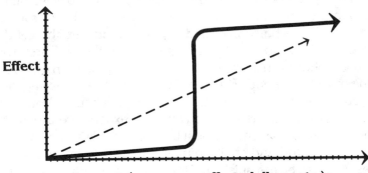

Amount (e.g., mass, effort, dollars, etc.)

Of course, many other basic kinds of curves depict life processes. But these (or minor variations of them) are two of the most significant, and they so clearly contrast each other. Let's consider examples of each one. Some people find that the amount of food they eat has an effect on their weight, which roughly follows the broken line. Or, the number of dollars you pay per month in rent may be directly proportional to the quality of dwelling in which you live. Or, the amount of time you spend studying for a test will have a direct, proportional effect on your test score. Of course, a more accurate depiction of many life experiences (approximating

90

the broken line) would be a curve. The line would rise proportionately at first, but the concept of diminishing returns would set in and the line would begin to curve and then flatten out.

It is interesting to note that the example of studying for a test will sometimes better fit the solid line. Suppose you are stuck in your learning by not understanding a particular key concept. If you study one or two hours, it may look pretty hopeless for the test tomorrow. Your score will be low and, furthermore, the difference will be very slight between having studied for one hour versus two hours. But imagine that it takes *three* hours to crack the difficult concept. Suddenly at the three-hour point that elusive concept becomes clear and now you have the insight to be able to solve what had seemed to be impossible problems. Your score now is likely to be very high. Additional study may help a little bit more, but not very significantly. To put this in a chart we have:

Hours of study	Effect (i.e., test score)
1	45
2	47
3	85
4	87

This would be a classic example of critical mass or threshold effect. There are other commonplace examples that we could experience. For instance, running water into a bathtub and measuring the amount of water that has overflowed out on the floor. For the first 10 minutes in which the faucet runs there is no spilling effect upon the floor. But suddenly the critical mass point is reached—in this case the 75-gallon capacity of the bathtub.

We might consider another example involving a critical number of people: a political election. Suppose that 100 million people vote in an election between a liberal presidential candidate and a conservative one. And assume that the effect which we are trying to measure is conservative fiscal policy coming out of the White House. What is the critical mass that can create that result? If the vote is 50,000,001 for the liberal candidate and 49,999,999 for the conservative one, we get no effect. (This, of course, assumes that we have just elected a very stubborn liberal president who refuses to moderate his stance in view of the narrow victory.) However, with a net shift of two votes in favor of the conservative candidate, we suddenly get a tremendous effect as we pass the threshold point.

In Cayce's estimation, the future of planetary consciousness will be shaped by a critical mass type of curve. What may be misleading about the political example just used is that in the philosophy of his readings Cayce never suggests that the future of the world is by majority vote. It will not take a bit over one-half of humanity in order to create a dramatic change in planetary awareness. This theory supposes that the critical mass effect can be initiated by a relatively small number of people. That "little leaven" which can lift consciousness in all humanity may seem to be just a handful of people compared to the earth's population.

The teachings of the Bible, as well as the philosophy of the Cayce readings, indicate that this has happened before. Recall the story of Abraham at the time just before the destruction of Sodom and Gomorrah? God warns Abraham that this destruction will take place because of the selfish consciousness of people in those cities. But what is Abraham's response? He attempts to bargain with God. He wonders, "If 50 righteous people can be found, would the cities be saved?" God's response is yes, that for the sake of the 50, the city will not be destroyed. And then Abraham proceeds to find out just how far God will go in His offer of mercy—45, 40, 30, 20, 10? Yes, even if only 10 righteous people can be found, the principle of critical mass will produce a saving effect on the entire populace of the cities. Ten was the threshold amount. Unfortunately it appears from the story that even those few could not be located.

In another illustration, the Cayce readings speak of the ancient Jewish sect called the Essenes as having served as a critical mass. Historians tell us little about this group of people who lived before and during the time of Jesus. Much more is known about the larger sects of Jewish thought in those times: the Sadducees and the Pharisees. In fact, were it not for the discovery of the Dead Sea Scrolls near the ruins of an Essene community, almost nothing would be known of them.

However, in Cayce's psychic vision of the past, the Essenes were said to have played a key role in the coming of the Christ. It was this group who prepared themselves as a channel for the Messiah's entrance. Over many decades of practicing physical, mental and spiritual purification, they became a leaven that acted upon the consciousness of the planet. According to the Cayce readings, it was largely through the work of this relatively small group that the Christ incarnated as Jesus. Apparently there were problems later. Jesus was not exactly the sort of savior they had planned for and there may have been a break between Jesus and this community as He reached adulthood. However, the point here remains that a threshold number of people—far, far smaller than any numerical majority—had an impact that was profoundly far-reaching.

And what, we might ask, are the numbers we are working with as we consider the possibility of "critical mass changes" in our own times? Perhaps the quantity will be similar to those of the past. How many Essenes did it require to create a channel for divine incarnation? Perhaps just several hundred. In Biblical times we have seen that just 10 righteous people were all that was required for a divine promise of mercy. Two passages of a Cayce reading mention numbers as threshold amounts for a quickening effect on the *mass consciousness.*

Why then the turmoil in the world today?
They have forgotten God! Not that it is merely a karmic condition of a nation, of a people; for, know ye not that the prayer of one man saved a city? 3976-25, June 23, 1940

Let thy voice be raised, then, as in praise to thy Maker; not in word alone but rather in the manner in which ye meet thy fellow men day by day. For the prayer, and the living of same by those sixty and four who are here gathered, may even save America from being invaded—if that is what ye desire.
3976-25, June 23, 1940

The first passage suggests that the threshold level for changing the future of one community is not even 10 people—it can be just *one* person who is attuned to God's will. The second passage is even more provocative. It was directed specifically to the 64 people gathered to hear a public reading at the yearly Congress of A.R.E. This passage suggests a way of influencing the future of a collection of people even as great as the United States.

In this case, it was the threat that America would be attacked or invaded. We should note that World War II was already under way, yet it was still a year and half before Pearl Harbor. Cayce seemed to be saying in June, 1940, that if even 64 people prayed *and lived* in attunement with God's plan, then the likely future for the American people (that is, attack and war) could be changed. Apparently the critical mass in consciousness was not achieved because the nation soon found itself embroiled in the war.

The story surrounding this reading has already been mentioned at the end of the third chapter. Recall the mood of the people at the conclusion of the reading. We might have hoped that their subsequent conversation would have centered on questions like, "What kind of prayer will be the right one?" or "At what time of day could we all be committed to praying?" However, in the recollection of one person who was present, that was not what was discussed. Instead the conversation focused on speculation as to where an attack or invasion might occur!

More than 40 years later, we look back on that incident and perhaps think of those people as having been foolish or fear-ridden. We wonder how they could have missed the spirit of what was being promised. We wonder how they could have failed to see and grasp the spiritual opportunity being offered them. And yet don't we often do the same thing now? The principles and numbers are still the same. The situation may be a bit different. World War II has come and gone, but today there are equally threatening prospects for our nation. But once again, 64 people can make the difference.

So what is *our* response? Do we wonder where the first earthquake will hit? Do we speculate on what kinds of riots will ensue if there is economic collapse? The opportunity is still there to be the little leaven that quickens the consciousness of the masses. This is a powerful concept which says that critical, threshold amounts of people can have a tremendous effect on the course of the future. It is an idea that bestows on us a sense of promise and a challenge of responsibility. And we are more likely to feel some hope and accept that responsibility if we see clearly just *how* the magic of "critical mass" *works* in the realm of human awareness.

A Mechanism to Explain Critical Mass

How is it that 10 righteous people or the prayers of just one individual could save a city? What forces and laws are at work to create such an extraordinary thing? Is it that God is placed in a dilemma? Perhaps in looking down on Sodom and seeing 10 righteous people, God felt "stuck." He could not afford to destroy

10 of His best followers, this line of reasoning would say, so He would have been forced to let everyone else off the hook.

However attractive this kind of argument may be, it has little merit. It reduces God to a befuddled being who dishes out punishment and yet is easily manipulated and placed in situations where He is forced to be merciful. We can do far better than this lame and naive explanation of how the principle of critical mass works on human consciousness. We can identify the universal laws which are at work and which naturally govern this process.

Let us begin with the universal law of oneness. It is the first key to understanding a mechanism which may allow the love of a few people to lift the awareness of humanity. One Cayce reading says that the law of oneness is so fundamental to the way the universe runs that it should be the object of study for the first six months in spiritual inquiry. We might wonder how we could ever study that law for so long. It seems as if we would merely agree that all force or energy is essentially just an expression of the one life force. Then we could move on to more interesting topics. In our impatience we might think that it all seems so simple. We might be satisfied to say that all life is one life; all minds are connected at some level in a cosmic unity. However, there may be much more than this to the notion of oneness. It may be much more profound an idea and have many subtle ways in which it directs our experiences.

For example, how does the law of oneness provide us with a clue as to how a threshold number of people can change the course of the future for all humanity? It begins by asserting that there are not two equal but opposing powers of good and evil which are battling for dominion of human minds. There *is* light and there *is* darkness, yes. Our experience tells us this and no abstract law of oneness can deny this experience which we all have. There are good works being done by some people, and there are evil-appearing, destructive works being done by others. The question, however, is this: What is the *relationship* between light and darkness, or between good and evil? Are they *equal* but opposite powers? If so, then we have majority rule when they clash, and nine units of good when confronted with ten units of evil will always result in a victory for evil.

But is that really what happens? When light confronts darkness what is the result of their interaction? If someone lights a candle in a darkened auditorium, doesn't the light permeate the entire room? Admittedly, that candle may illuminate the huge room with only a very dim light, but the fact remains that the darkness does not overpower the tiny candle flame. Light and darkness are not really equal but opposing forces. Darkness is better understood as an *absence* of light.

In other words, there is a fundamental oneness in the elements of what we observe in this example. There is the one force, which in its full manifestation is pure light. It is possible to experience diminished or dimmed expressions of that one force—or even the absence of its expression. But the darkness is not a power that is independent from the light and which could defeat it by superior numbers.

In the same fashion, the prayers of one person can work to save an entire community. The darkened consciousnesses of thousands of people do not constitute a power which can defeat a lighted prayer despite numerical superiority. Of course, that one person who lives in a community of fear and selfishness may be psychologically affected by his surroundings. He may feel discouraged, drained and stuck in the thinking patterns of his neighbors. He may forget to pray or may doubt the value of prayer. In this sense the darkness can "win." However, the law of oneness indicates that once that person remembers to pray and believes that healing work is being done, then the darkened consciousness of the masses does not block the widespread impact.

In addition to the law of oneness, there is a second universal law which helps us to understand the mechanism of how critical mass works. It is a principle with which we may be most familiar from physics: the law of resonance. Perhaps you will recall from high school physics the way in which tuning forks can demonstrate the action of this law at a physical level. What happens if you strike a tuning fork and set it to vibrating and then move it near another of similar structure? It will set the second tuning fork to vibrating as well. A process analogous to this physical demonstration may also happen at the level of human minds. It may well be that the vibration of consciousness can have a resonant effect upon other minds, recreating a sympathetic vibration or state of awareness.

Let us consider two ways in which the law of resonance may be operative in a mechanism for explaining critical mass. First, consider an idea which Cayce and many others have suggested.

Is it possible that there are many souls of advanced spiritual development who stand ready to help the earth in this time of transition? This aid may be through direct incarnation if appropriate parental channels can be found. Or it may be through the infusion of ideas and knowledge which could be telepathically transferred (perhaps even without the receiver being quite sure where that inspirational insight came from!). These ideas might be philosophical insights into the human condition, or they might be technological inventions which could help humanity deal with threatened physical survival. The law of resonance would give us one way of understanding how this assistance would be received. If a certain number of people made themselves into receptive tuning forks *of the proper structure,* then they might be set to "vibrating" with a conscious awareness which is quite extraordinary.

Another way of seeing this same possibility is that levels of energy for literally healing the planet would be the content of a resonant transmission. Instead of philosophical and technological *ideas* being transferred to receptive channels, it might be certain levels of *energy itself*—what some people have speculatively called new age energies. The channeling of such energies might be used to heal physical bodies or perhaps even to heal and purify our polluted and sick physical earth. We can only guess at what kind of help might be available from conscious beings in other dimensions of God's creation. Of course, we cannot passively await their intervention and expect them to clear up the mess we have collectively created. However, there may be significant validity to the law of resonance when applied to levels beyond physical objects like tuning forks. As we work to shape our personal "structure"—by meditation, exercise, diet, etc.—we may some day find ourselves set to vibrating with energies or ideas that seem to come from beyond ourselves and which promise to help the world as a whole.

In addition to this perspective on the law of resonance, there is another angle which is equally important in explaining how critical mass might work. It could well be that within every person there are many "tuning forks." One tuning fork within the mind of each person is the Christ Consciousness. Perhaps it has been buried away and forgotten in many people, but it is still there. However, it can be set to vibrating in one of two ways. The first is by conscious effort on the part of the individual—by seeking it out and making specific efforts to activate its vibration in physical life. It is probably safe to say that only a small percentage of the world's population is involved in doing this now. The second way is by the law of resonance. If someone nearby has set his or her own Christ Consciousness tuning fork to vibrating, it may create a sympathetic activity upon similar structures in other people.

And how would people *experience* such a secondary awakening of Christ Consciousness vibrations? Since they are not voluntarily at work on the spiritual path, how would they receive the impact of new vibrations mysteriously emerging from within themselves? It might appear as strange new feelings about themselves and others. It might come as dreams or intuitions. It could manifest as a change in physical health—for some as a healing and for others as a temporary illness (as the old ways of treating their bodies can no longer be handled by a newly sensitized body and mind). Or it might appear as some sort of cosmic or supernatural physical phenomenon in response to these inner events in man's consciousness. Some people expect an outer, physical reappearance of the Christ—a second coming—as the manner in which this global awakening would express itself.

Whatever the means or the appearance, we can expect that some people will be inspired by what they have received and proceed consciously to begin work on nurturing this newly realized spiritual dimension of themselves. However, others may be more frightened or stubborn about the process and they would reject what they feel happening to themselves.

Here, then, is one possible scenario for how human consciousness could be transformed in the coming decades. It does not deal with the impact which *outer* earth changes—like earthquakes, wars or weather changes—might have. It concerns how just a relatively few people could work to bring on a new age by the manner in which they deal with the inner level of earth changes. The scenario supposes that even a small group— perhaps only several thousand or hundred people—will begin to handle the inner changes in a loving, creative, responsible fashion. These people will not be sucked into the darkened consciousness of the masses, which is cynical and fearful. Instead they will attune themselves; they will make themselves of such a "structure" that new age energies and new age ideas will set their minds and bodies to vibrating through the law of resonance. They will receive aid from the Christ Consciousness within themselves and perhaps also from souls in other dimensions. When the number of this group reaches a significant amount, then a critical mass point will have been reached—a threshold level will have been achieved and a tremendous new effect will come into play.

A second type of resonance will be set in motion throughout the planet. Perhaps within a matter of months—although it could be years—resonant vibrations will begin to stir to life the Christ Consciousness in those who have not been seeking. This will be a remarkable event in human history. It will be a moment when humanity is on the verge of a quantum leap in awareness. If that moment coincides with a period of catastrophic *outer* change in the world, then the choices and responses made will be even more crucial. But this scenario supposes that very large numbers of people will be inspired by and accept the new ideas which they feel coming from within themselves. Remarkable dreams, intuitions and feelings will be encountered by millions of people— experiences which have not been consciously sought, but instead seem to be *given* from the inner self. Certainly there will be holdouts, those who may fearfully hold on to the old ways. But we will have turned the corner and the momentum will have become unstoppable. Humanity will be at the dawn of what Cayce and so many others have predicted for the 21st century—a new paradigm for human living based on cooperation and peace.

The Politics of the Transition

It has been said that politicians are the last to respond to changes in mass consciousness. The spirit of the times is usually felt in art, science and religion before it finds expression in the power games of the governing process. How, then, we might wonder, will the transition to a new paradigm overcome the blocks created by world leaders who want to hang on to the old system? How can enlightened souls have an impact on the decisions being made which affect all nations?

Undoubtedly, it is best for us to insist on some kind of explanation. There is no point in claiming that by magic several thousand spiritually attuned people can cause world leaders to alter the quality and direction of their decisions. Instead of relying on magic for an explanation, let us consider by what mechanism spiritually attuned people can create what Cayce called an "invisible empire."

The term "empire" is a blatantly political one. It refers to power and influence in human affairs which extend beyond the borders of any one nation. Historically, we might think of the Roman Empire or the Persian Empire, clear examples of political influences which spanned many regions and nationalities. When the Cayce readings refer to spiritually attuned people creating an invisible empire, they suggest that our work involves influencing the decision-making process which governs the nations. And "invisible" suggests that the influence will come at the levels of mind and spirit.

But how can we really have an effect upon the decisions which shape the world—such as the choices of war and peace, or the decisions on how national resources will be spent? The answer lies in first considering *who* it is that is *really* in control of the world.

Before you respond that it is the presidents of the United States and the Soviet Union, or the chairmen of Exxon and I.T.T., think about this principle: Only those who can truly control *themselves* (that is, their bodies, their attitudes and emotions) can claim to control things *beyond themselves.* And the indisputable evidence points out that most, if not all, of the so-called world leaders are actually *controlled.* This is *not* a matter of some conspiracy in which multinational corporations exert lobbying influences to mold the decisons of governments. Instead it is a matter of world leaders not being enlightened, spiritually free beings. And so, they are controlled, but the influence comes from their *own subconscious minds.* Their desires, fears, insecurities, and habits shape the nature of their decisions which, in turn, affect millions of people. Often those controlling influences from within themselves are hidden or only dimly perceived. Imagine, for example, how many important decisions are made by world leaders because of a feeling, mood or hunch. Suppose a national leader had to decide the next morning whether or not to invade a neighboring country. The quality and content of his or her dreams that night (remembered or unremembered) will likely leave that world leader with a particular mood or perspective in the morning which will largely affect the decision.

To the degree that world leaders are not yet enlightened beings who are free from the controlling influence of their own subconscious minds, *we* can exert a tremendous impact on their decisions. It is at the level of the *subconscious mind* that the apparent decision-makers are direct-able. If Cayce is correct and all subconscious minds are in contact with one another, then we have identified a vehicle for creating an invisible empire. From a dimension beyond the three-dimensional physical world, enlightened awareness has an influence. A world leader may never say, "I feel people praying for me and encouraging me to select the way of cooperation and peace." However, that may be exactly what is taking place.

In the past, patterns of fear or confusion may have existed within the subconscious mind of that leader which exerted a control and which led to choices of international tension and discord. But in the not-too-distant future, that same subconscious level may be the avenue by which the world leader is led to see matters a bit differently or to have new feelings and hunches about how to deal with old problems.

We *can* make a difference in the shaping of world events. *We* can make the difference. Just look at the arithmetic that can be extrapolated from the Cayce readings. Sixty-four people were once enough to change the destiny of the United States, and this nation is approximately one-twentieth of the world's population. If we multiply 64 by 20, we have approximately 1300 as a target number for the critical mass to change the destiny of humanity. Perhaps as few as just 1300 people who truly live and pray in attunement with God's plan will be the threshold amount to trigger global changes for healing.

If we will just understand the power to which we have access, this can occur. If we will but look deeply and see what power is really all about, then we can judge in whose hands it actually lies. Yes, we can make the difference. By the way that a few of us prepare for and deal with the *inner* aspect of earth changes, we will largely determine what *form* the *outer* earth changes will take. Just a handful of spiritually dedicated people can create a graceful, loving form of change in which all humanity will participate.

Chapter 6

Interpersonal Relationships in Times of Change

Beginning with this chapter we start on a new phase in our study of times of change toward a new age. The next several chapters will examine specific aspects of our life styles. They will propose elements of new age awareness which can direct us toward a different way of living with ourselves and with each other.

Probably no area of living is more challenging than close interpersonal relations. In this arena we continually are tested concerning how well we know ourselves, what are our values and priorities, and what have we to contribute to the world. Family relationships are often the most challenging; but similar, special opportunities are also frequently found on the community and vocational scenes.

In this chapter we will first explore some tools of consciousness which can be applied to almost any interpersonal relationship. These concepts and techniques are based upon insights and understandings of human nature which will most likely characterize a new age awareness. In the second section of this chapter we will take a close look at the meaning of marriage within a new age paradigm, with special emphasis upon balancing the masculine and feminine polarities within every soul.

New Age Tools for Relationships

We can well expect that in future societies there will continue to be stresses and tensions among people. Our visions of a new age should not be so utopian that we imagine interpersonal friction suddenly disappearing. What may change, however, is the variety of tools available to the consciousness of people who face a resentment, jealousy or other debilitating emotion. Perhaps we can develop techniques of awareness to transform and heal such reactions within ourselves. There are ways to meet at mental and spiritual levels the interpersonal problems which have usually been resolved at the physical level.

What will be proposed in this chapter is not a means of avoiding necessary human encounter. If you have a problem with a spouse or child or neighbor, the new age way of dealing with it is not necessarily to withdraw and handle it on your own. Too often our notion of the spiritual path is that we can just "meditate away" our troublesome emotional reactions. Even in a new age there will often need to be encounters and exchanges between people who are not getting along.

The question, however, concerns the attitudes and perspectives with which people try to work out such difficulties. The tools of consciousness which will be proposed in this chapter are not meant to be more sophisticated methods for suppressing honest emotions. Rather they are ways of *working with* those emotional energies, finding a place for them, and mixing them with understandings which can sometimes channel them into constructive directions. As one Cayce reading said, a person without the ability to get angry isn't worth much, but the person who cannot control his anger is worth even less. New perspectives of human living (or sometimes old perspectives which are to be recycled) can greatly aid us in this controlling or channeling process, bringing to us a deeper sense of joy and fulfillment in the interpersonal dimension of our lives, which is so important to all of us.

One such tool of consciousness is really an ancient one, although perhaps we can now see it in a new light. The theory of reincarnation is a powerful concept for understanding our interpersonal relationships. The idea that we have been here before (in *human* form only) strongly suggests that the interpersonal tensions, as well as harmonies, which we experience are at least partially the result of what has happened in a forgotten past. We have built and created patterns of thinking, feeling and acting toward particular souls, and, as we once again encounter them in this life, it is quite natural that some of those remnant patterns of consciousness would resurface. Sometimes the emergence of an emotion toward someone seems very bewildering to us. We cannot imagine why we feel or act in a certain way toward a specific person. We may be unable to account logically for our own reactions. The reincarnation perspective can be a valuable tool in these sorts of experiences.

Unfortunately it is not within the scope of this chapter to examine adequately important questions about reincarnation which need to be answered by each of us, as individuals, before we try to adopt this tool for dealing with interpersonal relationships. Each of us should wonder about problems like these:

What evidence is there to convince *me* that there is something to reincarnation?

How can reincarnation be reconciled with my previous beliefs (for example, are reincarnation and Christianity compatible)?

How do reincarnation and the laws of karma and grace work? There are a number of worthwhile books for the study of these and similar questions. Dr. Gina Cerminara's study of the Cayce readings is a classic in the field: *Many Mansions.* Joseph Head and S.L Cranston have compiled an excellent anthology, entitled *The Phoenix Fire Mystery,* which includes excerpts on reincarnation from numerous time periods and cultures. These and other books, in addition to our own dreams, intuitions and feelings, will help each of us to decide for ourselves whether or not we want to perceive life and relationships from the reincarnation angle.

If we choose to work with this ancient concept, what new age tools can be derived from it? In its essence the theory of reincarnation proposes at least three key ingredients for viewing other people and our interactions with them. *Responsibility* is one important element. This theory says that we ourselves are *at least in part* responsible for the quality and condition of our relations with others. Even if it appears that situations or feelings have arisen in a random, arbitrary way (that is, the neighbor who just happens to have moved in next door), there is actually a level of personal responsibility for us to accept in the kinds of people who are drawn into our lives. Through past associations, we have built tendencies to think, feel and act in specific ways toward those souls whom we once again encounter.

A second key ingredient in the theory of reincarnation is

purposefulness. It suggests that the interactions between us and other people happen for a reason. Something is being worked out—or, at least the potential exists for a healing to happen. There is purposeful opportunity, especially in the most difficult of interpersonal relations which we have to face.

And a third important element is the *continuity of life.* When we adopt a long-range time frame on our own lives and on the lives of others, then something can happen to our attitudes toward relationships. We realize that the tensions and difficulties which characterize even the best of relations have likely been a long time in the building. And for that reason it may take a little while for problems to be solved. The continuity of life—in *both* directions, past *and* future—can help us to be more *patient* with ourselves and others. If the theory of reincarnation helps us to overcome a tendency to be impatient with people, it becomes a valuable aid in working with our interpersonal relations.

With these three ingredients in mind, we can attempt to find practical ways to work with the reincarnation perspective. Unless there are tools to make applicable the concepts, then there is little direct value in even considering the idea of reincarnation. One of the most helpful techniques in this direction is creating past life scenarios which might explain why certain conditions currently exist in one's relationship with a particular person. Although this procedure could be used for a relationship which is going very well, it is especially potent when applied to a troublesome interaction with someone. What is required in this exercise is to use your imagination—to give yourself a type of past life psychic reading. What do you suppose Edgar Cayce would have seen concerning specific past life experiences you have had in previous incarnations with that soul?

Of course, some people protest that they are hardly likely to come up with actual past life data if they just use their imaginations, and that is probably true. But it misses the point of this technique. We will admit that the story you make up may not be precisely correct—in fact, it may be wrong on most all the details. However, the purpose of the past life scenario which you create is to establish a *clear visual image* in your mind's eye. Once you have a brief vignette from the hypothetical past clearly in your mind, you can use it as a *reminder.* Whenever you bring those images from the past life scenario to mind, they serve to recall the facts that (1) you are at least partially *responsible* for the current condition, (2) there is *purposefulness* in what is going on now, and (3) you need to be *patient* in working out this relationship because it may have been a long time in the building.

Consider an example which may make this process more understandable. Suppose a mother is having special difficulties in her relationship with a rebellious teen-age son. Some degree of frustration and hurt feelings on her part are probably quite normal. But how could the theory of reincarnation provide her with a helpful perspective? How could the new age consciousness technique of past life scenarios help her to shift her awareness? She might write out a hypothetical story based on the assumption that she and this soul are *repeating a pattern* from the past. Last time they failed to fulfill their purposes together, and now they are back working on it again. This is *one* manner in which the law of karma can work. Her story might read:

> Joseph and I lived together in Germany at the time of the Reformation. At that time also I was his mother. His father was very autocratic and harsh in discipline. I was afraid of my husband and failed to stand up for my son on those occasions when he was right—especially when he expressed very normal desires for independence as a teen-ager. A resentment toward me on his part developed and it carried through his adult years in that life.

This story has the main elements necessary to create a clear visual image for the woman: time period, country, the nature of the relationship (for example, father/son, boss/employee, etc.), and the quality of what went on between the two people. What is not especially important for this technique is whether or not the woman actually lived in that place and at that time. If reincarnation is true, then all we are concerned with are three things: that she realize personal *responsibility,* feel a sense of *purposefulness* in the midst of the current problem, and attain some feeling of *patience* about working this out. The hypothetical past life story can do that for her.

Try doing this for a troublesome relationship in your own life. If the idea of "repeating a pattern" doesn't seem to fit, try another way in which karma can work. For example, "role reversal" may feel right. This could be literal role reversal—such as, you were the boss and she was the employee last time, and now she is the boss and you are the employee. Or the role reversal could be the switching of characteristics and feelings. For example, maybe last time the husband was hypercritical and the wife got her feelings hurt easily. In this lifetime the souls maintain their gender, but characteristics are reversed: The wife is hypercritical and the husband easily gets his feelings hurt.

Once you have a scenario that seems to account for some of the current difficulties, here is how to use the images. When you are having a problem with your feelings toward this person, close your eyes for just a moment and let the past life images remind you of responsibility, purposefulness and patience. Those time-honored qualities of the spirit are rediscovered as a new age consciousness for healing interpersonal relationships.

In addition to the past life scenarios technique we can use another awareness tool for transforming our attitudes and feelings toward people. It is especially powerful for letting go of an old resentment or jealousy. This procedure is based on a new age understanding of how the mind works.

Common sense says that our minds can think only one thought at a time. We may be willing to accept the notion that there are multiple layers of consciousness, but it usually seems that our awareness can be functioning at only one layer at a time. Nevertheless, we occasionally have experiences to refute that assumption. For example, you may be driving down a highway with your mind lost in thought on some subject. Suddenly you realize that you have been driving for the last ten minutes without conscious recollection. You might even wonder, "Who was driving this car?" Or, in another example, there were many instances in which Edgar Cayce reported having a dream while he was giving a reading. In other words, it was as if one aspect of his awareness was functioning at the dream level and another at the superconscious state from which the readings came. These kinds of phenomena suggest that more than one level of mind is operating simultaneously, whether we are always aware of it or not.

Most likely a fundamental concept in a new age psychology will be that whenever a person is having an experience, many levels of his consciousness are taking it in simultaneously. *Conscious* awareness may be focused on just one level in a particular experience, but other levels are also recording it *and understanding it* in their own unique ways. Such a principle offers a technique for healing troublesome memories of old experiences—especially the unhappy emotional patterns of interpersonal relationships. The technique is based on the idea that an individual might learn to remember how other levels of his own mind understood that past event, an event which now creates such a problem.

To understand this more clearly, let us first consider an analogy. Suppose that three people were placed in a room in which a television was showing cartoons. Those three people included an eight-year-old child, an electrical engineer, and an aborigine tribesman who was unfamiliar with modern technology. How would those three experience and understand what was before them? The child might quickly become engrossed in what was on the screen, forgetting everything else but the cartoons. The tribesman might be confused or frightened by what he saw. The engineer might be relatively unaffected by the program on the screen and yet fully understand the mechanics of how a television set displays a picture.

Suppose for a moment that we identify with the tribesman. His reaction to the experience is fear and confusion. After leaving the room, he could carry that memory pattern with him for years. Whenever he thought of that room and the strange box with pictures and sounds, he might feel the fear and confusion again. However, what if he could get in touch with and actually experience how the other two people had perceived and understood the same event? Perhaps he would see that fear is not the only possible response to a television. The child would probably not be of much help to him, so his understanding would be no greater; but the mind of the engineer could help. If only the tribesman could "remember" what the engineer remembers having seen, then his fear and confusion might be healed.

In this analogy the three individuals are three levels of your own mind. In any experience they each perceive and understand what is going on from a unique point of view. However, your conscious awareness is usually focused on just one level within the range of mental possibilities. It would be quite remarkable if you could get in touch with the memories of how other levels of yourself experienced and understood events—especially events that caused resentments or jealousies in interpersonal relations.

For example, imagine that two years ago a close friend said something in a moment of anger which hurt you. It awakened in you a resentment which has since clouded the relationship between the two of you. You find it difficult to forgive, even though you know you should. Perhaps if you let go of the memory of how it hurt you, it won't seem as if you were being true to yourself.

But what is "yourself"? In a new age we will see that "self" is more than just the level of mind at which a person's awareness is currently focused. "Yourself" is just as much the levels of mind—*already within you*—which love and understand others. Even if those levels are still unconscious, that does not mean they do not already exist, nor does it mean that they fail to take in and record from their own points of view what you are physically experiencing.

In other words, according to this theory, we can predict that more than one genuine part of you "saw" the events of that day two years ago. A forgotten aspect of your mind—you may call it your higher self—*understood* why your friend said what he did, still loved him and quickly forgave. What would happen in your normal conscious mind if you could "remember" that day through the eyes of your higher self? It was actually there and understood the events.

Imagine the healing in interpersonal relations if we would learn the technique of multiple level recall. If we had that skill, then forgiving and letting go would no longer be a matter of being untrue to our genuine feelings. Feelings of love and forgiveness are just as genuine, and they are stored, too, within our memories. They are merely awaiting our skills at bringing them to the surface.

Our work in developing new age tools for healing relationships may involve specific techniques for training people in such multiple level recall. Meditation, when coupled with prayers for the healing of interpersonal relations, is one such approach. At the end of a meditation period, after having attained some measure of attunement, we can pray for a particular person. We might even imagine reliving an upsetting event with that person. However, in our meditative and prayerful fantasy we would see only the *events* as they previously happened, *not* the emotional reaction we had. We would *listen* in order to "recall" what other levels of our own mind, which were also present at the original event, may have felt and understood.

Or we might make a more careful study of our dreams when

trying to heal a festering problem with someone. Dreams are a likely stage for the forgotten levels of our mind to play out their perspectives, feelings and understandings. In the dream we may find ourselves adopting an unexpectedly loving attitude toward the person in question. Or we may encounter the symbol of some third party (actually a part of self!) who expresses great caring and understanding toward this person for whom we have been harboring bad feelings.

Another effective technique for awakening a multiple level recall of an event is journal-writing. This is a powerful technique for allowing muted voices from the unconscious to have their say. As we *write out* our feelings and thoughts about people and relationships, we can often get beyond the barriers of our habitual thinking. We have probably all experienced this in writing a letter to a friend. We may think about that letter for days before actually writing it. As we start to write, we suspect we know how it will look in the end because we have a pattern of thought about it. But what often happens? Unexpected things pop into our minds as we write. We get into ideas and feelings we had not expected to relate or did not even know were within us. This is what can happen by keeping a spiritual growth journal. In it we will record our failures and our successes in trying to learn how to love. And often it may be as valuable a tool as are meditation, prayer and dreams for "remembering" some troublesome event from a new point of view.

Soul Mates and Marriage in a New Age

Having explored briefly two fundamental tools for working with *any* interpersonal relationship, let us turn our attention to the topic most people think of when they hear the words "close relationship." We think of marriage. We think of the security and joy of mutual commitment to someone special. Almost every person feels a longing for companionship. At times we may understand this desire as a directive toward union with God; other times as a desire for union with another person.

Two principles come together in the material from the Cayce readings concerning the choice of a companion—particularly a companion for the marriage relationship. First is the notion that we are here in the earth for the purpose of growth and development in consciousness; furthermore, associations with some individuals

110

are more conducive to growth than are associations with others. This principle is probably easy for us to accept if we merely think back to the types of influences various friends and acquaintances have had on us in the past. A good marriage should be founded upon a shared purpose in life and the capacity to help one another to grow.

The second principle is the one of reincarnation: that we as spiritual beings (or souls) experience our growth in consciousness through a series of lifetimes in physical *human* form. In other words, we have likely been here before in the earth and, more specifically, have had close personal relationships with particular souls before. Attraction to another person and thoughts of marriage are very likely related to memory patterns (even subconscious memories!) of having been with that soul before. The readings suggest that often we are attracted to a particular person for marriage in this lifetime because of marriage relations at least once before.

But if reincarnation is a fact, we might expect that we have been married to many souls in the course of other incarnations. Which one of these partnerships is the best one to build upon now? Does a soul have only one other special soul that it is meant to be with whenever possible?

Many sources of psychic and metaphysical information have proposed concepts such as "soul mate" and "twin soul." The Cayce readings, although simultaneously raising some provocative questions, do shed some light on this topic.

A fundamental issue is the very nature of the soul. Is it male or female? Both or neither? The readings say the soul in itself does not have gender. "In the beginning, as was outlined, there was presented that that became as the Sons of God, in that male and female were as in one. . ." (364-7)

However, in order to learn and grow, a soul enters into the physical domain (characterized by such polarities as light/dark, positive/negative, thought/feelings) and chooses to incarnate into male or female expression. It is likely that in the long-range growth of the soul over many incarnations male *and* female experiences are needed. In selecting one gender over the other in a particular lifetime, a condition is usually created in which a balance or complement is needed, such as can be found in a marriage companion. This is not to say that important spiritual growth cannot be made during a life without marriage. Rather, the marriage relationship is *one* great avenue for development.

Perhaps this pattern of soul growth has not always been usual. Some readings suggest that in ancient prehistory, such as in the times of Atlantis more than 12,000 years ago, a soul could incarnate in such a way that male and female *qualities* were manifest simultaneously. It is not clear what form the physical body took in these cases. One person was told in a reading about an Atlantean incarnation: ". . .for then both male and female might be—desired so—in one." (288-27)

What, then, is a soul mate? Is it the soul one has married the most in past incarnations? Frequent marriage may be one factor, because apparently the soul-mate condition is built by shared physical experiences over a long period. However, it is more than this. A soul mate is a *complement* to self. One reading poetically describes it as "the tongue to the groove, the tenon to the mortise. . ." (1556-2) It is more than just a physical attraction; it is a *capacity to help each other* at the physical, mental and spiritual levels.

The condition of soul mates is also a matter of ideals. One important passage states: ". . .such as have in an experience found an ideal may be said to be soul mates, and no marriages [are] made in heaven nor by the Father save as each do His biddings." (275-38)

These criteria suggest that one could have more than one soul mate, although it is not clearly spelled out in a reading. We should no doubt be cautious about leaving a current marriage partner merely because of an attraction to someone else who might be a soul mate. Divorce is a complex issue and depends much on the ideals of the partners. However, those who come across the concept of soul mates *after* having already married can still rest assured that there is a purposefulness and opportunity for learning with the present partner.

For those who have not yet married and who would like to find his or her soul mate, what do the readings have to offer?

First, they suggest choosing someone who will help you to a "more helpful, more sustaining, more the well-*rounded* life. . ." (364-7) In modern expression we might also say that we are looking for someone who has the "right vibrations" for us. In fact, this is a phrase used by the readings in describing the kind of experience that might be felt between soul mates: ". . .with the union of two that vibrate or respond to those vibrations in self. . ." (364-7)

But even if we find someone who fits these criteria—someone who is perhaps a soul mate—this does not guarantee a good marriage. There will have to be *work* together in order that the great potential of the relationship may flower. This is what Cayce seems to suggest in the following answer. We might assume that the question, in effect, asked whether or not these two people were soul mates.

Q-7. Is this girl the type and quality of womanhood best suited to this man for a successful life?
A-7. May be made so in each. No one is suited exactly in the beginning, unless it has been foreordained through the ages of the mating of each. 257-15

This final statement is not clearly explained. We might understand "foreordained" to include a choice by the two souls before being born this time, or it may relate to very strong bonds built over many lifetimes of being married (that is, "the mating of each").

A concept similar to that of soul mate is twin soul. When Cayce used this term, he did not mean to imply that two souls were identical. Instead, it was a matter of two souls sharing a common purpose or ideal. The two souls would *not* necessarily have had previous marriage incarnations. In other words, the soul-mate condition is largely built in the material plane of existence (although, as has previously been mentioned, it has mental and spiritual components beyond sexual attraction). However, the twin-soul conditions evolve more from a commonality at the idea or ideal level.

An example of twin souls, according to the Cayce readings, is Mary and Jesus. One reading says, "In the beginning Mary was the twin soul of the Master in the entrance into the earth!" (5749-8)

Finally, we might ask, "Where does all this business of soul mates and twin souls take us? Is it our destiny to find and be reunited with some other special soul?" This is *not* the approach of the Cayce readings. They refer to Jesus' teaching that in the heavenly kingdom we are neither married nor given in marriage. As helpful as marriage relationships may be in the earth, beyond this material domain it is our destiny to find wholeness within our own souls. If one must think in terms of being destined to ultimate union with some other soul, then think of that other soul as the Christ Soul. One reading said, "But know, the soul is rather the soul mate of the universal consciousness than of an individual entity" (that is, some other particular soul). (2988-2)

The principles of soul mate and twin soul are therefore potentially both helpful and misleading. These concepts can help us understand some of the key factors in making a wise choice of a marriage partner and can remind us that some relationships are tremendous storehouses of love and helpfulness which can be reawakened. However, these concepts can be misleading either if we forget that our ultimate companion is the Christ, or if we use them to leave the responsibilities of relationships to which we have already committed ourselves in this lifetime.

Finding the Inner Partner

As we have already seen, one essential feature of the readings' philosophy of relationships is that the soul is both male *and* female. Most likely our capacity to experience a fulfilling relationship with someone else will be determined largely by how well we get to know both sides of *ourselves.* In other words, before marriage or any other deep relationship, we *already have* a profound inner relationship between polar opposites. We already *have* a partner before we go in search of an outer companion in the physical world. That companion is a little known aspect of ourselves. It is what John Sanford has so beautifully termed "the invisible partner," in his book* on achieving individual wholeness. C.G. Jung has also defined this concept in terms of the *animus* (the unconscious masculine qualities within a woman) and the *anima* (the unconscious feminine qualities within a man).

It is probably safe to say that our attraction to certain people and our desire to form lasting relationships with them is often profoundly affected by how well we have integrated the animus or anima into our conscious lives. The ancient teaching "Know thyself" is nowhere more applicable than in choosing a partner. Marriage is not an end but a beginning; and a couple's growth, as individuals and as a unit, is shaped by the more fundamental relationships which both of them have with this hidden side of themselves.

*John Sanford, *The Invisible Partners*. New York City: Paulist Press, 1981.

114

As the paradigm shifts in our times, as the assumptions change about so many things, what will happen to the meaning of close personal relationships and especially marriage? In the old paradigm of Western culture, the role expectations of men and women have been tightly defined. Clearly those assumptions are being shaken. Not only do men and women more easily take on roles which were formerly reserved for just one sex or the other, but the very notion of marriage is being challenged in many aspects of society. Each of us needs to think about and decide where we stand on some tough questions:

> Are there fundamental differences between men and women which should then be reflected in social roles and behaviors?
> Is marriage any more special from a spiritual standpoint than a couple just living together?
> Are there parts of myself I am afraid of—parts which are usually associated with the opposite gender?

How we answer these kinds of questions will be important in defining a new age paradigm for relationships. *All* of us need to think and pray about these issues because they will deeply affect the quality of our society in the centuries to come. Those people who have been married for many years under the traditional paradigm which is now being shaken are the very ones who perhaps should be most concerned. They are likely to be among the first ones coming back again—reincarnating in the 21st century—testing out the new assumptions for close relationships which we create now.

Whatever we choose and build together, one view seems clear. Cayce, Jung and many others agree that we need to find pathways for men to know better their feminine sides, and for women to know better their masculine sides. If we are ever to build a social structure that is not sex-biased, it must begin with a critical mass number of well-integrated, balanced individuals. It will be started by enough people who courageously complete the scary business of learning who they are all over again—people who are willing to explore and trust the opposite gender buried within them. And what, we might well wonder, will that entail? At best we can speak only in generalities, but even these broad guidelines can have an archetypal validity.

For a man it may mean the experience of several ways of living which traditionally have been associated with women. For example, he has *feelings* about things, not just logical analyses of them. Oh yes, men have almost universally known they *had* feelings (like they have possessions or maybe a nagging disease) but have they been capable of *being* those feelings and giving them expression naturally? Perhaps at a football game they have easily shown excitement or displeasure; perhaps occasionally in the privacy and intimacy of their bedrooms, they show feelings. But there is considerable room for growth and learning for most men by discovering the range of their feelings and their expression.

Likewise the *intuitive* path to knowledge is one of which men know but perhaps are less inclined to take. It is a feminine approach, whereas logic and rationality are more familiar and reliable avenues for most men. The *arts* are another area to be explored. Boys may have teased each other about doing "sissy" things like taking dance, painting or music lessons. Somehow there has developed in our culture the idea that the arts are primarily the domain of women, and this concept easily permeates the methods used to rear children. Certainly there are many examples of men who are at the top of their fields in the arts—great dancers, composers, artists, etc. Nevertheless, for mainstream adult males in our culture, direct participation in the arts is an uncomfortable task. Perhaps it is because the arts require more of one's feeling and intuitive side than most men feel competent to express. Perhaps men are more inclined to be embarrassed and ashamed of the awkwardness which usually accompanies trying to learn to dance or paint or make music. Whatever the answer, this area of human expression is an especially good one for many men to explore as they try to learn about that invisible partner within themselves.

The care of children is another type of experience which traditionally has been left primarily to women. It has been assumed that women are more naturally skilled at *taking care of children.* Of course, there are some biological facts which point in this direction, such as nursing an infant. However, there is no reason to suppose that a father cannot become aware of *and* express the nurturant talents within himself. Too often in the past men have wanted to *have* children but not to help rear them. Sharing equally in the upbringing of children will not only help mothers have the time to explore the masculine polarity of themselves, but will also be a blessing to fathers as they uncover important and beautiful aspects of themselves. We can well imagine that the new age model for the marriage relationship and for parenting will encompass this more balanced approach to child care.

Two final areas for men to explore in balancing the male-female polarities within themselves are *listening* and *sensitivity*. Once again we are dealing with levels of human experience which women traditionally demonstrate more skillfully. It is not that we lack adequate examples of sensitive men who know how to listen. But pointing to exceptional individuals does not contradict an obvious tendency within men. The masculine role has too often been relegated to making decisions, being assertive, leading, *telling* others how things are. However, there is an equally valid pole within every man that is skillful at receiving and listening. The balanced man, the man of our new age paradigm, will have explored and become more comfortable with both sides of this polarity and the other polarities which we have examined.

And what then for women? What are the levels of human experience which tradition says are primarily reserved for men? What areas have women thought to be outside the domain of their opportunities? One good example is the exploration of the logical, rational, *analytical pathway to knowledge*. The soul mind of a woman has just as much capability as that of a man to obtain knowledge by logical pathways. A woman's tendency may be to follow more intuitive or feeling-oriented avenues. However, to be balanced, integrated women of our new age paradigm, they must learn to trust and develop this other aspect.

Likewise women might explore their abilities to *master mechanical objects*. The job of maintaining the products of modern technology has usually been left to men: repairing automobiles, servicing broken appliances, etc. Once again we can see that there are certainly exceptions. We all know of some woman who tunes up her own car or another woman who can repair faulty electrical wiring in appliances. However, we are looking at the broad trends, the archetypal patterns of our 20th-century Western culture. And from that vantage point we see that little support is given to women in certain areas, little encouragement is given to them for getting to know the invisible male side within themselves.

This is true not just with developing analytical powers or

mechanical skills. It also involves *business responsibilities* and *leadership in community and political roles*. Women may, in fact, be our best hope to humanize these areas. They may become the greatest asset in the future development of new methods and a new image for the business world. The natural sensitivity of women may dramatically help to bring a new spirit to the politics of leadership—at the community, national and international levels.

The world needs the kinds of contributions which women can make in areas of life men have dominated—just as much as the world needs the contribution of men in areas which have seemed foreign to them. There is no doubt that a sex-bias exists in our old world paradigm, directed more specifically at women. But the effects of the biases on men have been subtle and damaging as well. Perhaps some measure of looking back is helpful. Maybe lessons can be learned from how the prejudices, biases and limitations developed. However, we cannot afford to get too caught up in recrimination and resentment. We need cooperation and good will between men and women in order to build a new kind of world.

Such cooperation and good will is created at the *personal* level first. That principle cannot be stressed too much. For example, if you are a woman and you are out of touch with the masculine archetype within your own soul, then it is most likely that your life will reinforce the old world paradigm. You will probably contribute to tension between the sexes and rigid role models for men and women. However, if you are in touch with your masculine qualities and comfortable with them, then you are able to contribute to the building of a new kind of world. And, of course, the parallel example holds true for men.

This is *not* to say the new age paradigm is to be a genderless social structure, although many people have reached this unnecessary conclusion. Many very feminine women are also balanced, integrated models for our new age ideal. They are comfortable and aware of their masculine side. They know their animus energies and can draw on them when needed, without a sense of fear or embarrassment. However, they may choose to express the feminine qualities most often in the key areas of their lives. The same sort of process is true of some men. It will be important for people to leave open the options of how far they want to venture in living out daily the opposite polarity within

Discover the wealth of information in the Edgar Cayce readings

Dreams
Soul Mates
Karma
Earth Changes
Universal Laws
Meditation
Holistic Health
ESP
Astrology
Atlantis
Psychic Development
Numerology
Pyramids
Death and Dying
Auto-Suggestion
Reincarnation
Akashic Records
Planetary Sojourns
Mysticism
Spiritual Healing
And other topics

Membership Benefits You Receive Each Month

EDGAR CAYCE FOUNDATION and
A.R.E. LIBRARY/VISITORS CENTER
Virginia Beach, Va.
OVER 50 YEARS OF SERVICE

BUSINESS REPLY CARD
First Class Permit No. 2456, Virginia Beach, Va.

POSTAGE WILL BE PAID BY

A.R.E.®
P.O. Box 595
Virginia Beach, VA 23451

themselves. What seems most crucial is personal awareness. Even if a man chooses to stay in the business world and primarily use his logical mind, he should have occasional experiences of the feeling, artistic, receptive side of himself. Even if some women choose to be homemakers and focus on child rearing, they should be aware of and occasionally experience the masculine archetype within themselves. With this expanded understanding of our *individual* natures, we will create a more balanced, harmonious model for close interpersonal relationships. A greater likelihood will exist for *understanding* and for helping each other complete the unique work each of us was born to do.

Finding an Outer Partner

Keeping in mind that getting married is not the end of a process but the beginning of one, it is all the more important to make the proper selection of a lifetime partner. It is hoped that in a new age more grace and attunement would be involved in our marriage selections and less karmic compulsion which thrusts people together but soon thereafter leads to discord or even divorce.

Some readers of this book will have the selection of a partner still before them. In many of these cases their situations involve the desire to form a better second marriage than was the first. The principles and concepts soon to be outlined may prove beneficial in finding the right partner. Most of the readers of this book are probably already married; and yet, it is still pertinent to consider what methods may be used to find a partner in a new age world. Very likely we will all be back (that is, reincarnated) in that new society and have chances to apply these approaches. What we learn in this lifetime does carry over—if not as a conscious recall then at least in terms of unconscious predispositions. We might even speculate that a soul who now sets ideals for how to choose a partner in the next lifetime will be attracted to parents in the next incarnation who will provide a similar sort of instruction.

The key element in a new age paradigm for choosing a marriage partner is setting *ideals*. (This topic will be examined in detail in the next chapter; let it be sufficient for our discussion of marriage preparation to say that the ideas in that chapter are important to apply.) By setting a spiritual direction for our lives, we set in motion an unseen selection process which attracts to us situations *and* specific people for the fulfillment of those ideals.

But more than one variation of the procedure of setting ideals is needed. Not only should we go through the general steps involved in setting a spiritual ideal and complementary mental and physical ideals for *current* situations and relationships; additionally, we might well formulate an ideal image of the kind of partner whom we think we would like to be with. What we need is a balance between specifics and a willingness to let go and trust that we may have left out some important factors. God wants us to be *involved* in the selection procedure. How else do we learn to use the will? How else do we come to understand our conscious and unconscious desires?

One way of understanding the soul's journey in materiality is the work of learning how to use the conscious, finite ability to make choices in a way that is in attune with divine will. By way of analogy, teenagers cannot grow into mature adults as long as the parents are making all the decisions. They must learn to exercise their own individual free wills. The same process holds true if we are to move into spiritual maturity. We must develop the God-given ability of conscious choice.

On a piece of paper write out statements about the ideal partner whom you desire to have in your life. If there are certain items which really do matter, indicate just that. However, be very honest with yourself. Don't worry about blocking God's plan for your life, because writing out this ideal image is not the last step in the process. Of course, in the end, we will need to say, "Nevertheless, Lord, not as I will it to be, but Your will be done." However, we misunderstand the way God works with us in our growth if we *start out* saying, "God, it is all up to You." So jot down your responses to these categories about the ideal partner for you (in this lifetime or in the next).

What sort of beliefs would this person hold?
What kind of family background?
What age (that is, compared to your own age)?
What personality characteristics?
What educational level?
What vocation?
What physical appearance: hair color, eye color, height, weight?
What attitude toward having children?
Been married before (that is, divorced, widowed)?

Once you have created your list, then put it away. Perhaps you might want to place it in your Bible. Now be ready for God's instructive work to begin with you. You can expect to be tested. This does not necessarily mean "tempted," because it is not God's intention to make things hard on us. Rather it may be that you will be given the chance to see for yourself whether or not your ideal image is really the one with which you want to stay. Most likely you will have the opportunity to re-evaluate several times the items you have put on your list as different kinds of people are drawn into your life.

Other levels of work can also be going on within you at the same time that your image of an ideal partner is being refined. One worthwhile exercise is to try to identify the patterns of acting, thinking and feeling which may have characterized previous and unfruitful relationships. Do you observe recurrent themes in the sorts of people to whom you are attracted when hoping to find that special companion? For example, some people recognize that they are looking for a substitute parent. Other people have observed a frustrating pattern of being attracted to members of the opposite sex who have problems and want sympathy. If you can recognize how you may have repeatedly frustrated yourself, it will be important to try to break that cycle. Getting past the old blocks is crucial to finding the ideal outer companion for this lifetime. It always means changing something about the way you respond to the world and people around you; and it usually means changing something about how you see yourself.

Another action you can take while your image of the ideal partner is being refined involves *becoming* that ideal. In other words, try living *yourself* the traits that you are looking for in another person. Something almost magical can happen when you do this. People are often drawn to others in whom they see a reflection of themselves. Sometimes that reflection involves aspects of themselves which they are unable to express adequately. In such an instance, we would see a couple who seem to be opposites but in whom this principle is still working. Both of them see something in the other which they know is within themselves, even if they are not proficient at expressing that quality. Sometimes the marriage is based on the hope of being able to help each other learn to manifest these hidden factors. Other times the marriage becomes a kind of unproductive

121

dependency in which both of the partners are saying, "I don't have to learn to express the qualities hidden in me because my spouse is so good at doing it for both of us."

Whichever way the concept is used, it is a significant part of the chemistry of close personal relationships. Using this idea you might wonder, "What would happen if I tried living the qualities I want to see in my future partner?" If you try this, you may discover the magic that was suggested: It may well be that when the soul best suited for your companionship comes into your life, he or she will recognize himself or herself in you and be attracted to you. In other words, if patience, kindness and a sense of humor are traits listed in your ideal image, try living that way yourself. If the day comes when that best person for you passes your way, he or she is likely to experience a self-recognition upon encountering you.*

A final exercise in preparation for marriage concerns an openness to revelation. In other words, we can receive guidance along the way in picking a partner. Through prayer and meditation we may get intuitions about these important decisions. In dreams especially we may gain important insights. However, always combine common sense and rational analysis with what appears to be guidance from dreams. Dreams can sometimes reflect fears or desires. Ask yourself before assuming that a particular dream is guidance from God, "To what degree does this dream just play back to me what I have been thinking or feeling in waking life?" A dream in which you are marrying someone *may not* be a revelation which spiritually blesses such a marriage, particularly if you have been daydreaming of such a match. The dream could just be a rehashing of your habitual train of thought.

A better way to use dreams as a guidance tool for marriage is to pray for a dream which gives you feedback on a tentative decision you've made. For example, you might ask your dreams to give you a precognitive look at where a relationship will tend to go if you follow the path down which you are currently headed. This approach to using dreams for guidance in your marriage choice also holds true for most any kind of interpersonal relationship and the aid you might seek from your higher self.

As we work with some or all of these tools for finding an ideal

---

*Credit for this idea about attracting the right partner goes to Charles Thomas Cayce. I tried applying his advice in my own life and I feel it was instrumental in helping me find my wife.

marriage partner—whether in this lifetime or in the next—we need to maintain an attitude of peace and faith. Nothing is gained by being anxious or compulsive. If we are driven out of a sense of loneliness to find someone, it may well be that no other person could ever solve that loneliness for us. There must be some degree of love for our own companionship with self if we are ever to be a good partner. For many of us, this affirmation holds true: "The kind of person I want as my partner is looking for someone who is not desperate to find a partner."

And even more important is the affirmation that if we sincerely seek a life of companionship and mutual service, there *is* a partner for each of us. Many people have found this prayer to be a helpful one: "Lord, send me that person whom I can help and love, and who will help and love me."

Conclusion

As a new age paradigm begins to emerge, the way in which people relate to each other will clearly be affected. We will be able to observe this in a variety of types of interpersonal relationships, but perhaps in none as clearly as the intimacy of marriage. The current day confusion which is so evident in our culture's attitudes and behaviors with marriage is evidence for how the old assumptions no longer seem to be serving us well.

Any new age life style regarding marriage will grow out of new assumptions of human awareness. We cannot act out effectively a different method of living unless there is a genuine consciousness behind it. Aspects of that new awareness will include the perspective of reincarnation, the realization of male and female poles within every soul, and the importance of ideals in selecting a partner. Setting ideals is the key for developing a harmonious relationship within oneself, the prerequisite of a good relationship with someone else. In the next chapter we will explore the meaning of ideals and the role they play in building a new kind of world.

Chapter 7

Creating a New World Through Ideals

No study of Edgar Cayce's vision of a new world would be complete without a description of how ideals can shape our future. Of course, Cayce is not alone in using ideals to formulate a picture of how the world is changing. Virtually every futurist either explicitly or implicitly identifies certain ideals which he or she recommends as guiding influences in building new ways of living. In fact, any prediction of the future which does not involve a shift in ideals for humanity is not really a creative vision at all, but rather an extension or extrapolation of the present.

What is it about ideals which is so crucial to our exploration of shifting paradigms and spiritual renewal for the planet? What does an ideal *do* at the individual level or at the level of humanity as a whole? In essence, ideals provide a way in which we can break out of the inertia of old patterns of thought, feeling and action. Ideals are the tool by which we break the momentum of where we are headed and chart a new course. The spiritual principle of ideals—along with the gift of free will—is the most helpful ingredient in the chemistry of these changing times.

Certainly not every ideal breaks the inertia of the old paradigm. The old assumptions which constitute that world view are themselves based on certain ideals. Nevertheless, any shift in assumptions which could subsequently lead to a new way of living *begins* with a change in ideals. In other words, ideals are the bedrock of the structure of human experience. Efforts to hold on to the old world are primarily attempts to maintain old ideals.

However, the universal laws which govern our lives and spiritual evolution continually present us with the opportunity to formulate new ideals and to set in motion a different kind of future—for ourselves as individuals or for the earth as a whole.

Definitions of Ideals

The principle of ideals is not one which easily lends itself to a single synonym. The word "goal" is often used interchangeably with "ideal," but the Cayce readings attempt to draw a distinction between the two. A goal can be understood to be a physical product which is desired. Usually we can observe material conditions and determine whether or not a goal has been reached. Examples of goals would include making at least a B on an upcoming test, losing ten pounds, fund-raising $30,000 for an organization, or becoming vice-president within five years. However, these would not really constitute ideals—even physical ideals—in the way that Cayce used the term.

An ideal has more to do with the unseen levels of our being as we live our lives and work toward our goals. It is not that we are to eliminate goals from the way we consider the future. Instead, we should just include a careful plan as to *how* we intend to pursue those aims. In other words, an ideal identifies the "why" and the "how" of our thoughts and actions, whereas a goal indicates the "what."

From the examples of goals just given, we might ask ourselves these kinds of questions in trying to formulate ideals:

The test:	Why is it important to me to make at least a B?
	What methods will I use to achieve that goal and what methods are unacceptable?
Losing weight:	Why do I want to lose weight?
	What is my attitude toward my body?
	How can I best lose weight?
Fund-raising:	Why is this cause important to me?
	What techniques for fund-raising will be consistent with the purposes of this organization?
Vice-president:	What are my attitudes toward my current position with the company?
	How do I achieve my goal?
	Why do I want to be promoted?

Using these questions and others like them we can readily see that two individuals could achieve the same goal but have different ideals in the process. For example, one person might have an ideal of greater responsibility and service in desiring to become vice-president, but another might have a purpose of wanting more power. Both might obtain the promotion in their own respective companies, but entirely different processes would have developed within their souls.

Besides distinguishing an ideal from a goal, the Cayce readings use other terms to characterize the nature of ideals. One is the concept of a standard of measurement, a *self-determined* criterion by which each individual can evaluate his or her experiences. The point of an ideal is *not* to make us feel guilt, which is certainly something which *can* take place when we evaluate ourselves. In fact, guilt is most often associated with measuring our thoughts and actions against a standard put upon us or accepted from *someone else.* The self-determining feature of an ideal may serve as a safeguard against unnecessary self-condemnation or guilt. For this reason, it is wise in the selection of an ideal to choose something which is a delicate balance between two poles. On the one hand, the ideal needs to stretch us to grow. On the other hand, the ideal needs to be something which is do-able. There should be reasonable prospects for success when picking an ideal. Even if it is not something which we are likely to be good at doing *every* day, it helps to reinforce our efforts if the ideal is something we are probably going to achieve at least occasionally.

Those of us who work with ideals as a tool for self-transformation in a new age do not want to be thought of as being "idealistic," with the negative connotation that word has assumed. We are not to be impractical, day-dreaming visionaries who have great ideas but can never apply any of them. If we set our ideals too high, we risk appearing to be "idealistic" to others and to ourselves. However, this cannot happen if we find that stimulating equilibrium between stretching ourselves to grow and change on the one side and putting success within our grasp on the other side.

In addition to the notion of a standard of measurement, an ideal also has the character of a motivation. In fact, if you wish to talk to a traditional behavioral scientist (for example, a psychologist or a sociologist) about ideals, you had best use the term "motivation." They will dismiss you as a mere metaphysical speculator if you refer to ideals but can talk to you for hours about theories of motivation. Actually the two terms are almost identical, the only difference being that motivational theories usually deal with the narrow domain of our drives to fulfill physical needs. Fortunately, there are a few respected theoreticians in the human sciences who recognize the levels of mental and spiritual need within us and who consider the inherent motivations to fill those needs.

A motivation tells us *why* we do what we do. Many individuals make it their profession to explain the motivations of others. However, this condition could not exist if people were not generally unconscious of the inner dynamics which control their thoughts, feelings and actions. Otherwise there would not be such a demand for professional motivation analyzers.

When we decide to work with our ideals, we are in effect saying that we want to bring the motivational layer of our being into the light of day. We want to see not only what has pushed and pulled us around through life, but we want to have a choice in what those influences are going to be. Perhaps setting an ideal does not immediately and automatically do away with the old motivational patterns which have controlled us; however, it is a powerful first step in taking control and responsibility for ourselves. It is the initial requirement for the development of a new age consciousness. As we *work* with those new ideals (because we are speaking of far more than just *setting* ideals!), the motivational influences begin to change.

A final aspect of our definition of the principle of ideals is the spirit in which we live. This concept is the clearest and most helpful one to many people as they try to understand how ideals work. We may have goals and aims in life, but *how* are we going after them? Will it be with aggression or with kindness? Will it be with resentment and a long face or will it be with joyfulness, hopefulness or faith? When we answer these questions, we are taking a big step toward selecting an ideal for our lives.

Whether you think of an ideal as a standard, a motivation or a spirit of living, it is important to keep in mind that ideals themselves are not something new. One Cayce reading has suggested that we all have ideals, whether we are conscious of them or not. However, what will be new is the way in which people work with ideals in a conscious manner. Once we understand the power of the mind to change our physical lives, we will begin to wake up to the influence which ideals have. Once we discover the spiritual gift of free will, we will see how crucial it is to choose our own ideals and not let any teacher or television program subtly determine them for us. As the foundation of human experience, ideals are the starting point in our attempt to develop a new age awareness.

Setting a Spiritual Ideal

Because we live in a three-dimensional state of consciousness, most people find that their work with ideals is best accomplished by working with three levels of ideals which correspond to three levels of ourselves: spiritual, mental and physical. Ideals are best set in that order, with the spiritual ideal chosen first. This was how we were created as souls: a spiritual creation initially, then the gifts of mind and free will, and finally a movement into matter. The *setting* of ideals follows this progression; however, the *application* and experiencing of those ideals best begins with the physical level and retraces those steps.

There has often been considerable bewilderment in the minds of people who have studied the Cayce readings on the spiritual ideal. Clearly those readings recommended to men and women that they set a spiritual ideal first. However, there seem to be contradictory statements in other parts of the readings which cause confusion. In some cases the readings state that we all have the *same* spiritual ideal—that in fact there is really only *one* spiritual ideal. And yet other readings seem to stress the individual quality of a spiritual ideal and encouraged people to pick their own. How are these two positions to be reconciled?

One theory is that this paradox can be solved only by seeing that the readings are speaking to two equally genuine but quite different parts of ourselves. To the soul there is really only one ideal. Every soul was created in the image of God and has that ideal written within itself. That single, universal spiritual ideal is the *experience* of the soul's oneness with the Divine and of the unlimited love and harmony which exists between it and its Creator. We might arbitrarily label this ideal the "Spiritual Ideal." It is given many different names but in every case it means that highest imaginable consciousness: Christ, Buddha, Creative Forces, Jehovah, Nirvana, etc.

And yet despite the existence of this consciousness within us, we are generally unaware of it. It is buried within the unconscious like a hidden and dimly felt pattern of the mind. We struggle to catch a glimpse of it. We speculate about its qualities. We make the best guess we currently have as to what that Spiritual Ideal is all about. And that guess or approximation which is made by our conscious, physical selves is what we might label the "spiritual ideal." In this sense, the spiritual ideal is different for different people because they are not at the same points in their understanding and experience of the Spiritual Ideal. In fact, what we are often doing when we choose a spiritual ideal is to select just one significant quality or aspect of the greater Spiritual Ideal. This is especially the case for those of us who set ideals that we can get a handle on, work with and have some prospects of being successful with. It is probably wise to set a spiritual ideal which is only one aspect or facet of the highest Spiritual Ideal.

With these concepts in mind, you might consider this specific approach: A first step is to affirm that a greater Spiritual Ideal exists within you. Even though you may have to admit that you do not know fully what it is like, it is important to be able to think in greater and more universal terms. Try giving it a name. What word or phrase comes to your mind to represent that highest consciousness toward which you move in your spiritual journey? Is it God, Jesus or Allah? Is it universal oneness or limitless love? What is important is that you select a word or phrase that feels right to you. This is the ultimate ideal—something your soul seeks in incarnation after incarnation. From one lifetime to another you may have called it by different names. What is the best word or phrase you have now?

Second, try to set a spiritual ideal which is much closer to home. The focused spiritual ideal will actually be one quality of that greater Spiritual Ideal. It will be some aspect which most directly challenges your current spiritual growth. It may be a word or phrase such as "patience," or "joyful creativity." It might be "understanding" or "freedom" or "faith." To get a clearer picture of what you are being asked to choose in the selection of a spiritual ideal, think about these two analogies.

First, imagine a huge superhighway which has fifty lanes headed in one direction. This a modernistic version of a spiritual path. The entire highway is analogous to the Spiritual Ideal. Each of the fifty lanes is a particular quality or characteristic of that highest Ideal. For example, one lane is labeled "tolerance," another is labeled "peacefulness," etc. Progress can be made in any of the lanes. However, at any given point in your soul's evolution there is one track which is the "fast lane." If you are working on that particular quality and growing with it, then your progress is especially quick. That "fast lane" is the best one for you to choose as your spiritual ideal. It is as if you were to say, "I know that if I pick this one, specific quality of the Divine and really work on living it, then I am really going to grow."

Of course, as this analogy suggests, it is possible to change lanes. And, in fact, people who are seeking do find a periodic need to switch the spiritual ideal. However, most people find that several months or several years may go by before such a change is genuinely needed. This is not to say that after "changing lanes" you no longer need to work on the former quality. If you move from the "patience lane" to the "faith lane" after a year's work of focused effort and growth, there will still be many opportunities to live and improve on your patience. The switch merely denotes a recognition of *which quality has now become the key catalyst* for moving you along most rapidly.

This principle is further explained by a second analogy. Imagine a beautiful gemstone with fifty facets. Each facet could be thought of as a specific quality that might be chosen as a spiritual ideal. The gemstone as a whole is like the Spiritual Ideal. However, at any point in your spiritual condition there is a particular facet of it which is special. When you look toward the center of the stone through that facet, it particularly allows you to see into the heart and the essence of that stone. Such is the function of a spiritual ideal, which holds the key to our lives. When lived fully, it provides us with a preview of the fullness of the spiritual heritage which we are in the process of claiming.

Understanding Our Spiritual Ideal

Take some time now and write down both the greater Spiritual Ideal and a more focused spiritual ideal, using words that seem best to you. Do this recording in something you will keep, such as your dream journal. You will most likely feel the limitation of words, but press ahead. The ideal is never a word itself, but the experience. The words merely serve to reawaken the experience. If you choose the words "selfless service" for your spiritual ideal, realize that the actual ideal is the feeling and the purpose you have as you live in such a way. The words can be a powerful tool for recreating that feeling and purpose.

Or you may sense a resistance to *writing down* these ideals. Your mind may say, "Oh, I already know what my ideals are, and I'll just keep them in my head." However, the committing of them onto paper is an important step: It is even a symbolic expression of your intention to do something about these ideals in physical, practical application.

A frequent experience in setting the focused spiritual ideal is that we are not really sure what the quality we have selected actually entails. For example, the word "forgiveness" might intuitively feel like the right word to one person. She might have a sense that being more forgiving would quickly transform many aspects of her life. It seems to be a key—the fast lane for her growth right now. But she is left wondering what forgiveness really means. How does it work and where does she begin?

At this point our dreams can be especially valuable tools for guidance. In fact, without having set an ideal we should probably be very careful about using our dreams for direction. Like a ship without a compass, it may be hard to tell where a dream is taking us. But with an ideal clearly stated, even if not yet fully understood, our dreams will begin to illustrate for us the meaning of that ideal in practical application and understanding.

For example, one woman who had studied the Cayce material for several years decided to set for a spiritual ideal the word "faith." Still a bit perplexed as to how she should try to live that ideal, she was encouraged to see how her dreams began to give her new insights within a few days. Here are two of her dreams:

(Dream #1) "I accompany a friend and my aunt to a mental institution. I thought I was going with them to be supportive, but I learn that I too have a mental problem and need help.

"We take part in various counseling sessions, and then go to a gym to be entertained by dancers and singers. I am standing by the wall watching when one of the singers—a lady—dances right up to me and sings in my face, 'You need to learn to love the world.' [By 'the world,' I understood her to mean 'nature.']

"I start to cry because I know that this is true, but I don't know how to do it. Then she thrusts a magazine in my hands, with a headline which reads 'Faith: How to Get It.' I open it up and leaf through the pages which read over and over again: 'You've got to believe first, then you'll have it.' "

(Dream #2) "I am at a carnival. My sister is to perform on the organ, and I am rushing around to find a good seat to hear her play. There is much confusion and disorganization. When the concert ends, I walk around, feeling very lonely in the midst of the crowds. I accidentally bump into a young man who turns and swears at me. That hurts my feelings so bad that I begin to cry.

"Then I notice that I am holding the hand of a small boy. A voice says to me, 'Don't be sad; I am always with you. You are not alone.' "

The dreamer interpreted the first experience to mean that she needed to start acting as if she believed first. *Then* the consciousness of faith would follow. Specifically she felt that she could start this process by acting out of love toward the natural world.

She interpreted the second dream experience to be giving her further direction on how to understand her ideal of faith. She wrote in her dream journal, "What faith means for my life now is that I am not alone—not only in the sense of people supporting me, but God always working in my life."

Setting Mental and Physical Ideals

As an aid to the application of your spiritual ideal, you can designate ways you intend to express that ideal through your thoughts and feelings (that is, mental ideals) and your actions (that is, physical ideals). Mental and physical ideals play supportive roles. They can serve as stepping-stones to the realization of the spiritual ideal. Oftentimes the spiritual ideal looks a bit imposing once it has been set. We may say to ourselves, "Where do I begin, how do I try to live this?" An effective answer is to choose just a few specific relationships or situations in life and to set supplementary, supportive, mental and physical ideals for each of those areas. Whereas the spiritual ideal is the same for all parts of life, the mental and physical ideals will vary from situation to situation, from relationship to relationship. This is not a matter of inconsistency but rather of flexibility, because life presents us with a variety of challenges in which each needs its own particular response.

Frequently the notion of mental and physical ideals has been misunderstood. A common misconception of Cayce's theory of ideals is that the physical ideal is what one really wants to have physically in his or her life. Using such an interpretation a person might make a list of "physical ideals" such as this: have an income of $30,000, own two late model cars, live in a four-bedroom house, and get the weight down to 130. Following this line of reasoning, the same person might list as mental ideals: become psychic, have a high IQ and be rid of all guilt and self-criticism. However, this is not exactly the approach the Cayce readings have recommended for setting physical and mental ideals.

The physical ideal is defined as those *actions* which will bring into expression the spiritual ideal. It is *not* a physical condition we desire, as some people would say. It is far too simplistic and spiritually naive to suppose that setting a physical ideal is merely imagining exactly what you want and then sending out that image to the universe so that it can manifest. Certainly that technique "works." There are countless stories of people who have discovered this power of the mind in relationship to the physical plane. But to label this a universal law of manifestation and to claim that this is equivalent to setting physical ideals is greatly misleading. In truth, the physical ideals must be *integrative*—they can exist only in the context of a spiritual ideal and ideal mental attitudes. They rest upon a sense of purposefulness and clearly defined motivation. It is true that clearly defined images of our physical desires will manifest, but to call this working with physical ideals is a distortion.

Instead, the physical ideal is your answer to the question, "What am I going to *do* with conditions as they currently exist in my life?" The physical ideals you write down for specific areas of your life will be *actions* which you have reasonable hopes of being able to accomplish if you apply your free will and invest some energy.

Here are some examples of physical ideals for certain areas of life.

Person #1: Spiritual Ideal/spiritual ideal= God/patience
relationship: my son
physical ideals = Spend at least 30 minutes daily in creative activities together.
Have bedtime prayers with him.

Person #2: Spiritual Ideal/spiritual ideal= Christ/understanding
area of life: school
physical ideals = Regularly attend class.
Get up by 6:30 and study for an hour.

Person #3: Spiritual Ideal/spiritual ideal= Universal Love/joy
area of life: job
physical ideals = Smile in interactions with fellow employees.
Be at work on time.

In each of these cases the person has identified actions which he or she feels will help to express the spiritual ideal previously chosen. Similarly, mental ideals should be selected for each of these areas. Mental ideals can be understood as patterns of thinking and feeling which are in harmony with the spiritual ideal. Like the physical ideals, they are best determined for unique aspects of our lives and do vary from relationship to relationship. In the three cases just cited, the individuals might set these corresponding mental ideals:

Person #1—relationship: my son
mental ideals = thankfulness kindness
Person #2—area of life: school
mental ideals = curiosity persistence
Person #3—area of life: job
mental ideals = appreciation self-confidence

Once again you are strongly encouraged to *write down* the ideals which you are willing to set. Using the same paper on which you indicated your spiritual ideal, make a record of supplementary mental and physical ideals. Keep in mind that ideals change as you grow in consciousness. You might want to write them down in easily erasable pencil. Most people find that mental and physical ideals change more often than does their spiritual ideal.

As a starter, you will probably find that about four areas of your life will be enough to get you going. You might want to designate one of them as *yourself*. In this instance, your physical ideals will concern how you want to act toward yourself (that is, how you treat yourself). Here is where you can list your intentions of diet, exercise, resting, etc. Your mental ideals in this case would be the best ways you could think and feel about yourself (for example, patience with yourself, confidence in your talents, etc.).

You may find that an even more specific relationship with yourself is crucial in the ideals-setting process. Since ideals can make you acutely aware of those times when you are failing to live up to the best you could be, it may be important to deal lovingly with yourself when this happens. In other words, *what is your ideal relationship with that part of yourself which occasionally messes up and fails to live up to ideals in other areas of your life?* Too often our attitudes and reactions make events even worse. Frequent reactions of the mind are guilt, self-condemnation, frustration and discouragement. And automatic behavioral responses may often cause us to lash out at an innocent bystander, to overreact self-destructively or to go watch television (that is, retreat into unconsiousness).

But what would be ideal responses for your relationship with your failing self? Mental ideals might be forgiveness, understanding, recommitment or humor. Physical ideals are a bit more tricky to determine. Some people decide to pray after having realized a failure to live up to another ideal. Other people try to relive these incidents in their imaginations to see what they hope to do next time the situation arises. Still others try to immediately go out and successfully accomplish an ideal in some other part of life so as to recreate a feeling of being able to live up to ideals. Whatever you may choose, consider this aspect of setting ideals as you select the key areas of your life.

Ideals and a New Age

What happens when you set ideals for your life? What is it about *consciously* working with ideals which makes it so crucial a process for helping to build a new age? One aspect of new age awareness and life style is the realization of energies and vibrations which come from beyond the three-dimensional physical world. As you work with ideals, you bring into play changes in these more subtle energies which profoundly influence your life.

A psychic who can see auras might provide us with a valuable description of just what ideals do to us. There is considerable evidence to suggest that these subtle energies and vibrations which characterize higher-dimensional reality can be found to surround the physical body. This so-called aura reflects both the physical health of a person and the conditions of mind and spirit within that individual.

But perhaps these auric vibrations do far more than just depict current conditions. They may very well serve to influence the situations which life brings to us. Although the physics of higher-dimensional energies is only beginning to be developed in human thought, we can speculate that a person's auric vibrations "attract or repel" particular situations and people (depending on *their* auric vibrations).

According to this theory, the process of *sincerely* setting new ideals immediately changes us. Having spent an hour writing down your ideals, you may not feel any different but things *are* different. If your efforts were genuine and not a mere paper-and-pencil game, then the auric vibrations around you will have changed. You may not be able to see it, but a good psychic might be able to recognize it just as clearly as if you had cut your hair or changed your style of clothes.

Even more importantly, that change in your aura will begin to alter the kinds of life experiences into which you are drawn. People and conditions will come to you which might not have appeared otherwise. They are *not* coming to *fulfill* your ideals for you; they are coming into your life because they will *challenge* you to see if you really want to live what you have set as your ideals. Some of these new people and situations will be beautiful and gratifying; others will make you uncomfortable. But working consciously with these laws of awareness and vibration is a hallmark of new age thought. Realizing and accepting personal responsibility for these challenging opportunities which come your way is a matter of expanding your mind to higher-dimensional sensitivity.

In fact we can imagine that consciously working with ideals is the beginning of *fifth*-dimensional experience! That sounds quite ambitious because our movement into a new age is usually characterized as humanity coming to understand *fourth*-dimensional reality. But no matter how ambitious or premature it sounds, it is crucial that at least a portion of humanity be actively involved with fifth-dimensional awareness while the greater numbers move into fourth-dimensional sensitivity. A small group must always be a step ahead of the larger group if the whole is to progress safely. For example, in pioneer days the wagon train would always send ahead a scouting party. Without it the settlers would have made many errors in their journey. The wagon train itself was a venture into something new. The scouting party was one step even more ambitious and bold.

Another analogy may be helpful to illustrate the necessity for some people to be an extra step ahead of what is developing. We have used the abstraction of geometry before and once again it provides an effective example. Although human awareness may be moving from three-dimensional perception to four-dimensional, we need to reduce the dimensions in our geometric example if they are to be drawn adequately.

Suppose a one-dimensional *line* is about to expand into a two-dimensional *plane.* In other words, initially there was only a sense of being able to go forward and backward along the line. Awareness is about to expand so as to include movement to the right and left.

However, there are *many* possible planes which can be created as an extension of that line. There is a horizontal plane, a vertical plane and many different planes tilted at various angles.

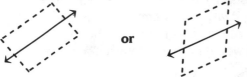

137

To a consciousness that only senses the two dimensions of forward/backward and right/left, all the planes feel the same. Only the awareness that perceives and understands a third dimension of up and down will realize the variety of possible planes. Only a mind aware of one dimension higher than the dimension being created can effectively guide that creation. Since an additional expansion of dimensions may happen in the future, some of the planes are "better" than others. In this case "better" means more suitable or fitting for the end product—and this can be measured against some universal law or standard. Since we may want to expand the plane into a solid figure, we might want to select a certain angle of plane to be the foundation of that later growth. For example, it is easier to build a house on horizontal ground than on a hillside with a 45° slope. We take into account the law of gravity in deciding that the horizontal plane is "better."

We must keep in mind as we move into a new age in the coming generation that this will not be the last "new age." It may take humanity hundreds of years to learn about fourth-dimensional awareness and to feel at home with it. But the time will come when the whole of the human family will be ready for another new age transition—this time into fifth-dimensional awareness. If we have not built in the 20th and 21st centuries an optimal foundation of fourth-dimensional understanding and experience, then the later transition will be more difficult. There will be many chances and temptations for people to use fourth-dimensional sensitivity in less than optimal ways. Those people who are already a step ahead and have at least some sense of what the fifth dimension is all about can provide the wisdom for the new age transition which is now before us.

To understand why ideals can be thought of as fifth-dimensional (a statement *not* specifically found in the Cayce readings), recall the best definition of the fourth dimension. Both Cayce and Carl Jung theorized that *ideas* or *thoughts* were the realm of fourth-dimensional reality. Since lesser dimensions need to be seen as projections or partial representations of higher dimensions, this theory fits well. It says that three-dimensional physical reality is a projection of thoughts and ideas. In other words, "mind is the builder." Any physical reality starts at the mental level and then can be projected into matter. Extending this theory beyond what Cayce and Jung said, it would hold that fourth-dimensional thoughts are the projections or partial representations of the fifth dimension. Nothing fits that description better than ideals. Every thought is the outgrowth of *some* ideal (not always a very spiritual one, but *some* ideal). If we have carefully selected our fifth-dimensional reality, then the projections of it which we experience in the fourth dimension will be harmonious and growth oriented. If we randomly or unconsciously allow certain fifth-dimensional realities to influence us, then we experience a hodge podge of confusion and disorientation at the fourth-dimensional level.

Without a core of people selecting a God-attuned, fifth-dimensional reality, humanity's movement into fourth-dimensional sensitivity is a dangerous transition. This sensitivity permits telepathy and psychokinesis; it awakens a person to how the mind creates physical reality. Imagine a world in which people easily experience fourth-dimensional abilities and yet have no clear sense of ideal and purpose. We might have the Pentagon focused on programs of psychic warfare; travel agents offering fantasy vacations using drugs or hypnosis; and marketing executives using the latest techniques of consciousness manipulation. (For example, could we tolerate commercials telepathically projected into our dreams?)

The expansion of consciousness in a new age should be a topic of concern for us. There are many different forms of three-dimensional experience because of the variety of fourth-dimensional thought patterns which do the building. In the same way there are many different types of fourth-dimensional experiences because of the variety of ideals and purposes from which they originate. In a new age we can use fourth-dimensional energies for psychic healing or psychic warfare. We can use the realm of thought forms to entertain us or to instruct us. The key lies in having learned something about the fifth dimension, too.

For humanity as a whole there needs to be at least a critical mass number of people who are experiencing a God-attuned aspect of the fifth dimension and who are helping to shape the quality of fourth-dimensional experience for humanity at large. As pioneers of new age thought, we need to accept the challenge and responsibility of working with conscious ideals. Our participation in that "scouting party"—our ability to be even one step ahead of what others think is new—is needed far more than we realize.

Chapter 8

Economic Healing and the Law of Supply

Many people are convinced that we are going through times of change primarily because of the pressures of a difficult economic situation. Pollution and inflation seem to be the two broadly accepted signs that the old system does not work well any more. Both of them deeply affect the quality of our way of life, but both of them can also provide us with positive lessons if we will listen to what they are saying to us. Obviously, the problems of a polluted environment say to us that we must befriend the earth once again—that we cannot abuse the soil, sea and air without expecting similar returns. But the worldwide problem of inflation is a bit more subtle, and people have been less inclined to perceive its lessons.

Inflation causes economic stress for almost everyone. When prices are going up more than wages, it can mean only one thing: We have to make do with less. Unfortunately many people who could do this without hardship won't do it. Instead, their usual response is to go deeper in debt, borrowing against the future. But when a person has borrowed against the future, then tomorrow looks more and more like something to be avoided. Hope, expectancy and optimism disappear because the future toward which we are headed looks even more debt-ridden.

The implication that many people could make do with less during times of inflation is not meant as a criticism of all people. Certainly many people already had less than their share before inflation came along. Many retired persons on fixed incomes have very little flexibility for dealing with these economic stresses. Nevertheless, there are large segments of our own society (probably a majority) for whom inflation can be a creative challenge.

The opportunity of these times is to rediscover that *God is the source of all supply and that by our own consciousness we create the degree of our access to it.* This principle is a lesson at the heart of current economic difficulties. And in this chapter we will explore how that principle can be lived. With such a new age awareness in our minds, there can emerge a life style which will keep us economically healthy.

Ideally we would live in a world guided by the principle that God is the source of all physical supply. It would be a world whose people were fed, sheltered and cared for medically. The personal and physical needs of every individual would be secure. But until the day comes when all humanity is prepared to adopt this type of consciousness, we can only work as individuals to manifest the law.

To understand the law of supply and how economic healing works, we must begin with a definition of "supply." We might think of it as physical resources for living, which would include food, shelter, money or anything else of the material world which we need. The Bible, the Edgar Cayce readings and so many other teachings all instruct us that God is the source of all supply. In other words, the physical plane of existence is a creation of the Infinite and is sustained by it. The life force and energy of food is a projection into matter of God's creative forces. The mineral kingdom—be it oil, gold or whatever—is a manifestation of divine energies of a higher dimension. Even money itself, which symbolizes a kind of earthly power or influence, is only a lesser-dimensional projection of God's power. This idea of power is reminiscent of Jesus' statement to Pilate that he had no power except that which God had allowed him to have.

The difference between "God as the source of supply" and "God as the distributor of supply" is a subtle but highly significant distinction. In fact, many people who try to work with metaphysical laws of economic healing say the words of the first phrase but understand them as those in the second phrase. This kind of thinking supposes God to be the *dispenser* of material goods and money. It suggests that if you are on good terms with God, then He will put material rewards in the pipeline for you. And you do not need to have an anthropomorphic notion of God to be thinking in this fashion. Even if you have a more sophisticated idea of God such as Universal Mind or Creative Forces or Cosmic Love, this sort of understanding can still control your thinking.

But this is not what is meant by God as the source of supply. God *is* supply. The energies and consciousness of the Divine are infinite, yet they manifest in the three-dimensional physical world. Those manifestations are everything we think of as the resources for material living. It is in *this* sense that God is the source of all supply; but we do not have to coerce Him into a willingness to give us our share. God is not the boss at work who must be convinced that a raise is warranted.

Instead it is by our own consciousness that we create our access to supply. *We* are the dispensers and distributors of the Infinite Energies as they manifest in materiality. By the patterns of our thinking, feeling and acting, we determine as individuals the amount of physical resources to which we have access and responsibility: money, food, energy, shelter, clothing, free time, etc. Contrary to one of the old-world paradigm assumptions, there is *not* a *limited* amount of supply which can accommodate only a select few. Certainly there may appear to be current shortages in some specific *forms* of supply. But the resources of physical living are obtainable for every person of planet Earth if our consciousness is properly attuned—as individuals and collectively.

However, sometimes our experience seems to contradict the fundamental principle which has been proposed. Sometimes it doesn't seem that by our consciousness we create our access to supply. We all know of people who seem to have a highly attuned, loving spirit and yet they still seem to experience material shortages. Some of us may be good examples of this ourselves. To understand what is going on, we may have to look more deeply than the conscious patterns of thinking. The matter of economic healing and supply is the concern of the *soul* and necessarily involves unconscious levels of the mind, especially memory patterns from the present lifetime and past lifetimes. Simply put: We often must be patient in achieving *economic* healing just as we would with *physical* healing. We might prefer a quick metaphysical trick to make us rich. We might be tempted by simplistic positive thinking which promises instant riches. But that is the same sort of motivation which desires a pill to take care of illness instead of having to make deep changes of body, mind and spirit.

Many souls have chosen to meet in this lifetime certain karmic patterns from the past which express themselves as the challenges and tests of shortage. Certainly a good first step toward healing those conditions (especially the *inner conditions* of the soul) is a positive conscious outlook, even the expectation of better times. If material levels of supply do not alter instanteously for such people, it is not because the spiritual principle is wrong. Instead it is because unconscious distortions of mind and emotion from the distant past may be changing slowly.

Keeping in mind this need for patience, let us consider some of the ways in which we create our access to supply. We can actually go further than viewing God as the source of supply. God is also to be understood as a God of *abundance.* By the way in which we understand and respond to this divine characteristic of abundance, we are creating a key aspect of our consciousness toward material supply. The Bible beautifully illustrates God's intent to express Himself abundantly. The story of the loaves and fishes is an excellent example. Not only did Jesus manifest enough food to feed everyone who was there that day, there was such an abundance of food that tremendous quantities of leftovers were collected.

But what does abundance have to do with painful shortages which we may now be experiencing? By a twist of irony, the spiritual law is that our access to supply today is at least in part created by what we have done with abundant conditions in the past. In other words, we may be facing difficult challenges of material shortages to help us grow and change previous tendencies to misuse abundance.

Observe two circumstances in which we have a problem with supply. One is when there is not enough; and we experience discomfort, pain or frustration. Of course, when there is just exactly enough—when supply perfectly matches need—then none of these problems exists and everything is fine. But a second circumstance exists when there is *more* than enough. It is an often overlooked difficulty which is created when the amount available exceeds the need. What do we do with what is left over? How do we deal with such abundant conditions? The degree to which we deal responsibly and lovingly with the extra amount may clearly depict our real ideal toward material supply.

To understand how this process may have been working in your life, consider some of the categories of supply and some questions about how abundance might affect each one of them. Some of the most important categories are not ones we immediately think of when we consider material resources, but which are still significant aspects of physical life and the gifts granted by God to a soul in its incarnation.

1. *Money.* What do you do when you have a little extra money? How is it used? What desires is it used to fulfill?

2. *Free time.* What do you do with your extra time in the day? Do you waste it or use it creatively?

3. *Energy.* How responsible are you with energy when you are not paying the utility bill? For example, when you stay in a hotel, how conservation minded are you? Since this is a situation where you seem to have all the heat, lighting, and hot water you want at no extra expense, how do you react in such abundant conditions?

4. *Food.* How careful and responsible are you in taking only the food you genuinely need—or will even be able to eat—when you visit an "all-you-can-eat" restaurant?

5. *Talent and skill.* What do you do when the job you have to perform requires of you less talent or skill than you already have? Do you do just the minimum acceptable standard or do you fully use the abundance you have and produce a better-than-expected result?

The answers to these and similar questions will help you get a sense of how you deal with abundance. It may give you a clue as to what kind of consciousness you are creating for access to supply in the future. In observing this process you should realize that effects can be produced *across categories.* In other words, misuse of abundance in one area of life can create the need for lessons of shortage in another category. Fortunately, the principle also works in a more positive way, too: Responsible use of abundance in one area of life can produce proper supply in another area.

Collectively we seem to be experiencing the working of this law as a nation. We were blessed with an abundance of natural resources and yet have not been ecologically responsible in our stewardship. Current problems such as pollution are, in turn, creating difficulties for us in maintaining the previous levels of energy, clean water and safe air. The same process can be at work for an individual soul. The waste or misuse of resources may have developed in this lifetime or a past one. In either case, it is a pattern of behavior which runs counter to the evolutionary flow of the soul, and it is the soul itself which chooses and creates shortages to stimulate the learning process.

That learning can be straightforward and efficient if the individual chooses to try a new attitudinal and behavioral approach. Or it can be protracted and painful if the shortage is blamed on others and violently resisted. This is not meant to be a call for passivity in the face of poverty. There *are* social injustices in our world which foster poverty. But for any individual soul the work to change such conditions of shortage must begin with personal responsibility and motivation. It *can* be done and *has* been done by specific individuals; and largely by their courageous efforts and example will the acute material shortages of great segments of humankind be transformed.

Prosperity Consciousness and the Standard of Living

What alternatives do we have in trying to achieve material prosperity in our lives? One set of possibilities are those techniques suggested by business-wise people who have studied economic laws at work. They can teach us when to get in or out of the stock market, how to make a good real estate purchase or how to get the highest interest yield on savings. There is nothing inherently wrong from a spiritual standpoint with following the advice of such teachers. We may not want to adopt their value systems but that does not preclude our being practical and using common sense. We live in the society of a material world, and it is expected that we try our best to function within it. We can be "*in* the world but *not of* it." Sometimes this is tricky, but it can be done. Anyone who doubts the idea that the Cayce readings hold this view should look closely at the readings given to businessmen. There are dozens of readings in which Cayce gave specific business advice to people (for example, helping them to interpret their dreams about the stock market).

However, most traditional financial counselors do not have a big enough picture of how the law of supply works. They can describe what will take place at the three-dimensional level, but they may not take into account the forces from other dimensions which can affect materiality. They do not provide a complete picture of the laws which are at work to govern our experience with supply. It is not so much that traditional economists are wrong but instead that they are seeing only part of what is going on. A good analogy is found in physics. Einstein did not so much prove that Newton had been wrong in his theories of motion and gravitation; rather Einstein showed that Newton's theories were only a special case of a much broader theory. The Newtonian concepts had served mankind well for hundreds of years, but the more inclusive, new theories made possible many additional discoveries.

A second alternative exists with which we can attempt to achieve satisfactory supply. It differs sharply from the business-wise techniques already mentioned. It is the "prosperity consciousness" approach recommended by many schools of metaphysical thought. This philosophy clearly embraces the idea that higher-dimensional realities are involved in our access to material supply. And it is admirable to see that this approach has a profound appreciation for how the mind is the builder of experiences. Nevertheless, there often seems to be a naiveté to the way in which prosperity consciousness is taught. Spiritual law is meant to be simple, yet it is rarely simplistic. In other words, the rules which govern the universe are straightforward and consistent. However, we can fully understand those laws only if we are willing to look deeply at all the levels of reality which are involved. Too often the teachers of prosperity consciousness take a shallow approach to the human mind and soul. Far more is involved in the workings of the law of supply than merely what we consciously desire or want to have.

It may well be that much of this distortion is in reaction to a previous mistaken notion: The idea that poverty is next to godliness is an error. Seeing this concept as a mistaken one, some people have pushed the pendulum back to the other extreme and assumed that God really wants everyone to be rich. But the Bible, the Cayce readings and many other spiritual teachings say nothing of this sort. They show that God wants *only one* thing for us: to become fully conscious of our spiritual nature. For some people to take the next step in this direction, an experience with shortage is required. For other people the lesson lies in being responsible for the proper use of an abundance of supply.

There is, nonetheless, considerable truth in the teachings of prosperity consciousness. Certainly we can expect that thoughts of fear, doubt and worry about supply will most likely create experiences of shortage for us; therefore, an attitude of expectancy and hopefulness is a good first step toward economic healing. However, God cannot be manipulated. We gain the best access to material supply *not only* by thinking it will come.

The following joke shows how the tenets of prosperity consciousness can be misleading: "A politician and an economist found themselves trapped in a pit. The large hole was far too deep to jump out of. It had smooth, vertical sides. Yet the economist was confident that he could get them both out. When asked by the politician what they were going to do now, he answered, 'It's easy—first we'll assume we have a ladder.' " This is, of course, poking fun at the tendency of theorists to assume preconditions which verify their theories. But the same criticism might be directed at those who propose simplistic solutions of prosperity consciousness. The economist in the joke wanted to assume there was really no problem. And many teachers of prosperity consciousness want us to assume that the only problem is our belief that there is a problem. However, the issue may be deeper than this. There may have been a problem in the past, a problem created by our attitudes or use of material supply. It could have been in a previous lifetime or earlier in the present lifetime. Its karmic implications will have an impact on us in the present. And through *patiently living an ideal* do we heal that memory and genuinely obtain the optimal access to the resources we need.

Such patient efforts to live an ideal probably begin with a careful analysis of the current conditions. This self-study includes not just what we possess externally but what our inner mental expectations and desires are. In other words, let us evaluate not merely our standard of living but also our "standard of standard of living." By what *criteria* do we measure our lives and the physical resources of living? For example, does it increase or decrease our standard of living to have three color televisions instead of one? Is the quality of life really diminished by having to live in a smaller house which forces greater interaction between family members? Personal answers to questions like these are keys to our understanding and cooperating with the law of supply.

Clearly the consciousness of our nation as a whole is slow to think in these terms. We find it difficult to rationalize that our standard of living has not been diminished when we have to drive compact cars instead of gas guzzlers. We feel a bit humiliated that oil-exporting countries can force us to lower our thermostats in the winter (even though that lower setting may be more healthful for us!). Or we see books for sale with titles like *Going Broke on $100,000 a Year*.

Edgar Cayce and his family certainly faced difficulties with material supply. In fact, it seemed very ironic that in the late 1920s his psychic readings were helping some people become wealthy from the stock market, yet he and his family continued to just get by. When the readings were asked about this apparent problem, the answer came back that it was a matter of the standard of standard of living. The real needs of the family were being provided. If the proper perspective of material life was used, then situations would actually look all right.

During the Depression an especially significant passage from one reading pointed out the importance of the criteria by which we measure material life. An end to the worldwide economic disaster was primarily a matter of values and ideals.

Q-1. What is the cause of the great economic depression and when may conditions be expected to become normal in the United States?

A-1. . . .When there are, then, the greater number that would see that the *IDEAL* is again *made* the *STANDARD*, then may *conditions* be *expected* to improve. This is not as *men* count improvement, in dollars and cents, but in contentment and understanding—and *one* is the fruit of the other! 3976-8

In other words, a change in the standard of living (that is, dollars and cents) would take place in *response to* a change of values, a different way of evaluating material life. A sense of contentment and understanding had to come first, and then outer, material conditions would change. Most likely the same principle holds true for modern-day economic problems at a national and international level. And it is certainly applicable as well to each of us at the individual level.

A Program for Balanced Supply

Having already examined the basic aspects of the law of supply, we can formulate a systematic program for working with these principles. Such a program is not a method for manipulating God; rather it is a systematic way to create change in the elements of consciousness which determine our access to God's supply. (Recall our basic assumptions that God *is* supply, but that we are the dispensers of it.) These five progressive steps can be applied toward most any type of material resource for living (such as money, talent, skill, bodily energy, free time, etc.). In fact, at particular points in working through this program, it is required that we examine all the significant areas of supply in our lives.

1. *Set ideals and purposes.* We should not be surprised that a theory based on the Cayce readings begins at the level of ideals. This step involves setting ideals both for specific areas of supply as well as for our life in its entirety.

When applied to personal finances, these steps with the law of supply are called "economic healing." There is a good parallel between efforts to achieve physical health and those of economic health. Both start with setting ideals and purposes. Both require an answer to the questions, "Why do I want to be healed?" and "What would I do with my life if I were healed?" There is little reason to be healed of a physical ailment if our intention is to go back to ways of living which originally caused the disease. Similarly, there is no purpose in attaining economic healing if our desire is to return to attitudes and actions which previously led to the financial problems.

The word "healing" provides another significant parallel between physical health and personal finances. Cayce's definition of healing is the attunement of body, mind and spirit. If we are to experience an economic healing, then we probably need to work at the material level in our attitudes and emotions *and* in terms of our spiritual ideals and purposes.

If your primary area of shortage is *not* money, this first step of setting ideals is *still* crucial. For example, if you feel that you need more free time in your life, you might need to answer important questions about how you would use that extra free time if you had it. Or, if you feel that you need more friends in your life, it would be good to set ideals for how you intend to treat those friends once they are drawn into your experience. Although we much more frequently hear of "economic healing," we could just as easily speak of "time healing" or "friendship healing" or "talent healing." In all of these areas the basic definition of healing which Cayce gave should be a starting point for our work. *Attunement* is what is needed and the first step in attunement is setting ideals and purposes.

2. *Identify the lesson in the shortage.* If you are experiencing a shortage in any area of your life, there is a purpose and reason for that condition. Life is not arbitrary. When you develop the skill to see life from the assumption of purposefulness, it puts you in harmony with universal law. In our five-step progression of understanding the law of supply, the viewpoint of purposefulness frees you to make needed changes. If you are caught up in feeling sorry for yourself, you will never be able to seize the personal responsibility which is required so that a change in outer conditions might manifest. However, something very promising takes place when you see the shortage as an opportunity to grow.

Any shortage in the resources for physical living creates discomfort. But that discomfort is a challenge. It is an invitation to some specific quality within you to come forth, to be drawn to the surface of your personality. For example, if the shortage is money, the challenge may be for the characteristics of better planning or more faith to come forth. Or, if the shortage is in terms of talent or skill, the challenge may be to develop greater determination or self-confidence. If the shortage is in free time, it may create the opportunity to learn greater self-discipline or time management.

Identifying the positive growth opportunity presented by the shortage does not in itself solve the problem. What it *does* do is to shift your perspective on the situation. It allows you to feel a sense of purposefulness to what is going on. It moves you into a state of mind where the next steps in the program can work more effectively.

3. *Use well what resources are already at hand.* There is a strong cultural inertia against applying the spiritual principle to use what one finds at hand. A basis of high-pressure advertising in the media is to create in the viewer's or listener's mind the notion that we have a need and that something we do not yet have is required to meet that need.

Rather than blame others for this incessant obstacle, we must be willing to take some of the responsibility for its existence and then move on with our growth in spite of it. Our own impatience to have material goods and our own desire patterns have created a climate in which such media barrages have been able to expand and have influence. It can become a type of vicious circle. Our own initial restlessness and impatience to have more was fertile soil for an advertising strategy in our culture which says in effect, "Don't use what you have, buy something new." This strategy, in turn, tends to influence many people even more strongly in that direction of desire.

At some point we need to get off that downward spiral. We need to realize that current conditions often present the resources needed to fulfill our needs. Certainly we can hope for more and better things. However, they come to and are used by us most optimally if we have first used well what we already have.

It can be fun and rewarding to try meeting a need first with what is already available rather than running out to obtain something new. Admittedly sometimes there is no way around the fact that a key ingredient or tool or resource is missing and has to be obtained. Nevertheless, there will be other instances where our own ingenuity discovers a way of adapting and a way of channeling an old resource into a new application.

As we do this at a material level first—in cooking, with home repairs, etc.—something exciting happens. The process carries over into psychological and spiritual areas of life as well. We discover new ways to use talents and resources of our minds and spirits. Learning to do this insures that with each new gift that does come our way, we will be more likely to experience it in the fullness and variety that it offers us.

4. *Give if we would receive.* This is a spiritual law; but we must be careful not to think that we can manipulate it and use it to fulfill any desire. This law describes far more than action; it includes what is in our hearts as well, that is, our purpose or motive. For example, suppose that I aid someone with a difficulty, knowing that I am going to be needing help with something of my own soon. Is my attitude that I am now making an investment so that what I want will be forthcoming later? The purpose speaks louder than the action. Here is what I might expect in the future: Someone will be available to aid me, but he will be willing to help only if he is paid back in some way.

The area of personal finances is another one in which the application of this law can be illustrated. It is a principle of economic healing that one must give in order to receive. Because of this, tithing of our income is recommended. But what is our consciousness toward tithing? As we give that money, is it for the purpose of getting more back? What is in the back of our minds and behind our behaviors? Most likely the economic healing does not work if our motive in giving is just to get more back. The trick is to give without thought of return—*to find our joy in the very act of the giving.*

On the other hand, when we do give with the proper spirit, the law works to bring the supply back to us. But what is behind *how* the law has worked? It follows this principle: We draw to ourselves experiences to confirm or reinforce the consciousness we have developed for ourselves. For example, imagine a chart which listed all people's income from top (highest income) to bottom (smallest income). My position is likely to be neither at the very top nor the very bottom; let us imagine it somewhere near the middle.

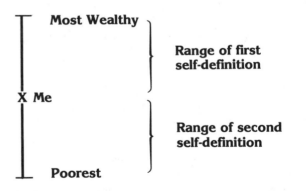

When I fail to give to others, I define myself in terms of those on the chart above me. I say to myself, "I'm barely making it; I cannot afford to give things away." I have a consciousness of being at the *bottom* of the segment of the chart; I define myself as poor, relatively speaking.

However, when I give to others who have less, I now am considering another segment of the chart and have defined myself as relatively well-off, when compared to those who have greater need than I. I have a consciousness of great supply and am likely to draw now to myself experiences to reinforce that consciousness. So it is not God's cosmic accounting system of debits and credits, but the simple working of a law of self-definition, consciousness and purpose.

For many people who are trying to work with this step at a financial level, *tithing* is a regular practice. Although it is a matter of personal decision, most people try to work with tithing from their *net* (versus gross) income. A person who feels unable to give 10% regularly might well try to start at some lower percentage. And it should certainly be kept in mind that giving is an important process which extends far beyond just money. We could think in terms of tithing free time or talents, for example. There are numerous reports of people who experienced healing in one area of material life only after they had started giving freely with *another* area of supply.

Nevertheless, most people find that giving some of their financial income is an irreplaceable part of maintaining economic health. For many of these individuals, it is not the commitment which is difficult, but the problem of how to keep simple, accurate records. Too easily when we intend to keep track of our tithing with periodic estimates kept in our imagination, there is one predictable result: We never really give as much as we thought. A simple procedure can remedy this: Use the last 6 to 8 pages of the small accounting ledger in your checkbook. Keep a running total of how much money is in your tithing account. If you write a check for a contribution, enter that check in your usual record-keeping area, then turn to the back of that ledger and also make a record of your gift. Conversely, when you receive some income (such as a paycheck) make an entry of how much money has been added to that tithe fund.

Many people find it important to work with a variety of categories in their giving. One category is friends who have a special need. Whenever possible it is probably best to make such gifts anonymously. Remember that that portion to be given away is not your money, it is God's. When you make the commitment to tithe you are saying that 10% of your income does not directly belong to you. You are only responsible for the wise distribution of it. Oftentimes the person receiving your gift does not understand it that way, even if you try to explain it. If you are reluctant to send cash through the mail, remember that a personal check is not the only recourse. The anonymity of your giving can be retained with a certified check from your bank.

Another category of giving includes spiritual or humanitarian organizations which you feel exemplify the ideals you hope to see expanded in the world. Churches would be one example of this sort of giving, along with food relief programs and animal assistance groups, but there are many other candidates. A third category of giving can be directed toward community affairs, including the local rescue squad, youth athletic activities, and dozens of other possibilities which are available wherever you live. What is needed in your giving program is a balance among different categories with which you feel comfortable. And most importantly, take time to feel joy and pleasure in the act of giving. The biggest reward to "tithing" (at any percentage level and with any form of material resource) is not something which comes back to you weeks later, but the experience of love which is present in your act.

5. *Be open to receive from unexpected sources.* A basic spiritual principle is that the material supply we are able to receive is deeply tied to our willingness to give. An important corollary to this law is that the return of what we give very often *does not come from the same source* to which we previously gave. If I contribute $100 to a charity, I can hardly expect that charity to send me back $100 next week. In the same way, if I give love and attention to a person in need I should not expect that that person will necessarily be the direct source of what comes back to me. This sense of openness to receive from wherever it comes is crucial. Too often we decide just how we want to be loved and by *whom,* and our rigidity may blind us from seeing just what is being presented.

In a similar fashion we must truly be *open* to receive. Being "too proud" to receive from others can block the law of supply from working harmoniously. Here are some of the negative affirmations in our thinking which need to be *removed* and healed if we are to complete this fifth step in the process:

It's okay to give, but I shouldn't receive from others unless I've earned it.

I'm unworthy of receiving.

I don't deserve it.

Conclusion

The law of supply is very simple, yet it is profoundly challenging in its application. It tests us to know ourselves and to set ideals which will benefit self *and* others. We *can* express attitudes and actions about material supply which will be in harmony with the spirit. It is not always easy, especially in times of crisis when shortages create such fear. But an attunement of action, mental outlook and spiritual purpose is possible in our dealings with everything material. That attunement produces health: *economic* health and health at the level of every other resource for physical living.

The test during the times of transition is to live in harmony with the law of supply *in spite of* stresses which make it all the harder to do so. We all know that it is much easier to have faith and to give when there is plenty. Unfortunately, we are strongly tempted in periods of shortage to eliminate giving as the first method for successfully balancing our budgets.

But if enough of us will understand and on a small scale *live* the universal law of supply, then very different world conditions may arise in the 21st century. In a new age we can well imagine a human family in which everyone is adequately fed, clothed and housed. It is within God's plan for the earth for such a situation to be created. It is within our capability personally to live with an awareness that makes such a vision possible.

Chapter 9

Elements of a New Age Awareness

The times of transition in which we live can be viewed primarily as a period of consciousness transformation. There will likely be many alterations in human behavior and life style as well, but the fundamental change will be in mental outlook and perspective. In previous chapters we have already looked at a number of potential characteristics of a new age consciousness: ideals, faith in the law of supply, and reincarnation, to name just three. In this chapter we will explore several more elements which might well be a part of human awareness in the coming century.

The Development of Psychic Perception

Extrasensory perception and a new age seem to go hand in hand for many people. This is probably because psychics have most frequently delineated a hopeful picture of the future. However, this association is not necessarily the proper one. Just because psychics claim to see the future does not mean that most people who live in that future will be psychic themselves. Rather, we can predict that ESP experiences might be commonplace in a new age because they are a natural outgrowth of something else which has been predicted: attunement. If we imagine a world in which most people are consciously making efforts to align the body and the mind with the spirit, then we have a society ripe for psychic development. In the view of the Cayce readings, psychic experience is of the soul; it is an expression of the spiritual forces

156

manifesting in the material world. When people meditate regularly, watch their dreams carefully and sincerely try to be of service to each other, then the stage is perfectly set for the flowering of ESP.

However, with the blossoming of these latent abilities come challenges and potential difficulties. We need only to read the biographies of many modern-day psychics to notice that the development of psychic perception has created problems for the individual. The predicament in which they found themselves was not due only to the skeptical society in which they lived; they had to wrestle with inherent difficulties when their gifts of telepathy, clairvoyance or precognition were awakened. For what purposes should such abilities be used? How should intuitive, nonrational sources of information be combined with logical common sense? We might expect that these kinds of questions will be as frequent in 100 years as are questions about inflation and the gasoline shortage today.

The theory of psychic perception found in the Cayce readings is extremely valuable to present or future efforts to place ESP in a balanced, helpful context. The first principle, as already stated, is that psychic experience can be fully understood only in the framework of a physical, mental *and* spiritual human nature. Add to this a significant second premise: Psychic awareness is a normal and natural response of the mind to the desire to be of service to others. One Cayce reading referred to this orientation as the *love intent,* acting as a catalyst upon the unconscious mind and opening it to conscious awareness of the ever-present connection between all souls.

Both of these fundamental notions are rather metaphysical in nature. They depend upon our willingness to think in terms of nonmaterial reality. However, at the same time, the Cayce readings further suggest that ESP should be a practical, down-to-earth sort of experience. Unless we can find ways to use it productively and in materiality, it is of little value—for example, healing baffling diseases (as demonstrated in Cayce's own work) or offering insightful vocational guidance to seekers. But whatever form it takes, it needs to be applicable, in a three-dimensional physical sense.

This brings us to a distinct challenge of how we will respond to awakening psychic abilities within ourselves. What do we do with impressions we receive about others, which we suspect may be accurate extrasensory information? What is the next step if out of love you are praying for someone and unexpectedly get a strong feeling for what that person should do? It is rather disconcerting to imagine that in a new age we will have everyone walking around giving unsolicited readings for each other. We must have a balanced way of sharing this information without seeming pushy or invading the privacy of others. If, in fact, psychic experience is to become commonplace in a new age, then it is crucial that we find such approaches for sharing impressions.

A part of the answer may lie in a willingness to communicate impressions without forcing the issue. In other words, we can relate our inner experiences in such a way that we simultaneously admit that they may not be telepathy or clairvoyance at all. A dream or meditation experience can be related in such a way that the listener can comfortably refuse to see it as a psychic impression about him or her. For example, suppose you have a dream in which your next-door neighbor appears as one character; and you feel that this is a psychic dream about him. The Cayce readings encourage you to share the dream with him, *but* in a way that makes it easy for him to respond that your dream must surely be only about yourself. However, in telling the dream the possibility always exists that it *may be* psychic in nature and may be received gratefully and used for benefit. One reading put it this way:

Q-5. Are the messages that come for individuals when seeking for them, in my dreams and meditations, of the spirit of truth? and should they be given to these individuals?

A-5. As has been indicated, as ye hold fast to Him, knowing all power is of Him when not turned to self in any manner, to be sure these should be given—whenever they come; but force never the issue. Let the Spirit of the *Christ* guide thy hand. Let that thou hearest, thou sayest, come as *His* message to such seekers— through *thee* only as a channel of blessings!   540-3

Related to the same issue is how we treat information which seems to be precognitive in nature. This is a tricky and subtly misleading topic. What do you do with impressions which appear to be "guidance"? Sometimes that information comes in response to prayers asking for direction in a decision. Other times it may come without your particularly seeking it. In either case, what is needed is a delicate balance between obedience to the inner reality and plain common sense. God wants you to use your logical, intellectual mind—but *not exclusively* that level of mind. To do so entirely is to become skeptical, rigid and uninspired. On the other hand, the plan for our spiritual evolution does not involve blind obedience to every subjective impression which comes into awareness.

Nothing cuts off a discussion faster than the statement, "Well, it was my *guidance* to do this." With these words—spoken or thought—the dialectical process by which we learn and grow is shut off. Perhaps the word "intuition" is often a better term for the inner direction which we seem to receive. When a person says, "My intuition is that I should do this," it has two important connotations. First, it says that the source of the information is from within one's own soul. This is in contrast to claims of "guidance," which implies some force or entity outside of oneself who is calling the shots. Second, the term "intuition" suggests that the impression is not yet a closed matter but will still be combined with logic and common sense.

In a number of readings, Cayce recommended a specific exercise for developing one's psychic perception in making practical life decisions. We can well imagine that in a new age a technique such as this would be frequently employed. One reading describes some of the steps in the following way:

Q-11. Give detailed directions for developing the intuitive sense.
A-11. Trust more and more upon that which may be from within. Or, this is a very common—but a very definite—manner to develop:
On any question that arises, ask the mental self—get the answer, yes or no. Rest on that. Do not act immediately (if you would develop the intuitive influences). Then, in meditation or prayer, when looking within self, ask—is this yes or no? The answer is intuitive development. On the same question, to be sure, see? 282-4

Here is a more detailed outline of the steps in a decision-making procedure that, by helping you learn how to receive intuition from universal awareness, can stimulate increased psychic development:

1. *Set your spiritual ideal.* You have already been instructed on how to do this in a previous part of this book.

2. *Pose a question*—one that can be answered yes or no—concerning some decision you must make. In working on this exercise, you may choose a simple question or problem that you are currently facing in life, or you may choose one that is of profound significance to you. Whatever problem you decide to work on, write out a question that describes a current decision you are faced with. Be sure to phrase it so that it can be answered by a yes or a no. For example, the question, "Should I go back to college?" is much easier to work with than "What should I do now that I have a lot of free time?" would be. The latter is too open-ended and avoids a consciously made choice. Part of our growth in consciousness as souls involves learning how to make decisions properly that are in accord with divine will.

3. *Make a conscious yes-or-no decision* in answer to the question you have just posed; in doing this, take into consideration all the information you consciously have access to. Be sure that your decision is one you would be willing to carry out.

4. *Measure the decision by your spiritual ideal.* Ask yourself, "Could I follow through on my decision and still be true to my spiritual ideal?" If the answer is yes, you could be true to your ideal, go on to step 5; if it is no, go back to step 3 and try the opposite decision. Occasionally a person finds that neither a decision of yes nor one of no will allow him to remain true to his spiritual ideal. In that case, the person is not really ready to make a decision on the problem, and he should turn to consistent prayer and a deeper analysis of the decision being faced.

5. *Meditate*—not on the question, but for *attunement.* With this step we are beginning a process whereby we will seek a confirmation of our conscious decision from within. This confirmation (or denial) is likely to be accurate only to the degree that we have in meditation attuned ourselves to universal awareness. Do not let yourself be tempted into dwelling on the decision during meditation. Put the question aside and have a period of silent focus upon an affirmation.

6. At the end of your meditation, *ask the question and listen for a yes-or-no answer from within.* This "listening" sometimes elicits a response from an inner voice; at other times, the answer comes as a hunch or an inner impression. Occasionally a person will get nothing at all during this period. In that case, he will want to

extend the "listening period" and pay special attention to his dreams. If this is done, a precognitive dream frequently follows, saying, in effect, "If you follow through on the decision you've made, here are the likely results." One can then consciously judge whether or not the likely consequences are acceptable. If they are not, a change in the decision is called for.

7. *Measure the decision by your spiritual ideal.* After receiving a confirmation or denial, either at the end of meditation or by way of a dream, one should once again check to make sure that the latest understanding of the proper choice does not violate the nature of the spiritual ideal.

8. *Act on the decision.* No form of psychic or intuitive development has much meaning unless we act upon whatever we receive. Be sure to do this in relation to the specific situation on which you have been working with the previous seven steps.

After going through this exercise you may want to repeat each of the steps, especially if the decision you face is an important one. At the end of the procedure, you might wish to record your question, decision and resulting action, as well as your feelings about this exercise.

In addition to the question of guidance and decision making is another feature of psychic development that is particularly noteworthy. Many people who have tried to speculate about the future predict that a new age will offer a much greater understanding of the process of physical death. People will not fear death as they do now. The development of a certain form of psychic perception may play a great role in such a change of consciousness. If large numbers of the human family evolved clairvoyant abilities, imagine what might be the result. Perhaps people would begin to "see" and communicate with those who had passed on. Using the same type of expanded sight which allows someone to see auras, people in a new age might perceive the after-death bodies of friends and loved ones. Such a development would have tremendous impact on the values and awareness of humanity. So much of human behavior is motivated by a fear of death. If it was a common *experience* to know that death is merely a transition to a new way of living, we can guess that efforts for peace and cooperation in the world would be enhanced.

This speculation dovetails nicely with a Biblical prophecy about times of change. Certain verses from the Bible seem to predict that the reappearance of the Christ is to be associated with a period in which the dead will be resurrected. But how probable is it, we might wonder, that corpses will crawl out of the graves? Another interpretation is that *experientially* it will be *as if* the dead have been resurrected. In other words, to those of us still alive in flesh bodies, it will be as if the dead have come back to life—because we will see them and communicate with them in their astral or etheric forms. Perhaps the Biblical prophecy means that the reappearance of the Christ will come when humanity has developed its spiritual sensitivity to the point where other dimensions of life can be readily sensed and experienced. This is an exciting possibility and it puts the concept of a Second Coming of the Christ in a different light.

Understanding the Nature of Paradox

Although psychic ability is a more glamorous and sensational topic, a new age understanding of the paradoxes of life is probably an equally important evolution in awareness. The contradictions of living have long been stumbling blocks for those who have sought to find meaning and purpose in material life. Paradox, in the many varieties in which it is encountered along the spiritual path, is the great obstacle to our understanding. We want everything to make sense and be orderly, but the self-contradictory nature of paradoxes teases and frustrates us. And yet, ironically, this ancient nemesis of the seeker can be a friend and can provide a spring-board into the higher-dimensional awareness of a new age consciousness. Universal truth *is* orderly, but not always on the terms with which we are familiar. Properly understood, the nature of paradox stretches us to see a new order of reality.

First, let us define what we mean by paradox. A situation can be called paradoxical when two of its aspects both seem to be true and yet they contradict each other. Consider, for example, some pairs of statements which create paradoxical conditions:

1. a) Light is made up of particles called photons.
   b) Light is made up of vibrations or waves.
2. a) I am an outgoing person.
   b) I am a shy person.
3. a) Seek and you shall find.
   b) Let go and let God.

Paradoxes are found throughout life. Science confronts them in studying the building blocks of nature. That fundamental energy we call light seems to have dual, self-contradictory characteristics. Sometimes it behaves as if it were made up of small particles; in other instances it seems to be clearly a wave-like process. Depending on which way a physicist designs an experiment, it will allow one characteristic to emerge but not the other.

Our own personalities are often paradoxical. When we do not understand how this can be the case, the internal self-contradictions can cause confusion or disorientation. However, it is quite possible and normal to be both outgoing *and* shy. Perhaps these characteristics do not manifest at the same time, but they can both be true of a person. Think about the paradoxical human qualities which are often evident in people. Some examples are listed below. One or more of them is likely true for you. In addition, you can probably think of other paradoxes that make up your unique personality. The people who *really* know you are the friends who don't think that you are just one way, but who recognize, understand and accept self-contradictions.

self-reliant/dependent
trusting/questioning
critical/tolerant
affectionate/cool
creative/habitual
organized/spontaneous

Spiritual teachings are another example of how we confront paradoxes. In virtually all world religions key concepts about the spiritual life seem to be self-contradictory. The tensions between seeking and trying hard versus letting go and allowing is one such paradox. Many of the parables of Jesus also contain a paradoxical quality. A good example is the story of the laborers in the field. (Matthew 20:1-16) On the one hand, God is portrayed as universal justice. On the other hand, the story depicts Him as one who would reward a laborer for only one hour's work the same amount as one who had worked all day—hardly our idea of what is fair.

An apt description of spiritual law as paradox is found in Michael Murphy's book, *Golf Is the Kingdom*. Murphy relates his encounter as a young man with a certain Scottish golf instructor named Shivas Irons, who taught spiritual law to people via the game of golf. One especially pointed lesson of Shivas Irons was that the barometer of a person's spiritual enlightenment is how that individual deals with a paradox. The reason that this is such an appropriate criterion lies in the very nature of paradox itself. To understand how paradox can happen is to catch an insight of a higher reality.

One way to explain paradoxes is to begin with the assumption of the existence of multiple levels of consciousness, each with its own value and reality. Anyone on the spiritual path knows this, even if it is only from the common altered state of awareness which we call dreams. But there are many other levels of consciousness as well. In fact, as we consider the many altered states available to human awareness we are left to conclude that reality is more deeply textured than our physical senses tell us. There must be dimensions beyond the three-dimensional physical world. The best way to understand how a paradox can happen is to realize that these added dimensions are the key. Even if there is only *one* extra dimension—a fourth dimension—we have sufficient building blocks to construct a theory of paradoxes.

The basic principle of this theory says this: When a fact or condition of one order of dimension (that is, a fourth-dimensional truth) manifests itself into a lesser dimension (to human, three-dimensional, rational awareness), it may appear as multiple and contradictory expressions. This principle may sound a bit wordy and complicated, but a couple of illustrations will help to make sense of it.

First, consider how this principle is depicted in mathematics. It may have been a long time since many of us took algebra, but the basic ideas will come back to us easily. Recall that algebra is a tool for solving equations, for determining the numerical value of an unknown quantity. Here is an example of a simple algebra problem: $8 = 4 + 2X$. Without too much difficulty we can arrive at the conclusion that $X = 2$. That is the *only* value of X which will make the equation true.

However, what happens when we increase the depth of the problem? What happens when we add an extra dimension to our mathematical equation with something like this: $2X^2 = 8$. The term X^2 (meaning X multiplied by itself) is analogous to one dimension greater than problems which contain only values of X itself. The basic principle for understanding paradoxes makes a prediction for what will happen when we try to take a higher-dimensional fact

($2X^2 = 8$) and determine how it will manifest into a lesser dimension (that is, $X = ?$ for that problem). The basic principle says that we will get a paradox, that we will get at least two manifestations that are true but which contradict each other. In fact this is exactly what happens, because we find that X can equal 2 *and* −2. Both values for X make the equation work. But obviously the two solutions cannot be simultaneously true from a logical standpoint.

Perhaps a more graphic way of illustrating this theory of paradoxes is to work directly with dimensions. We have done this several times already. Let us imagine that a two-dimensional, flat surface is our three-dimensional physical world. (By dropping the dimension by one in that fashion, we have something that is easier to imagine when we start to deal with a fourth dimension.) Suppose that on that two-dimensional surface there are two-dimensional people who are trying to understand the nature of higher-dimensional reality. They hope to grasp the truth about *three*-dimensional facts or creations.

Imagine that we are "spiritual teachers" to these two-dimensional people. As three-dimensional creatures ourselves, we readily understand our own world but feel challenged to explain it to these beings of more limited awareness. Suppose that we begin by trying to explain to them the nature of a soup can, which is cylindrical in shape. Our technique of teaching is to "project" objects into their world by using a light which will cast a shadow. The shadow which is cast into their world gives these two-dimensional beings a way of understanding a higher reality. However, our problem as teachers is that more than one type of shadow can be cast by the soup can, depending on how it is positioned relative to the light source. Here are two of the possibilities:

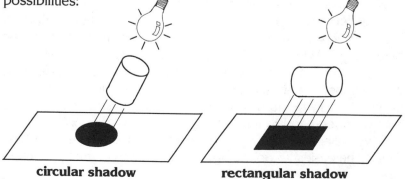

circular shadow   **rectangular shadow**

If we hold the soup can in one way it casts a circular shadow and we might say to our two-dimensional students, "Here is how you can understand the nature of soup cans." Their response is likely to be, "Oh, we can understand that—higher reality isn't so hard to grasp after all!" But then we must add—perhaps reluctantly because we know how this will confuse and frustrate them—"But just a minute. What you are about to see is *also* the nature of a soup can." So we change the position of the soup can relative to the light source and it now casts a rectangular shadow onto the two-dimensional world.

How are our two-dimensional students to understand what they now see? They have experienced the reality and truth of a darkened circle. And just as clearly and truly they now see the darkened rectangle. These two shapes contradict each other because they are being told by their teachers that these two shapes are the same item: a soup can. How is this paradox to be understood? Only the student of the two-dimensional world who can *think* in terms of a third dimension (even if he does not immediately experience that third dimension) will be able to grasp what is being presented. Translating this analogy to the actual human condition: Only that person who can imagine a dimension of reality higher than the one in which the paradox presents itself will be able to understand its real meaning.

If a new age is to be a time of human enlightenment, then we can expect that paradoxical situations will be treated in a fashion quite different than has been our tendency to treat them in the past. We will be able to do a sort of "double think," which is really not just a high tolerance for illogical things but a breakthrough in human consciousness: the capacity to perceive, experience and consciously create within an extra dimension.

What have been our alternatives for dealing with paradoxes? If our tendency has been, in fact, to handle self-contradictory situations in ways that lack spiritual enlightenment, what are the better ways? At least four broad categories of response exist from which we choose each time we run up against a paradox. As these are described, we should keep in mind that paradoxes most often confront us in terms of human personality characteristics (our own or others) and in terms of spiritual laws.

1. We *reject one side* of the paradox and embrace the other. This is the easiest to do. It might lead a person to think, "I cannot

handle being both a self-reliant person *and* a dependent person. It's all too confusing. I'm going to have to deny or suppress my dependent side." Of course, some of this thinking process may be at a nonconscious level of the mind. In another example, imagine a person dealing with two universal laws which seem to contradict each other. That person could choose to reject the principle of "opposites attract" and work with only the law "like attracts like."

2. We are *immobilized* by the dilemma created by the paradox. Sometimes the whole matter is so confusing to us that we freeze, unable to act or make any decision concerning what we believe. If the paradox concerns two contradictory personality characteristics within oneself, a person may be unable to decide who he or she really is. If the paradoxical qualities are within another person, we may stop interacting with that individual because we cannot handle the inconsistency. Or, if the immobilizing dilemma happens with spiritual laws, people have been known to get so frustrated that they give up on the spiritual path.

3. We can try to *force* the contradictory issues together. This is another version of the denial process. However, this time a person does not deny one condition or the other (as was the case with alternative #1), but rather tries to deny that any contradiction exists. Often using complicated and even circular logic, an individual can try to convince himself that no paradox really exists. In the analogy of the two-dimensional students and the soup can, they would claim that no really significant difference exists between a circle and a rectangle.

4. We can learn to *discriminate* and properly apply both sides of the paradox. The enlightened response is to see that both statements or both characteristics are true, but that they cannot be applied in the three-dimensional world of daily living at the same time. Enlightened awareness does not only permit an expanded vision of a higher dimension, it also sees the optimal way to apply each side of the paradox as it manifests in a lesser dimension. For example, we might wonder how an enlightened inhabitant of the two-dimensional world would deal with the paradox of the soup can. First, that person would grasp the three-dimensional fact that the circle/rectangle paradox makes sense. And just as significantly, that enlightened awareness would perceive whether it is best to deal with soup cans as circles or as rectangles.

In a new age, this breakthrough in human awareness will have far-reaching effects. It will permit us to have more peace of mind about the spiritual path. It will make us more sure and more sensitive to the right application of universal laws. This key aspect of new age consciousness will also allow us to love ourselves *and* others more deeply. We will not have to pretend that we love one part of a person while denying or ignoring an equally important part. And lest we think we "have it made" once we understand paradoxes created by fourth-dimensional truth, we can keep in mind that another exciting opportunity always lies ahead. Fourth-dimensional awareness will be challenged to deal with paradoxes created by fifth-dimensional laws. In other words, the *process* of dealing with paradoxes is *inherent* to the journey through ever-increasing dimensions. But once we learn that process, then its application can forever be with us.

Lucid Dreaming*

A third important aspect of a new age consciousness is the experience of lucid dreaming. Just as there are a number of people who already have psychic perception or an understanding of paradoxes, some individuals have already developed the ability to dream lucidly. In fact, most people have had at least one experience of this unusual form of dreaming. What we can expect in a new age is a dramatic increase in the frequency with which people dream in this way.

A lucid dream is defined as an experience in which the individual, while still in the dream state, realizes that he or she is actually asleep and dreaming. This self-reflective quality is usually missing from our "normal" experiences and its onset is experienced as a dramatic shift in consciousness. Sometimes the lucidity is so startling that it wakes us up. In those cases in which the dream state can be maintained in the presence of this ability, a wide variety of options are open to the dreamer.

We need to realize that in a lucid dream the *will* is suddenly brought into play. In "normal" dreams we are in a *subjective,* reactive position relative to the events of the dream. We rarely stop to think about choices; we are subject to what is going on around

---

*Note to readers: The author wishes to hear from those who are willing to share accounts of their personal lucid dreaming experiences *or* who may be interested in on-going, home-study research with lucid dreaming. Letters should be addressed to Mark Thurston, c/o A.R.E., Box 595, Virginia Beach, VA 23451.

us. For example, another person or an animal may threaten us in a dream and it is our automatic reaction to fight back or to flee. It doesn't occur to us that there are other choices—that this person or animal is just a dream image and could be encountered in other ways. But with the onset of lucidity in the dream, choices occur to us. Free will is much more evident. We move into an *objective* relationship with the symbols and events of the dream. In other words, the awakening of the will allows a discrimination between what is oneself and what is outside of oneself. In "normal" dreams, generally when we lack the use of will, we make little or no distinction. We are *caught up* in what is going on, never realizing the ability we have to separate ourselves from the events and to respond lovingly, with healing.

The introduction of free will in this fashion is not without its dangers and temptations. Nearly everyone who has had lucid dreams has experienced manipulating the dream—that is, using free will in conjunction with the creative powers of mind to change the dream. For example, one option available to us as lucid dreamers is to change with our desires and thoughts that threatening animal into a beautiful woman or a handsome man. However, this is a procedure that should be avoided if we are to make the best use of the special opportunity which a lucid dream provides. It is far better to use the will to *change our own response* to the original dream content from that of fear to that of love. What we may find is that the dream symbols and events *then* begin to change as we *first* alter our reactions. Resisting the temptation to manipulate or concoct dream images allows the integrity of the dream process to be maintained. That process is often being directed by higher levels of mind which see the necessity for certain scary or uncomfortable events or images to be confronted.

Lucid dreaming is either a literal or a symbolic experience of the next evolutionary state in human consciousness. If it is merely symbolic, then it suggests to us (or allows us to rehearse) "waking up" from a sleepy stupor. It may well be that we are almost "asleep" as we go about our daily affairs. Perhaps in a new age, human awareness will have awakened. The shift would be just as dramatic as the one we feel when suddenly becoming lucid in a dream.

But even more exciting is the possibility that lucid dreaming is itself an experience of the next evolutionary step. The progress to be made by such a development is akin to the dawning of self-reflective consciousness *in materiality,* which theorists say happened thousands of years ago. There was probably a time in human history when man's awareness of the world around him was very similar to our awareness in dreams today. He was basically unable to distinguish between his own responses and the world around him—he was in a subjective state in relationship to the natural world. If we were to place this point in history along the timeline of the Edgar Cayce epic of creation, it might well be the point at which souls were most deeply engrained in matter and had most fully forgotten their spiritual heritage. But then the *will* began to awaken (or reawaken) and the sense of personal identity emerged. There developed a self-reflective quality that created an objective consciousness.

In his excellent treatment of this subject, Scott Sparrow points out the similarities between this ancient shift in human awareness and the modern experience of lucid dreaming. In his book *Lucid Dreaming: Dawning of the Clear Light* (published by A.R.E. Press), he proposes that humanity may be going through an identical process; but this time not at the level of material reality but at the level of dream reality. If this is so, then the shift in awareness could have just as dramatic an impact on humanity as did the emergent self-reflection in natural life thousands of years ago.

A remarkable parallel to this theory can be found in Rudolph Steiner's writings. Steiner was a contemporary of Cayce and shared his holistic vision of human nature. Although his inspiration and spiritual insight came in a method different from Cayce's (Steiner consciously received information and did not go into an amnesic, altered state of consciousness as did Cayce), there are very significant parallels in philosophy.

In his book *Cosmic Memory* Steiner describes the next evolutionary stage for human awareness. He calls it "self-conscious image consciousness." This term can be translated in such a way that lucid dreaming becomes *at least an example* of this next state. The dream itself is an example of "image consciousness." In dreams we confront the thought form images we have created. The "self-conscious" ingredient is well illustrated in the self-reflective quality of a lucid dream.

Although not quite as direct a parallel, the teachings of J. Krishnamurti also provide an insight into the importance of

170

learning to dream lucidly. In Krishnamurti's teaching about the nature of the mind, he encourages us to develop the capacity to have thought observe its own movement. One application of this principle might be in the dream state (although he clearly had in mind our learning to apply this principle in waking life, too). When we realize that the dream images we experience are representations of our own thought patterns, then lucid dreaming can be seen as a kind of objective self-observation of the movement and flow of our habitual thinking process.

But perhaps the very notion of "evolution in consciousness" needs to be examined more carefully. What does it mean to say that human awareness is evolving over the centuries? And even more important to a theory of lucid dreaming, what might be the next quantum leap into a new age awareness? At least two significant factors may interact to produce consciousness change: quantity/quality and perception/processing. Using combinations of these polarities we can observe four different types of transformation in awareness. With a matrix chart we can depict this interaction and give an example of each type. The four cells are numbered for easier reference.

	quantity change	quality change
perceptual change	1. move from two-dimension to three-dimension perception	2. healing of color blindness
processing change	3. a two-year-old watching a movie vs. a 25-year-old	4. developing greater patience in one's personality

The change in consciousness of the first and second cells of the matrix involves perceiving information from the surroundings which wasn't consciously available in the past. That change can be quantitative, such as the imaginary two-dimensional man who "sits up" to discover a third dimension. Or it can be qualitative, such as a color-blind person who suddenly sees the true color quality of objects.

But another type of consciousness change does not involve having more information or externalized experience available. It has to do with a new way of processing or understanding the data which has been perceived all along. For example, you might have watched a movie at age two and understood little of its complicated plot. Years later when you are 25, you might watch the same movie again (that is, same information being perceived) but you would process and understand it quite differently. Primarily it would be an increase in the *quantity* of the details in the movie which you are able to process effectively. Between age two and 25 your personal consciousness had evolved.

The fourth cell of the matrix illustrates another way in which a change in processing can be called an evolution of consciousness. In this instance, it is the quality of processing. A classic example of this is the development of a patient inner response to outer circumstances which formerly caused anger or frustration. The development of patience is not a matter of more information being processed but rather the quality of the way in which events are arranged and interpreted.

Into which of these four categories would we place lucid dreaming? Some examples of heightened consciousness have characteristics of several or all of the possibilities. However, lucid dreaming seems to fit best into the fourth cell of the matrix chart— a change in the quality of how information is being processed. Usually the quantity of detail which makes up the momentary experience is not appreciably changed by becoming lucid in a dream. The enhanced dream vividness can sometimes cause us to see certain elements of the dream that had gone unnoticed, but for the most part the "dreamscape" and dream events keep happening just as they did before the moment when lucidity suddenly emerged.

Why, we might wonder, is lucid dreaming not better placed in the first category? Isn't it the direct experience of moving from three-dimensional perception to fourth-dimensional perception? The answer is generally no. The lucid dream still *looks* three-dimensional, just as the everyday physical world. No appreciable increase exists in the quantity or dimensional *texture* of what we perceive. In fact, this is usually what startles us when first becoming lucid: We are amazed by the *similarity* of the dream world to the physical world with which we are familiar. We may even say to ourselves *in* the lucid dream, "This is just as real and solid as normal waking life!"

However, an exciting conclusion remains in this theory of evolving consciousness. Lucid dreaming may not be the direct *perception* of four dimensions, but it *is* fourth-dimensional *consciousness*. The difference can be easily understood by considering the analogy of a square and a cube.

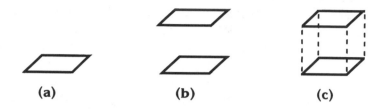

(a)   (b)   (c)

In condition (a) we have only a two-dimensional square. In condition (b) we have added another two-dimensional square but we still do not have a three-dimensional cube. The cube is created in condition (c) by the vertical dotted lines. The principle is this: The consciousness of the next higher dimension is created by forming a relationship between two independent examples of the original, lesser dimension. *The conscious capacity to relate two separate, three-dimensional worlds creates fourth-dimensional consciousness.* In effect the relationship *is* the next dimension. The dotted vertical lines *are* the third dimension.

In our analogy, the first square is our everyday, material awareness and the second square is dream awareness (*not* necessarily lucid). They are very similar. Both are made up of images, objects and stimuli that affect our seeing, hearing, tasting, etc. However, when lucidity emerges, a remarkable event has occurred: The fact that we realize we are dreaming means that we realize there are other, equally real, three-dimensional worlds. In effect, by remembering that there is another three-dimensional world where my body is asleep in bed, I have created a conscious *relationship* between the two worlds. That relationship is the beginning of fourth-dimensional consciousness. Actually, the *idea* which says, "This is really a dream," *is* the fourth dimension. This is what Cayce meant when he defined the fourth dimension as an idea. In a sense, any idea relates the physical world to any imagined world of possibilities. But nowhere is the power of an idea to create fourth-dimensional consciousness more dramatic than the idea that one is actually dreaming.

All of this can be said in a much more direct way (and some readers may wish all the abstractions had been skipped and the point come to more quickly): In a new age of fourth-dimensional consciousness, people will know that there are other spiritual worlds. There will be no fear of death. People will have consciously experienced these other worlds and be able to relate and make applicable their experiences in those other levels. For many people lucid dreaming will be the safe and direct way to make that quantum jump in awareness and evolve into fourth-dimensional consciousness. For other people, that development will come through an exploration of awakening psychic abilities. For still others it will come as a new understanding of how the paradoxes of life are created. By whatever means an individual uses, this new age awareness of the nature of reality will lead to new visions of our life style in a physical world.

Chapter 10

Visions of a New World

Throughout the previous chapters of this book we have explored prophecies and speculations about the immediate future. Each prediction created an image—a possibility—of what may come. The two primary sources of those images have been the Cayce readings and the author's own intuitions. And yet the occasional reference to other writers and teachers suggests that more than just these two sources have been blended in the chemistry of creating this book. One purpose of this final chapter is to examine more explicitly two of the most significant parallel sources which have affected the philosophy and direction of the previous chapters. Another purpose of this concluding section is an attempt to tie together some of the "loose ends" created by the vast scope of our journey through new age topics.

Visions of a Cultural Historian

In looking back we can sometimes see the trends of the past. If those trends are extrapolated to create a vision of the future, they often create a valuable insight into what may lie ahead. This principle can be applied to major cultural transformations in history. Recurrent themes appear on what happens when society experiences a shift in paradigm. Not only can we learn from these historical periods, we can also formulate predictions of what may lie ahead for us.

One especially noteworthy cultural historian who has tried to do this is William Irvin Thompson. Dr. Thompson has taught at MIT, York University and Syracuse University. In 1973 he founded the Lindisfarne Association, a contemplative educational community devoted to the study and realization of a new planetary culture. In a number of his books, particularly *Darkness and Scattered Light* (Anchor Books, 1978), Thompson examines the alternatives for the future—choices which he predicts will face us based on recurrent themes of major historical changes.

A summary of his ideas about these times of change fits nicely in our exploration of new age visions. In many ways his theories closely parallel the concepts in the Cayce readings, although they are often much more explicit and detailed in a discussion of new age life style. Like the Cayce readings, Thompson sees the latter portion of the 20th century as a likely period for a paradigm shift at least as great as the Renaissance 500 years ago. In his words, the change will be from civilization to planetization. Civilization is to be understood as a world order which focuses on material production and consumption. Planetization is a world order whose *priorities* are contemplation, consciousness and ecological balance. Not that production and consumption will cease to be relevant issues in a planetized society, rather the change is in priorities—or in Cayce terminology, new *ideals.*

The particularly difficult times of change, which Cayce foresaw for 1958 to 1998, are designated by Thompson as an initiation period for the earth. Using the three classic stages of initiation in mystery religions of the past, Thompson provides a framework for viewing both recent current events and future predictions. In other words, the ancient concept of spiritual initiation for an *individual* seeker may be acted out collectively by *all* of humanity. The traditional challenges and difficulties faced by the individual initiate may be analogous to the ones humanity will confront during these times of testing. Briefly, here are the three primary stages and, in Thompson's interpretation, the way in which we collectively may experience each stage:

1. The illumination of one's darkness or shadow side. The individual initiate might expect to face terrifying images from his own unconscious—the destructive, selfish potential within his own mind. Facing this inner demon can be not only frightening but also discouraging. There are likely to arise feelings of doubt and

unworthiness in seeing this shadow side of ourselves. This testing is felt most acutely by the initiate's ego.

When this state is applied to humanity as a whole, it is easy to see some recent examples of the illumination of humanity's dark side, such as the war in Viet Nam and the ecological disaster caused by the misuse of technology. In Thompson's theory it is especially the elite of the society (that is, the "ego" of a civilization) which experiences the humiliation of this first stage of initiation.

2. Discovery of the edge of one's sanity. For the individual initiate, this is the point at which he realizes that all the old definitions of reality no longer work. The old images of the ego no longer hold together. A breakdown in the sense of oneself and in the sense of reality results.

At a collective level, considerable evidence indicates that our society has entered this second stage of testing. The old systems and approaches upon which we used to depend no longer work. Many perplexing national problems seem to have no solution, and so many proposed solutions create even bigger problems while trying to solve the original difficulties. As one article in the *Washington Post* observed, no new ideas are around and the old ones no longer hold things together like they used to.

3. The defeat of the ego. It is at this point in the individual initiation process that the seeker lets go. In that instant of openness and vulnerability, a new self-identity can be born. Our society has not yet reached this point. It may be years or decades away. As long as the leadership of a society convinces its people that the old ideas and identity still might be made to work again, the courage to surrender and let go will not be present.

These three classic stages of initiation are the archetypes of transformation which historically have been known to only a few. The alchemy of consciousness change is about to make a quantum leap—from the level of the single person to the level of humanity as a whole. As these three stages are enacted for the masses of the planet, Thompson predicts that they will affect different segments of society at different times. In his view, the changes will be felt first in the spiritual/religious community. This is not the group of religious leaders who hold stubbornly to the old paradigm. Rather, it is those who are genuinely open to a mystical *revelation* of what is being born in the world. Thompson cites Teilhard de Chardin as a good example of this process.

The second segment is the artistic community. The new spiritual vision is given new life in art. Through art a great portion of humanity can sense the imaginative possibilities seen by the mystic. For Thompson, the third segment of society to feel the impact of this new vision is science. Whether it is the architecture of people like Buckminster Fuller or mystic physicists like Fritjof Capra, the original vision of the attuned spiritual community finds expression for the masses in science. In fact, many modern-day physicists sound more like mystics than most ministers and priests of traditional Christianity.

The final segment of society to feel the change is the political faction. In effect, the political process is the last area to reflect transformation. It is the hardest to change, the most likely to depict our past rather than our future. Thompson summarizes these four stages of cultural transformation in this way:

> The stages [of planetary cultural transformation] are part of a sequence in time, but from another point of view they are all going on at the same time, like the voices in a fugue. But for the sake of simplicity, it is easier to separate [them]. . .The first stage is religious. The second is artistic. The third is scientific and technical. And the fourth is political. The political transformation is the last stage. . . Most people tend to think that only politics is real and the cultural transformation has finally come into being when it has become political; but from my point of view, the cultural transformation is pretty well over by the time it has become politically implemented. (*Darkness and Scattered Light,* pp. 39-40)

In Thompson's writings we find a description of various cultural forces at work to reshape the planet. One force is the emergent sense of world community. Even if we are not yet able to cooperate very effectively with other nations, the inescapable fact remains that our future and well-being are tied to that of other countries. The "planetization of the nations" is being felt first in its uncomfortable aspects—problems in one part of the world almost immediately create problems worldwide. But as a force for cultural change, this development could just as well nurture a sense of world fellowship. The days of a nation choosing isolationism are

178

over. The planetization of the nations is ultimately a force for transformation which requires a choice between cooperation or suffering.

A second force at work upon our world is the decentralization of cities. In other words, there is a trend away from urbanization and a growing new respect of smaller communities as optimal places in which to live. As large urban centers of America (particularly the older cities of northeast America) decay, we shall be faced with hard choices about rebuilding them. Cultural forces at work point toward smaller and more manageable models for living instead of the urban centralization which has characterized the industrial age.

Thompson writes that the miniaturization of technology is a third force for transformation. At first glance it would seem that technology has been a part of the problem in the old paradigm. We might wonder how a product of technology could constitute a force toward a new set of assumptions for living. It is indeed ironic that the most remarkable of achievements of the old world order would create an impetus and an assistance to a new life style. However, this is exactly the effect that the miniaturization of technology has. Observe what has been made possible by computers or medical equipment so small they are portable. For example, on a desk top a businessman can now have an information retrieval system as powerful as one 20 years ago which required a thousand times the space. When the technological tools for living become portable, the decentralization of population centers becomes possible. We no longer have to live in unwieldy urban centers to have access to the technological, medical and communications resources we need. The miniaturization of these tools for living open up new options in life style.

A final, crucial force at work to change our world is the interiorization of consciousness. With this fourth force as well as the first one (that is, the planetization of nations) we find the most direct parallels between Cayce and Thompson. As humanity begins to look for the source of the good life within rather than without, value systems begin to shift. A contemplative culture can emerge which finds new meaning in meditation, dream study, mythology and the arts.

In Thompson's view these four cultural forces work to create a new model for living, what he calls the meta-industrial village. The prefix *meta* means *beyond,* so the meta-industrial village is an evolutionary step *beyond* the life style models of industrial life. The idea of village life may sound like a retrogressive step; it conjures up images of America in the days of George Washington: semirural communities with no electricity, no plumbing, no modern communications devices. But Thompson goes to great lengths to explain that this is not his vision at all. Although some proponents of "back to nature" would like to see us return to 18th-century life styles, he proposes a return to the village *scale* but incorporating the technological breakthroughs of science. Communities of like-minded people—perhaps several hundred residents per village—can become models for new age living. Each such meta-industrial village would include:

1. Energy self-sufficiency, using a combination of replenishable energy sources, such as solar, wood and wind power.

2. Agricultural self-sufficiency, using organic or biodynamic methods for growing food which respect the delicate ecological balance.

3. Cottage industries for the production of salable goods. Such small-scale production could range from hand-crafted furniture to farm implements to microcomputers. The sale of products for the village's cottage industries would provide a source of income or a means of bartering items manufactured in other communities.

4. Education of body, mind and spirit for village members of all ages. Thompson beautifully describes this ideal in which "the entire village would be a contemplative educational community," with its basic way of life being "the adventure of consciousness. . . Everyone living in the community would be involved in an experiential approach to education, from contemplative birth. . .to contemplative death. . .And at the various stages of life in between, the entire community would function as a college, in which children and adults would work together in gardening, construction, ecological research, crafts, and classes in all fields of knowledge." (*Darkness and Scattered Light,* pp. 96-97)

The concept of the meta-industrial village is the end-product of Thompson's theories and visions and an impressive contribution to speculations about the future. It seems to be quite consistent with the ideals and spirit of Cayce's perspective on a new age, but it is far more detailed and specific in its description than is any life style model proposed in the readings. There appears to be no requirement in his vision that everyone live in such a village. We can well imagine that major cities will continue to exist into the 21st century. However, the quality of life and the security to be found in the meta-industrial village would likely attract many people— perhaps a majority—to this new model for living.

Visions of a Modern Mystic

Among the many teachers and sensitives who have written about a new age, David Spangler is a unique contributor. For several years he served as a formulator of educational development for the spiritual community Findhorn, in Scotland. More recently he founded the Lorian Association in America and has been active in lecturing and writing about the emergent new world order. He describes his own method of receiving information on this theme as an attunement to both a universal consciousness and specific discarnate souls in other dimensions of reality. Spangler is not a self-styled psychic, as the term is popularly used. Rather he is a broadly respected teacher of our times, whose method in some ways resembles that of Rudolph Steiner.

Among his various books, *Revelation: The Birth of a New Age* best expounds his ideas about these times of transition. An essential feature of that book is the notion that a new age is already here, but its current existence is simultaneous with that of the old world. The idea of two worlds may at first sound confusing, but if we look with sensitivity at what is going on within and without us, we may recognize that this is exactly the state of things in these changing times.

In Spangler's view a new age is born first in the formative etheric energies of the planet. A major shift has *already* occurred. Nevertheless, the old world's momentum perpetuates its apparent reality and produces a seeming inertia to the change in etheric patterns. For centuries, old world assumptions have guided the creative dimensions of higher realities, which have in turn manifested as the physical world we have known. Even after the creative impulse is removed from these old etheric patterns they continue to have their effect for some time. But they will necessarily play themselves out. They have within them the seeds of their own demise. An effective yet admittedly distasteful analogy is a chicken whose head has been severed but who continues life-like movement for a while. Spangler describes the two worlds in this way: ". . .with the translation of etheric energies to a higher level, the thought-pattern of the old etheric was left behind as something analogous to a corpse or a memory. This is certainly the creation of two worlds. . ." (*Revelation: The Birth of a New Age*, p. 157)

When we take this concept a step further, it suggests to us a strategy for building a new age. Our forces should not be in conflict with the old. The old world will fail of itself—primarily, Spangler feels, because the creative input at the etheric level no longer exists. Our job is to be a part of the new world, to be attuned to a new age which already exists and to learn to manifest its reality. Spangler puts it this way:

> To know the new, one must *be* the new. To engage in conflict with the disintegrating patterns is to be at one with them, just as to use violence to stop violence is to defeat one's essential purpose. The old will separate itself naturally, as we have seen; it need not be the task we take unto ourselves. (*Revelation*, p. 170)

These principles are some of the key concepts presented in Spangler's book, which merits our study. It constitutes a remarkable parallel to the ideas found in the Cayce readings and in Thompson's writings.

Prophecies of a Second Coming

Perhaps no vision of a new age is more dramatic than the possibility of a direct, physical interaction of the Christ in human affairs—an intervention that would be perceived by humanity as a whole. Nothing better expresses our hope that a new age would include a spiritually renewed consciousness within the human family. It is not presented as a certainty in the Cayce readings, nor are there specific details as to timing or appearance; rather it is a possibility—perhaps even a likelihood—*if* the "way is made passable" by preparatory work on our part.

The need for efforts to make the way passable is not the result of some inadequacy on the part of the Christ. It is not a matter of an inability of the Christ to appear in materiality without our help. Instead we might think of it this way: Unless a sufficient portion of humanity lifts itself into a new awareness, then a reappearance of the Christ would confuse us or be easily misunderstood by us. The Christ will come again only when such an intervention will be truly helpful in the spiritual evolution of which we are a part. It is out of the profoundest kind of love that any widescale, directly physical appearance of the Christ is delayed.

Among the Cayce readings on a Second Coming, several are especially noteworthy. Cayce clearly thought of the Christ as both a universal spirit that could be seen in all world religions *and* as the soul we call Jesus. However, the Christ nature of Jesus was attained over many lifetimes—according to the Cayce readings—culminating in Jesus who became one with the Christ Consciousness. In these passages about the reappearance of the Christ, the readings suggest that the soul we call Jesus will be the expression of the Christ in these times.

Q-10. He said He would come again. What about His second coming?

A-10. The time no one knows. Even as He gave, not even the Son Himself. *Only* the Father. Not until His enemies—and the earth—are wholly in subjection to His will, His powers.

Q-11. Are we entering the period of preparation for His coming?

A-11. Entering the test period, rather.   5749-2

Q-3. What is meant by "the day of the Lord is near at hand"?

A-3. That as has been promised through the prophets and the sages of old, the time—and half time—has been and is being fulfilled in this day and generation, and that soon there will again appear in the earth that one through whom many will be called to meet those that are preparing the way for His day in the earth. The Lord, then, will come, "even as ye have seen him go."

Q-4. How soon?

A-4. When those that are His have made the way clear, *passable,* for Him to come.   262-49

Q-4. Is Jesus the Christ on any particular sphere or is He manifesting on the earth plane in another body?

A-4. As just given, all power in heaven, in earth, is given to Him who overcame. Hence He is of Himself in space, in the force that impels through faith, through belief, in the individual entity. As a spirit entity. Hence not in a body in the earth, but may come at will

to him who *wills* to be one with, and acts in love to make same possible.

For, He shall come as ye have seen Him go, in the *body* He occupied in Galilee. The body that He formed, that was crucified on the cross, that rose from the tomb, that walked by the sea, that appeared to Simon, that appeared to Philip, that appeared to "I, even John."   **5749-4**

We may well wonder what kind of an expression of the Christ we are to expect. What scenario seems most likely? These readings predict that it will not come in the birth of a baby, as Jesus did 2000 years ago. Instead He will manifest in the very body that He resurrected long ago. Having so purified the flesh body and attuned it to the mind and spirit, Jesus the Christ can manifest that body in any plane or dimension at will. The pattern of incarnation by birth has already been established. So what might we expect for a new age?

At least three broad scenarios have been suggested. One is the spectacular, *mass appearance*—the Christ seen by millions of people in all His glory. In this type of scenario the populace of the world is quickly humbled, and the Christ reigns in a spiritual and political sense. Many branches of fundamentalism in Christianity expect some version of this scenario, often coupled with cataclysm and punishments to befall the earth just prior to the reappearance.

A second hypothesis is that the Christ will reappear in much the same manner He did just after Easter. This scenario involves the direct *physical* experience of His Presence by individuals and small groups. Recall the way in which Jesus ate fish with the disciples in Galilee just after His resurrection. In this case and in others, He clearly was perceived in a physical way in the outer world. Might this kind of contact with numerous *small groups* be the most likely possibility?

A third scenario is that the so-called Second Coming will be at nonphysical *inner levels of awareness*. Already there are individuals who claim to have had such a direct experience, and perhaps the Second Coming implies a dramatic increase in the number of people who experience this. The inner contact (via meditation, prayer, dreams, etc.) could well be with the resurrected body, mind and spirit of Jesus who became the Christ. Such a personal contact by millions of people could be expected to have a dramatic and uplifting effect on the attitudes and life styles of people worldwide.

Whichever scenario seems most likely to you, an important factor to keep in mind is the necessity for openness to the new. We must avoid repeating the *process* of what happened in Jesus' times. He was rejected, misunderstood or missed by so many people because they held narrow, old notions of what the coming of the Messiah was to be like. The Christ will come again only in the spirit of that which is propelling humanity's evolution forward, and hence will appear as something unexpected and new. In *Revelation: The Birth of a New Age,* David Spangler states this beautifully. It is a principle worth keeping in mind as we work to make the way passable for the coming again of the Christ into the physical plane:

> The concept of the Second Coming is past oriented for many people. It links the mind with an expression of the past and leads to an expectation of a repetition of that expression. It does not take into full account the possibility of a much greater manifestation of the Christ presence, revealing aspects of Divinity not previously known by man. Indeed, just as Jesus was rejected by many who felt that he did not fit into the classical expectations of a messiah and who could not perceive the fullness of what he represented, so the Christ manifestation for this new age could go unrecognized and rejected by many who are thinking of a Second Coming as a repetition and reinforcement of the past. We are in a new age. (p. 190)

Will There Be Religions for a New Age?

One of the characteristics of a new age which has been described is a closer personal attunement to the Creative Forces or God. In fact, when Cayce was asked to define human consciousness for the Aquarian age, he said that it would be the full realization of our capacity to communicate with God; that is, each individual may have the experience of direct access to the spiritual world within. We may wonder whether or not religions would be required in such a future.

Historically, many of the great world religions *began* as communities of people who were drawn together by their common spiritual experience. It was natural to want to meet in a regular and systematic way with others who were having similar inner experiences. As communities, they might celebrate in symbolic form the spiritual truths they knew and maybe to stimulate in each other additional—perhaps deeper—experiences. This archetypal first stage of religious development does not involve a hierarchy of authority that characterizes later stages. For example, in early Christianity the community of believers was bound together in small groups—much like a spiritual study group. Although there were some itinerant teachers such as St. Paul, these small communities were not focused on outward authority and hierarchy but rather on direct inner experience and application.

In later generations and later stages of developing a religion, a loss of much or all of this direct experience is likely. In its place may arise rituals with forgotten meanings and a hierarchy of leaders who theoretically make the attunement with the Divine *in place of* the community.

Perhaps in moving into a new age, a spiritually renewed world society, we will once again be at the first archetypal stage, and the meaning of religion will dramatically shift from what it has most recently become. An analysis of the dynamics of the current religious scene can point out both the crucial factors involved in such a shift and the potential pitfalls to be found in a new age religious development. By way of example, the analysis will be presented in terms of modern Christianity, but a similar process may be observed in Judaism, Islam or other world religious movements.

Two essential ingredients in our analysis are a pair of polar opposites. Each constitutes a choice that a religious movement must make. One pole or the other is invariably stressed. Although it may seem ideal to take the exact middle path between polar opposites, experience shows that one pole is emphasized somewhat more than the other.

The first pair of polar opposites is faith and works. A religious group must decide which to stress. Is it the works which they do in the three-dimensional physical plane? These may be deeds of service or they may be efforts to win God's favor. *Or* do they emphasize their faith in the divine intervention of higher forces into the material world? In this case, they are likely to be acutely aware

186

of how feeble human effort can be. Most great religions have some amount of each pole; and yet virtually all movements will stress one a bit more than the other.

A second important pair of polar opposites is duality and oneness. Again, a religious movement tends to emphasize one or the other of these two. With what perspective is life and the stage for spiritual evolution viewed? Those who adopt a dualistic outlook pay special attention to the tensions of a good and an evil. They point to abundant evidence in the material plane which suggests the dualistic nature of life (for example, positive and negative, light and dark, mind and body, etc.). Those who choose the approach of oneness in their religious outlook see a profound inter-relationship between all aspects of life. Not denying the *appearance* of duality, they claim that it is more fruitful to experience the underlying oneness behind the appearance. Broadly speaking, the religions of Western culture have been more inclined toward the dualistic notion while religions of the Eastern world have been characterized by an emphasis upon oneness.

Since a religious movement has two choices to make (that is, faith or works, and duality or oneness), four possible categories result. They are depicted here in a matrix form with examples listed for each category.

	Duality	**Oneness**
Works	Dry periods **Liberal Christianity** Brother's keeper	Manipulation **Technological Metaphysics** Trains the will
Faith	Bigotry **Fundamentalism** Simple devotion	Passivity, lukewarm **New Age Religion** Divine co-creativity

Each of the four categories has a dark side and a light side. In other words, each category has a way in which the choices made by the religious movement can create confusion and retard spiritual growth. However, each category also has the potential to make a meaningful contribution to spiritual progress. It is important to see both opportunities inherent in each box of the matrix. A word or phrase to describe the dark possibility is in the upper left-hand corner of each matrix box; the light possibility is in the lower right-hand corner.

An emphasis on duality and works is found in modern, liberal Christianity, admirable in its commitment to social action. Many examples of socially involved Catholic and Protestant churches exemplify the ideal that we are our brother's keeper. However, the dark side of the choices of a liberal Christianity is lack of spiritual experience by its constituents.. A spiritual dryness characterizes many liberal Christians. They have forgotten how to make direct inner contact with the spiritual world—or more likely they never learned how to go about it.

In contrast, fundamentalism in Christianity does not lack spiritual experiences. Laying on of hands, speaking in tongues and visions are commonly reported occurrences. In choosing faith and duality (that is, a strong emphasis on Christ vs. the devil), people of this category have chosen conditions which create other light and dark opportunities. On the positive side, fundamentalism nurtures simple devotion, which is a significant asset to spiritual evolution. However, on the other side is the temptation to fall into judgments and even bigotry. Many so-called new age thinkers see only this dark side of fundamentalism. Offended by what they feel is the narrow-mindedness and biases of fundamentalists, they may fail to see the important contribution of devotion which this category of people is making to our culture's religious thought.

The third category is created by a combination of the oneness perspective with an emphasis on personal efforts and works. It has become a loosely organized religious movement in our times which we might call "technological metaphysics." It is technique oriented. Making use of meditation, biofeedback, macrobiotic diets, prosperity consciousness and a host of other techniques, it tells us what we need to *do* in order to *achieve* enlightenment. Its dark side is that its motivations can become manipulative. It can lead us to think that God is required to give results if we complete

188

certain procedures. Technological metaphysics too easily leaves out love (for God and others) and devotion, too easily combines ancient spiritual approaches with Western impatience and preoccupation with achievement. Nevertheless, this religious (or quasi-religious) movement has an important light side: It makes the crucial contribution of teaching people how to use the will. Spiritual evolution is largely a matter of learning how to use the soul's birthright of free will. Without the excesses of impatience, manipulation and overconcern for achievement, this category can help many people to progress in spiritual growth.

The final category is what we might imagine for a new age religion. It is created by seeing the essential oneness of life and putting trust and faith in God. It does not deny a physical world with dualistic concepts, but it always tries to work with duality in the context of oneness. A new age religion will deal with the challenges of being a man or a woman, keeping in mind always that the soul is a combination of both sexes. It will deal with the problems created by what appears to be evil in the world, but it will remember that evil is essentially goodness misconstrued or misapplied.

In the same fashion, the emphasis on faith does not preclude personal effort and works. But those works are effective only in the context of faith and inner direction. Human effort by itself is feeble and can do little. Spirit is the real power. However, our works in response to faith-inspired intuition can accomplish much. The light side of this category is, therefore, divine co-creativity. The dark side of which one must be ever mindful is passivity: a faithfulness which forgets to act. (In The Revelation this is called "lukewarm." It is the fault of the seventh church, which corresponds to the highest spiritual center in man.)

In these times of transition we will observe change in all four categories. Important *internal* struggles will be happening for people within each category. The movement into a new age is not merely a matter of everyone shifting into the fourth category. Perhaps several generations from now, the primary religion(s) of the world will have the essential characteristics used to describe "new age religion." But during this time of transition, from 1958— 1998 and perhaps well into the 21st century, we can anticipate that all four categories will be active with many followers. The challenge for each area will be to express its light side instead of its dark side. In so doing, significant contributions in building a new age can be made by all people sincerely working within the form of the spiritual growth they have chosen. The real new age religion will include the light side of all four areas and each area needs people to bring its best qualities into expression.

Conclusion

No one can know the future. By its very definition it is that which has not yet occurred. However, we sometimes slip into thinking that the future is something which already exists on an imaginary timeline—something which already *is* but merely cannot be readily seen. This point of view leads us to psychics, economic forecasters or futurists, hoping to get the jump on the future before it shows itself. But no prognostication is a view of the future. Each one is rather a statement about the present. Even the best of predictions is actually just a way of saying, "Here is how things are going to be *if* they continue along the path they are now on."

What distinguishes the rare psychic whose prophecy proves to be accurate is a characteristic which sounds paradoxical: That individual saw the *present* better than others did. If Edgar Cayce or anyone else proves to have been accurate with prophecies of a new age, it will be because of his clarity of vision in seeing his *own* times. We reach this remarkable and ironic conclusion when we realize that almost all of us live in our minds in the past.

One of the most challenging Cayce readings says that that which appears as materiality to our senses is really the past. In other words, from a higher spiritual consciousness, physical life is meeting past karma in concrete form. For example, when we feel automatic emotional responses they are actually perceptions of our past.

Our own physical bodies are mere representations of past thoughts, feelings and actions. We have built our bodies and now we experience the results. Our behaviors and our material possessions are also projections into the three-dimensional physical world of what we have mentally created in the past. The problem in all this arises because we are tricked into a misperception of what is happening around us. We think that what we view in the world is the present, but seen from a spiritual standpoint it is better understood as a picture of the past.

It is not that the material world is not "real." To say that physical life is an illusion does *not* mean that automobiles, physical bodies,
190

houses and everything else of daily living is a fantasy. What *is* illusory is our *understanding* of all these items. We think they are the present and we often suffer for the mistake.

The enlightened spiritual teacher, and sometimes the gifted psychic, has awakened from this confusing slumber. The Edgar Cayce readings were probably more literal than we care to admit when they say that the soul is asleep while in material life. And that sleep makes us think that the past is the present, while the actual present is hidden. But the potential for soul awakening is always there. To do so is to begin to see and to understand what the present moment really is.

What is happening right *now* is our *creative response in consciousness* to what is physically before us. Awareness is the present; physical appearance is the past. For example, what is your inner reaction to reading the words on this page? This book and these words are not really the present moment when you view life from the perspective of an awakened soul. These words are a mere representation of the past, a picture of the creative impulses and ideas that the author had months or years ago. What is happening right *now* is the inward effect they may be having on you.

Or consider another example. What happens when your body is ill? The temptation is to fall into the old illusion that the illness is what is happening now. However, that sickened condition is more accurately understood as a representation of how you have treated your body in the past. Not that the aches and pains are a fantasy. It is rather a matter of awakening to the realization that your response in consciousness to the aches and pains is what is going on in the present.

If we extend this example, we can think about society and the world in which we live. In many ways it is ill. To listen to the news each evening is to hear the highlights of its pains. The suffering is real, but it is of the past. It is a product of the old world, and it is the creation of what people have thought and done in the past. Our job is to take note of the past and yet to keep our attention on what really is the present.

This is how we become visionaries of a new age, by seeing deeply into our own times. It is to recognize what is really going on in the present moment—to perceive what souls are creating in consciousness by their response to physical conditions. This is where a new age (no matter how beautiful or frightful) will be built.

However, the work of the visionary is not merely having a more subtle and more awakened *observation* of life. It is also a responsibility to be an active and self-reflective *participant* in that creative process.

In our final analysis we can see that Edgar Cayce knew no more than *you* can know now about a new age for the 21st century. If anything, you can have a clearer vision than Cayce did as he gave readings in 1935. Your clearer view is possible simply because humanity is further along in the building process. And even more importantly, you can still have a direct impact on the creating of what that future will be.

We have every reason to be hopeful about what lies ahead. Admittedly it is discouraging to see that stubborn human tendency which refuses to change until the old ways become too painful. It suggests that the birth of anything new will not be without discomfort and suffering. However, the real visionaries are at work in creating a great gift for all humanity. Those few people (hopefully the critical mass or threshold number required) who have freed themselves from the illusions of the past are doing a creative work in consciousness. They are building a new order of world society. Their efforts are a gift because they will reflect to humanity the unrecognized purity and beauty within each person.

It is the timing that is hard to judge. How long will it take to create that gift? And then how long will it take for it to be gratefully accepted? Are the times of transition to be the 40 years from 1958 to 1998 or the next 400 years? When we catch the truly cosmic vision of the soul's journey through materiality, the problem of timing does not seem quite so crucial. These questions seem to fade in importance when we remember our long, long history in the earth and the timeless prospects ahead of us. What matters is that the vision of a Christ-centered world exists in human minds. What matters is that the active work of creating such a new age is going on and that each of us is invited to play a unique and special part.

Here is an affirmation given by Edgar Cayce for those who want to help the transition into a new and better world:

Lord, here am I! Use me in the way, in the manner Thou seest fit; that I may ever be that Thou has purposed for me to be—a light shining as in darkness to those who have lost hope, from one cause or another. **3976-26**

Appendix A

A Geologist's View of Earth Changes

by John Peterson

The power of the earth is especially evident when its surface changes dramatically and rapidly. When Mount St. Helens erupted, it destroyed a two-hundred-square-mile area and blasted 1,300 feet off the top of the mountain. The event affected the entire northwestern portion of the United States. However, this effect was small compared to previous volcanic eruptions; for example, when Tambora, a mountain in Indonesia, exploded in 1815, it killed an estimated 12,000 people and affected the entire world. The event propelled enough ash into the atmosphere to create the "Year Without a Summer," 1816.

In addition to volcanic eruptions, earthquakes have destroyed large regions and have killed many millions of people. The 1976 Tangshan, China, earthquake killed an estimated 650,000 people. Closer to home, the 1971 San Fernando quake, of moderate intensity and of short duration, killed 58 people and caused approximately $500,000,000 damage.

Seismic sea waves, commonly referred to as tidal waves, have also changed many lives and nations and destroyed many cities and regions. The 1896 seismic sea wave that hit Sanrika, Japan, killed an estimated 26,000 people. When the volcano Krakatau exploded in 1883 in the East Indies, it produced a sea wave 115 feet high, which washed away 165 villages and killed more than 36,000 people. That wave was recorded around the world and was even detected in the English Channel.

Plate Tectonics

To understand these earth changes, a brief discussion of plate tectonics ("the study of the earth's crustal structure and the forces that produce changes in it," *Webster's New World Dictionary*) is necessary. The surface of the earth is broken up into ten major segments or "plates" and many smaller ones. Plates are approximately fifty miles thick and span over many thousands of square miles. In fact, the entire United States is but a portion of the North American Plate, which extends from the middle of the Atlantic Ocean to the San Andreas Fault in California.

These plates actually move about independently, and as they move energy is stored and released, causing the earth changes which affect us. Three basic types of margins occur between earth plates: (1) *collision* as two plates strike each other; (2) *separation* between two plates as they move away from each other; and (3) *lateral* or horizontal movement between two plates as they slip past each other.

Plate movement can generate many types of earth changes; some of the changes we might expect in the future include: (1) volcanic eruptions, (2) earthquakes, and (3) seismic sea waves (tidal waves).

Volcanoes

Volcanic activity can be triggered when one plate is being subducted (pushed down) under another plate. The energy produced by this activity melts the surrounding rocks which then rise to the surface. The Cascade volcanoes, and notably Mount. St. Helens, in Washington and Oregon are examples of this activity. These volcanoes have been created by the downward movement (subduction) of a small plate, Juan de Fuca, under the North American Plate.

The other plate boundary that causes volcanic events is two plates moving apart. Hot melted rock flows up into the resulting gap between plates and rises to the surface. Volcanic activity generated by this type of plate movement is restricted to certain zones on the earth; for example, along the Mid-Atlantic Ridge which divides the American Plates from the African and Eurasian Plates. This zone has a high number of active volcanoes, as also seen in Iceland. In this area, the island is actually being split in two and new crust is continually being generated.

One other type of activity is thought to produce such volcanoes as those in the Hawaiian Islands and Yellowstone National Park. These areas are thought to be caused by a "hot spot" in the mantle of the earth, that is, an area of intense heat within the earth's mantle under a moving plate. The hot spot gives rise to volcanic activity directly above it and builds a row of volcanoes as the plate moves across the relatively stable hot spot. The Hawaiian Island chain is an example of this with its distinct line of submerged and exposed volcanoes extending past Midway Island. This chain was created as the Pacific Plate moved toward the northwest over the hot spot.

Each type of volcanic eruption has its own particular characteristics. Variations in the rock in different areas contribute to two primary kinds of eruptions: the explosive eruptions, such as those in the Northwest, and the relatively quiet ones, such as those in the Hawaiian chain. In the Hawaiian Islands, the melted rock (magma) which is extruded is more fluid and contains less vaporized water than the magma which occurs in the Pacific Northwest. The volcanoes in the Pacific Northwest, which contain more vaporized water, are more dangerous for people to live near than those in other areas, such as Hawaii, because of the explosive type of volcanic eruption.

Earthquakes

People had just gotten off work and were heading home when the first shaking began. The time was 5:36 p.m. on Good Friday, March 27, 1964. By the time the earth had stopped shaking, an estimated 77,000 square miles of Alaska had been deformed. The earthquake had caused $300,000,000 in property damage and killed 130 people in a land which is almost deserted. For over thousands of square miles, the shaking was so severe that people were thrown from their feet and some became ill from motion sickness. This earthquake was one of the largest of recent times and now seismologists (who study earthquakes) are predicting that a quake of similar magnitude might occur in California.

To better understand earthquakes and how to prepare for them, we should first review the basic mechanics, causes and results of this type of earth change.

Earthquakes are geophysical events caused by a release of energy as one land mass moves against or past another. Plate movement is slow, normally not exceeding several inches per year. But as the years go by, the potential energy accumulates until it exceeds the amount of friction which can hold the rocks together. At this point an earthquake results along a fault or fracture in the rocks. The quake releases the stored energy in the form of earth shaking. Following an earthquake, the energy is again slowly stored up and a new cycle begins.

Along the San Andreas Fault zone, hundreds of earthquakes happen every day. Most are very small and cannot be felt by the people living in the area. In such areas, the amount of friction which is holding the fault from slipping is small, and because of this the amount of energy which stores up is also small. Hollister, California, located on the San Andreas Fault, is known for frequent small daily tremors. In such an area, a large, destructive event is unlikely, whereas in an area like San Francisco a great amount of friction appears to be holding the fault together, blocking movement. Since the last movement in 1906, the energy has been stored up, and the potential offset might be as much as thirty feet. Now, when an earthquake does happen, it is likely to be similar in magnitude to the 1906 quake.

The San Andreas Fault area is a major system because it separates the North American Plate from the Pacific Plate. The Pacific Plate is moving toward the Northwest relative to the North American with its movement averaging four to five inches per year. The history of this type of plate movement shows that California and the West Coast are not likely to fall off into the Pacific; it might move northward, but large-scale vertical movements are extremely unlikely. While this type of plate margin normally does not produce volcanic activity, frequent earthquakes do occur.

This type of earthquake zone (horizontal slippage of one plate past another) normally produces shallow-focused earthquakes, that is, of a depth of less than one mile. These shallow-focused quakes are responsible for about three quarters of the total energy released from earthquakes throughout the earth.

In other areas, earthquakes occur at depths of up to 400 miles. Deep-focused quakes are prevalent along plate boundaries wherein one plate is being pushed under another. In such areas, earthquakes are occurring along the margin of the two plates as they collide. Along the western edge of the South American continent, the continental plate is moving toward the west, colliding with a large oceanic plate in the Southern Pacific. As this occurs, the heavy, dense rocks of oceanic plate are forced down under the lighter rocks of the South American Plate, triggering a high number of earthquakes. The 1964 Alaskan earthquake was a result of this type of activity as the Pacific Plate was pushed under a portion of the North American Plate.

In addition to earthquakes along plate margins, quakes can also occur *within* plates, not being related to plate margins. These types of earthquakes are normally small and infrequent, although they have occurred in several locations within the United States. One of the largest was the great 1811 New Madrid, Missouri, earthquake. This one caused considerable damage in the area and was felt as far away as Washington, D.C. This type of quake is thought to be caused by localized forces related to readjustments within the rocks.

The magnitude of a quake is measured in one of two ways: (1) a direct measure of the *energy released* or (2) the relative degree of *movement* felt by people in the area and the amount of *damage* produced by the quake. The scale which measures absolute energy released is the Richter scale. This is the most commonly used method in measuring and comparing earthquakes and was developed by Charles Richter in 1935. The method measures wave heights as recorded by a seismograph (a machine designed to monitor earth movement). Because the size of earthquakes varies enormously, the scale is based on the logarithm of the height of recorded earthquake waves on the seismograph. An increase of one unit on the scale indicates a ten times increase in the earthquake waves. Also when the reported magnitude of an earthquake increases by one, the amount of *released energy* has increased *30* times. The Richter scale is open-ended with no upper or lower limit. Highly sensitive seismographs can record earthquakes with a magnitude as small as minus two.

The largest quakes measured in modern times were of 8.9 magnitude. With the upper limit to the magnitude of earthquakes determined by the strength of the rocks, the present theory in seismology is that 8.9 is the largest magnitude possible, because most rocks are not capable of storing greater amounts of energy. The Richter scale is a direct measure of the energy released and an indirect measure of the amount of damage produced by a quake.

The extent of damage and injuries resulting from a quake is measured by another scale, the Modified Mercalli Intensity Scale. This is a relative scale from one to twelve and its reading is dependent upon many factors. As an example, if a quake was felt by everyone and caused considerable damage to poorly built or badly designed structures and only minor damage to well-built structures, it would rate a seven on the scale. Since this is a *relative* scale, a magnitude seven earthquake in one area might only be magnitude five in another, basically because of the type of rocks in the areas.

The magnitude of an earthquake is measured at its focal point, or epicenter, defined as the point on the earth's surface directly above the initial point of movement. Normally most damage is done at or around the epicenter because this is the point closest to the energy release. Less and less damage occurs farther from this point.

Seismic Sea Waves

Another significant earth change to consider is the seismic sea wave, commonly referred to as a tidal wave. The term "tidal wave," as well as the Japanese word, *tsunami* (Japanese for "tidal wave"), are misleading terms, because tides have nothing to do with this type of wave.

Seismic sea waves are generated by a large pulse of energy either from an earthquake, a large landslide or a volcanic eruption. In normal ocean waves, the influence of the wave is less than one hundred feet below the surface. In a seismic sea wave, the influence extends many thousands of feet below the surface. Because of this, the wave while in the open ocean is normally only several feet high, but as it reaches shallow water, the energy becomes focused upward, causing the wave to grow higher. The largest seismic sea waves have been recorded at heights exceeding 150 feet.

In the open ocean, seismic sea waves travel between 400 to 450 miles per hour and can cross an ocean basin within half a day. While traveling on the open sea, the wave loses little energy until it impacts against a land mass. The energy is then quickly released, creating the coastal devastation commonly associated with this type of earth change.

Even though a seismic sea wave might reach a peak of one hundred feet, it usually does not travel very far inland. Damage is restricted to the extreme lowlands and river mouths. However, because of the dense population centers on the coast, a large seismic sea wave could have a tremendous impact on an entire country.

Pole Shift

Two types of pole shifts are possible: (1) a magnetic pole reversal and (2) a rotational pole reversal. The magnetic and rotational poles are actually physically separate, located several hundred miles apart. Because of this, the north arrow on a compass does not point toward true north, but toward the magnetic north pole.

Many magnetic pole reversals have happened in the past, averaging roughly one every million years. However, in the last four to five million years, the *average* has increased and a shift is occurring approximately every 300,000 years. Interestingly, the last shift was about 700,000 years ago, meaning that we are now overdue for one.

If a magnetic reversal were to occur tomorrow, what could we expect? Is there some evidence to support the theory that not much would, in fact, happen? A volcanic rock unit in Arizona, formed during one of the more recent magnetic reversals, recorded the direction of the magnetic poles by the alignment of certain minerals. These directions can be measured and indicate that the reversal occurred over *many years*—actually, several hundred years was required for the 180° shift of the magnetic pole. Because of this and because of the weak nature of the magnetic field, this type of pole shift is not thought to be capable of producing major earth changes. It might act as a *minor trigger* for some changes which are already set to occur, but we would not expect this type of shift to produce the major earth changes that are being predicted.

The other type of pole shift—a rotational one—would, however, produce major changes. Within the science of geology we have *no solid* evidence that a rotational pole shift has happened before. We do know that a great amount of energy is associated with the rotation of the planet. Because of this, it would take a tremendous amount of energy to disturb the present state of equilibrium. Many

199

ideas have been presented by various authors on what type of event could cause this to happen. One possibility would be a shift triggered by a large astral body passing nearby or actually colliding with the earth.

Edgar Cayce, in trance state in 1934, stated that a shifting of the poles was to occur. This reading appears to indicate that the future pole shift would be rotational, not magnetic.

There will be upheavals in the Arctic and in the Antarctic that will make for the eruption of volcanoes in the torrid areas, and there will be the shifting then of the poles—so that where there has been those of a frigid or the semi-tropical will become the more tropical, and moss and fern will grow.

3976-15, January 19, 1934

Conclusions

There has been considerable talk during the past several years about major earth changes in the near future. Edgar Cayce's readings describe a forty-year period from 1958 to 1998 during which major economic, physical, political and spiritual changes are to transpire. We are now more than halfway through that period and we have seen some physical changes, including volcanic eruptions and earthquakes, but are they of the scope his readings envisioned?

When the information about earth changes from the Edgar Cayce material is compared to the science of geology, many similarities emerge, including the troubled lands on the west coast of America and the safety lands of the northerly midwestern states. However, the science of geology does not support the possibility of the submergence of the west coast of America as it was indicated in Edgar Cayce's dream (in 1936). *In geologic terms, it is impossible* for a large area including the Sierra Nevada Mountains, the Rocky Mountains and the Colorado Plateau to sink thousands of feet in a short period of time. These areas have been rising slowly for many millions of years and for them to sink thousands of feet in several years is *highly unlikely.*

What can we expect in the future? If the key to the future lies in the events of the past, we can expect more earthquakes and volcanic eruptions in the areas in which they have already occurred. It is likely one or more major earthquakes will shake

California. It is also likely that Mount St. Helens will remain active for a time; but I believe this to be a normal, rather than abnormal, cycle of events.

The one major event which could change all the rules would be the rotational pole shift. But because it would require some tremendous event to bring this about, a rotational pole shift is highly unlikely.

As a geologist, I do not believe that catastrophic earth changes will occur in the near future. In 1939, Cayce gave reading 1602-3 in which he said these changes from the Piscean to the Aquarian age will be *gradual, not cataclysmic changes.* I believe this is correct and that worldwide catastrophic changes are not likely to occur, at least in the near future.

Whatever does happen in the future, it is important that we do prepare for this time, but it is equally important to live our lives to the fullest *now.* Doing the best we know to do today, tomorrow will take care of itself.

John Peterson, M.S., is a consulting hydrogeologist from Reno, Nevada. Both his B.S. and M.S. in geology were earned at San Diego State University. John's study of the earth changes material includes an integration of current geologic data with the Edgar Cayce readings and other psychic sources.

While completing his geologic studies in San Diego, he was an active A.R.E. Study Group and Team member, lecturing extensively on meditation, reincarnation and earth changes for radio, television and interest groups. His hobbies include scuba diving, skiing and mountain climbing. In addition to climbing Mount St. Helens in 1970, he has climbed extensively through the Sierra Nevada and Cascade ranges.

Appendix B

Proper Nutrition for Times of Change

by Bonnie Jenks with Karla Peterson

Introduction

The body of each entity is the temple of the living God.
2981-1

If the statement above, taken from the Edgar Cayce readings, is true, we should each take some time to reflect upon its meaning, especially how it pertains to these times of change.

A temple is a structure. In good weather, we would want our dwelling place to be strong, beautiful, and functional so that we would be safe and happy within it, and so that we might be proud to share it with others. In times of harsh weather or adverse conditions, any structure we inhabit would probably be fortified and strengthened to withstand and resist any damage which such changes might cause.

Of the many areas upon which the readings touched, that of diet and health is perhaps one of the most widely used. Much of the information the "sleeping" Cayce imparted on this topic was later accepted by nutritional science, and each day, it seems, more nutritionists are advocating what Cayce shared over 35 years ago.

With the help of Karla Peterson, long-time A.R.E. expert on the Cayce diet and health readings, a public health nutritionist and a registered dietician, I would like to share with you what we consider to be the most important aspects of this material for living healthfully in times of change or stress, and to examine how Cayce's recommendations compare with modern nutritional science. We will cover:

Balance in the diet (specifically acid-alkaline balance),

Food sources (what to eat, where it comes from, and how to prepare it), and

How to deal with stress through proper diet and health habits.

Balance in All Things

What did the Cayce readings emphasize most with regard to personal nutrition and diet? The most basic principle is balance:

Study, then, those charts pertaining to keeping well balanced in the chemical forces; not as to become a human pillbox but rather knowing the law and keeping same.   **2981-3**

According to the readings, a balanced diet is described as:

. . .have rather a percentage of 80 percent alkaline-producing to 20 percent acid-producing foods.

Then, it is well that the body not become as one that couldn't do this, that, or the other; or become as a slave to an idea of a set diet.   **1568-2**

In *The Edgar Cayce Handbook for Health Through Drugless Therapy**, Dr. Harold J. Reilly lists the acid- and alkaline-producing foods, according to the information given in the Cayce readings:

Alkaline-Forming Foods

All fruits, fresh and dried

Except large prunes, plums, and cranberries, with this exception: "The prune and pieplant juices [rhubarb], of course, are acid—but with cereals [whole grain] are *more* alkaline reacting. . ." (305-2)

All vegetables, fresh and dehydrated

Except legumes (dried peas, beans, and lentils).

All forms of milk

Including buttermilk, clabber sour milk, cottage cheese, and cheese.

---

*Macmillan Publishing Co., New York City, N.Y., 1971, pp. 79-80.

Acid-Forming Foods

Animal fats and vegetable oils
  Large prunes, plums, cranberries, and rhubarb are included here.

All cereal grains
  And other such products, as bread, breakfast foods, etc., rolled oats, corn flakes, corn-meal mush, polished rice, etc. (Brown rice is less acid-forming.)

All high-starch and protein foods
  White sugar, syrups, syrups made from white sugar (starchy foods in combination with fruits or proteins are acid combinations and should be avoided).

Nuts
  Peanuts, English walnuts, pecans, filberts, and coconut.

Legumes
  Dried beans, dried peas, and lentils.

Meats, poultry, and visceral meats
  Beef, pork, lamb, and veal; chicken, turkey, duck, goose, guinea hen, and game; heart, brains, kidney, liver, sweetbreads, and thymus.

Egg whites
  Yolks are not acid-forming.

This list alone, however, cannot give the complete picture of the Cayce diet recommendations regarding the acid-alkaline balance. To this we must add the recommendations about certain foods eaten in combination. For example, if you plan to increase your alkaline intake in the morning by adding a glass of orange juice to your breakfast menu of cereal and milk, Cayce had this advice:

Q-3. What foods should I avoid?
A-3. Rather is it the combination of foods that makes for disturbance with most physical bodies, as it would with this.
. . .do not combine also the [alkaline] reacting acid fruits with starches, other than _whole wheat bread!_ that is, citrus fruits, oranges, apples, grapefruit, limes or lemons or even tomato juices. And do not have cereals (which contain the greater quantity of starch than most) at the same meal with the citrus fruits. **416-9**

Orange juice and milk are helpful, but these should be taken at opposite ends of the day; not together.   **274-9**

Another principle to keep in mind concerns our life style and the acid-alkaline balance. It seems that many men and women have taken a renewed interest in exercise and physical activity. However, many people work at sedentary jobs, and participate in little or no additional exercise. What you need to keep in mind is your own life style in order to adjust the balance in your diet accordingly. We find this advice in the readings:

. . .in all bodies, the less activities there are in physical exercise or manual activity, the greater should be the alkaline-reacting foods taken. *Energies* or activities may burn acids, but those who lead the sedentary or the non-active life can't go on sweets or too much starches—but these should be well-balanced.   798-1

We have been examining what the Cayce readings tell us about dietary balance, but what does modern nutritional science have to tell us on this topic?

In a standard textbook for students of nutrition, the acid-base ("base" is equivalent to "alkaline") reaction of foods in the human body is explained in this way:

> The usual mixed diet contains a good balance of acid and basic factors. The basic elements, sodium, potassium, magnesium, and calcium may occur as salts of inorganic acids, such as phosphates, sulfates, or chlorides, or as organic acids. The mineral elements are sometimes referred to as 'ash' because they do not 'burn' up. When foods are metabolized in the body, the mineral elements are released to function in maintaining the acidbase balance; the organic acids are oxidized mostly to carbon dioxide and water. Foods are said to be acid or basic according to whether the acid or the basic elements in the ash predominate. Most fruits contain organic acids combined with basic inorganic compounds. When such compounds are oxidized in the body, they leave an alkaline ash. Some other foods, such as cereals and meats, not at all acid in taste, yield end products that are strongly acid.

Thus, potential acidity or alkalinity of foods refers to the reaction that they will *ultimately* yield after being oxidized in the body.*

If you have ever wondered or tried to explain to someone else why Cayce said citrus fruits—which we all know have citric acid—were an alkaline food, you now have the answer, direct from modern nutritional science. However, that is all the support which the Cayce emphasis on acid-alkaline balance with regard to diet has received thus far. This same source goes on to state: "Conclusive evidence is not as yet available [scientifically] in regard to the practical importance of the acid-base balance of foods in relation to health." *(Nutrition in Health and Disease)*

Another aspect of a balanced diet is implied in the readings but not specifically emphasized. No one food can meet all of a person's nutritional needs, nor can any 10 or 15 foods, to which many people tend to limit themselves. If you choose the same foods over and over again, chances are your body will be lacking in some vitamin(s) or mineral(s). Seek to be creative and explore new vegetables, grains, and legumes. For example: Jerusalem artichokes (recommended in the readings especially for diabetes and obesity), winter squash, salsify, kale or kohlrabi; millet or barley; black beans, garbanzo beans, lentils, azuki beans. Experiment with recipes from other countries and cultures. Be open-minded in your cooking and eating; share recipes and food with friends.

And finally, the point on which the Cayce readings and modern nutritional science agree completely, variety and moderation are the keys to a truly balanced diet in these times of change.

Food Sources

To return to our analogy of the body as a temple: If you were building a temple where you were to spend the rest of your life (which, by the way, you are), it seems reasonable that you would want to know as much as you could about the origin and quality of any building materials which you purchase. What type of wood is this lumber; where was the marble quarried; has any of this been dyed, or is this the natural color? And then you would have to

---

*Mitchell, et al., *Nutrition in Health and Disease* (16th edition), Philadelphia: Lippincott, 1976.

decide: How should I prepare this material for use in building, how sturdy do I want my structure to be, what should I do to give it the most resiliency and the best aesthetic appearance? The questions would go on and on before beginning your project and throughout the work. It seems only logical to do the same with the food that builds our bodies.

The readings time after time alluded to the importance of being aware of the source of the food which we are eating. Many city and suburban children believe that milk comes from a bottle, rather than from a cow. Many adults think this is amusing. Yet, how many of us know the background of even a small percentage of the foods with which we nourish ourselves each day?

Throughout the readings, Cayce recommended eating only those foods which were grown in one's local area.

Have *most* of the foods that are grown in the area where the body lives, as much as practical. 337-27

Use fruits, nuts, berries of all natures or characters that are grown in the environ of the body. . . 1771-3

. . .plenty of both raw and well-cooked vegetables, and those that are grown the more in the environ in which the body finds self. 2066-2

This suggestion was made to keep the body in tune with the natural growing cycles of various foods. In an era when many families move from place to place due to business priorities or personal preference, this particular reading may be of special import in maintaining personal health:

The body can adjust itself. As we have indicated bodies can usually adjust themselves to climatic conditions if they adhere to the diet and activities, or all characters of foods that are produced in the area where they reside. This will more quickly adjust a body to any particular area or climate than any other thing. 4047-1

Another advantage of locally (and especially home-grown) fruits and vegetables is that of vitamin retention. One reading tells us:

[This] depends upon preparation of same, the age, and how long gathered. All of these have their factors in the food values.

As it is so well advertised that coffee loses its value in fifteen to twenty to twenty-five days after being roasted, so do foods or vegetables lose their food value after being gathered—in the same proportion in hours as coffee would in days. 340-31

A home garden was recommended by Cayce, as was eating raw vegetables when possible:

Include in the diet often raw vegetables prepared in various ways, not merely as a salad but scraped or grated and combined with gelatin. . . 3445-1

Have at least one meal each day that includes a quantity of raw vegetables; such as cabbage, lettuce, celery, carrots, onions, and the like. . .
Do **have plenty of vegetables [grown] above the ground; at least three of these to one below the ground. Have at least one leafy vegetable to every one of the pod vegetables taken.**
2602-1

Cayce gave several suggestions for the cooking of food. Frying was to be completely avoided:

Beware of all fried foods. No fried potatoes, fried meats, fried steaks, fried fish, or anything of that nature. 926-1

. . .the preferable way to prepare such [vegetables] would be through cooking the vegetables after tying them in Patapar paper. . .or in a steam steamer, so that only the juices from the vegetables may be obtained—and no water added in the cooking at all. . .
. . .A little later the body may begin with stewed chicken, or broiled chicken or broiled fish. . .Even. . .the chicken or fish would be better cooked in the Patapar paper or a steam cooker.
133-4

The basic recommendations for a general diet as given in the readings consist of what has been mentioned here, along with the eating of only whole grain breads and cereals, a low amount of fatty foods, little sugar or sweetened products, avoidance of red meats (too difficult to digest) in favor of poultry, fish, and occasionally lamb (never pork), and six to eight glasses of water per day.

The above sounds somehow modern, doesn't it? It should. In the 1979 report of the Surgeon General's office entitled "Healthy People" the conclusions reached were that:

Americans would probably be healthier, as a whole, if they consumed:
1. only sufficient calories to meet body needs and maintain desirable weight (fewer calories if overweight)
2. less saturated fat and cholesterol
3. less salt
4. less sugar
5. relatively more complex carbohydrates such as whole grains, cereals, fruits and vegetables
6. relatively more fish, poultry, legumes (for example, beans, peas, peanuts), and less red meat.

Dr. George Briggs, of the University of California at Berkeley, has estimated that improved nutrition might cut the nation's health bill by one-third.

Modern nutritionists agree that fresh, locally grown produce is preferable to the canned or frozen varieties. The prevailing opinion seems to be that in-season fruits and vegetables purchased locally are likely to be more fresh and thus higher in nutritional value than produce which has been in cold storage (such as tomatoes, cucumbers, and zucchini in the winter, or apples in the spring and early summer).

We are also told that vegetables should be cooked in very little water, and as quickly as possible, to preserve the nutrients, although most vegetables that are best for the body are eaten raw.

More and more is found in the nutritional science literature about the necessity of fluids in the body to digest food, to carry nutrients to the cells, to flush out waste products, and to perform other bodily functions. It is recommended that a person drink about 8 glasses of water a day, and use water as an inexpensive substitute for coffee or tea, both of which have a high caffeine content.

At this point, it does seem that the information in the Cayce readings and modern nutritional science have reached many points of agreement. One final point of concurrence is that of the use of vitamin and mineral supplements.

There has been, in recent years, an incredible surge of interest in "natural" or "health" foods. Vitamin supplements, once an item for "faddists," are now made in the shape of cartoon characters and peddled through the mass media. The Cayce readings express a firm preference for obtaining vitamins from natural food:

So, keep an excess of foods that carry especially vitamin B, iron and such. Not the concentrated form, you see, but obtain these from the foods. **1968-7**

There is no supplementary to green foods in the real way or manner. . . **1158-11**

We hear the same thoughts echoed from nutritionists. They tell us, as Cayce did, that in certain cases, occasional use of supplements may be helpful, but should not be routinely depended upon to make up for a less than optimal diet.

Food, fresh and healthful, must be the building material for our temples beautiful in this time of change. On that we all agree.

Handling Stress Through Nutrition

Webster's dictionary tells us that stress is: "A physical, chemical, or emotional factor that causes bodily or mental tension and may be a factor in disease causation." What events can produce stress? There are many types of life changes with which we are all familiar; however, researchers at the University of Washington have compiled a "Stress Rating Scale," which is now quite well known and which does contain events generally not associated with what most people term stress. Among these are: marriage, marital reconciliation, pregnancy, change in a family member's health (for better or worse), change to a different line of work, buying a home, outstanding personal achievement, starting or finishing school, change in residence, change in recreational habits, change in church activities, change in eating habits, and vacation. *Any* change at all may produce stress! However, proper nutrition can ease us through these times, by fortifying our temples to keep us strong and healthy throughout.

The body's specific response to stress varies according to the type of stress placed upon it. The typical response is one of increased adrenal activity. The outpouring of adrenal hormones causes a mobilization of the body forces: Fat stores are broken down, muscle tissue breaks down, the liver's supply of carbohydrates is mobilized, and many vitamins and minerals are called into action. The mechanisms involved are complex, yet the consequence is simple: To provide energy for action, the body's nutrient stores (proteins, carbohydrates, fats, vitamins, minerals and fluids) are depleted. If the stress is short in duration and the body is well nourished, the individual is able to bounce back and rebuild its reserves quickly. If, however, the stress is prolonged or if the body is not well nourished, the body reserves become depleted. A weakened defense leaves the body more and more susceptible to infection, illness and, as Cayce put it, dis-ease.

The nutritional implications of stress are obvious: The body must be well nourished to withstand stress of any kind. The diet must supply ample amounts of protein, complex carbohydrates, virtually all of the B vitamins, and vitamin C, many trace minerals (such as zinc and magnesium), and the proper amount of fluids. Activities which may be part of our normal routine, such as smoking, drinking alcohol or use of birth control pills, are stressful nutritionally and cause a more rapid utilization of certain nutrients.

The safest way, according to modern nutritional science and the Edgar Cayce readings, to insure a strong defense system and optimal nutrient reserves is to provide the body with high quality foods and beverages. Eating whole, minimally processed, fresh foods as mentioned earlier will give the body the best resources possible.

Aside from physical preparation, Cayce mentions mental attitude as being of utmost importance in dealing with the maintenance of health, especially in times of stress. Overeaters Anonymous (an organization founded on the principles of Alcoholics Anonymous) advises what is called the H.A.L.T. principle for eating, that is, eat only when you are *H*ungry, never when you are *A*ngry, *L*onely, or *T*ired—all of which are conditions of stress. The Cayce readings say much the same thing:

True, the body should eat—and should eat slowly; yet when worried, overtaxed, or when the body may not make a *business* of the eating, but eating to pass away the time, or just to fill up time, not good—for it *will not* digest, as the body sees.   900-393

Especially to this body there should not be food taken when the body is overwrought in any manner, whether of high-strung conditions or that of wrath, or of depressions of any nature. . .preferably take water, or buttermilk—*never* sweet milk under such conditions.   **243-7**

To overload the stomach when the body is worried, or under any general strain, is a great *detriment* to the better physical functioning. To make for the taking of foods whether there is felt the need or desire of same is equally as bad for the body.
                                                                          277-1

. . .never, under strain, when very tired, very excited, very mad, should the body take foods in the system. . .   **137-30**

Although there is little in the nutritional science literature dealing with diet and stress, there is some mention in medical literature of how to deal with stress in a constructive physical manner. At times of emotional stress, the body responds as it would if it were in physical danger—energy, triggered by the release of the adrenal hormone available in the form of glucose and free fatty acids, fills the body. For continued physical health, the body must find a way to use this energy *constructively!* One theory states that if this energy is not burned off or utilized, fat deposits on the lining of the arteries may result; this, in turn, is believed to increase the risk of cardiovascular disease. A rational solution to this physical dilemma: when upset, exercise! Take a run or a quick walk around the block, walk up and down the stairs, pull weeds in the garden, clean out a closet (vigorously!), go for a swim, or climb a mountain. As the excess energy is burned off, the muscles also loosen up, the feeling of tenseness associated with stress is diminished, and a feeling of well-being should return. Of course, the ability to get up and get out to exercise will be dependent, to some extent, on the dietary input which your body has been receiving up to that point. Cayce often recommended walking as the best form of exercise for the body to maintain balance.

Present nutritional practice often emphasizes the use of certain vitamins to augment the diet during times of stress. In extreme cases, these will be prescribed in supplement form. Most practitioners, however, encourage their clients to simply increase their intake of foods containing both vitamins B and C. Foods often recommended are:

Sources of B-vitamins	*Sources of vitamin C*
lean meats, poultry, fish, eggs, legumes, peanuts, nuts, whole grains, potatoes, green leafy vegetables, mushrooms, bananas	citrus fruits, strawberries, cantaloupe, tomatoes, sweet peppers, cabbage, potatoes, kale, parsley, turnip greens

Although Cayce did not specifically mention these vitamins for stress, he did say:

B and B₁ supply the ability of the energies, or the moving forces of the nerve and of the white blood supply, as well as the white nerve energy in the nerve force itself, the brain for [force?] itself, and the ability of the sympathetic or involuntary reflexes through the body. Now this includes all [such energy], whether you are wiggling your toes or your ears or batting your eye. . .In these [B vitamins] we have that supplying to the chyle that ability for it to control the influence of fats. . . 2072-9

With this description and what we know about the physiological effects of stress on the body (previously discussed), the use of the B vitamins does indeed seem in accord with the Cayce principles as well. The same reading says of vitamin C:

In C we find that which supplies the necessary influences to the flexes of every nature throughout the body, whether of a muscular or tendon nature, or a heart reaction, or a kidney contraction, or the liver contraction, or the opening or shutting of your mouth, the batting of the eye, or the supplying of the saliva and the muscular forces in face. 2072-9

It does seem that the readings give some basis for the use of this vitamin in the easing of stress.

Maintaining the Temple Beautiful in the New Age

We began this study with an analogy of building a physical temple. In the readings of Edgar Cayce we have available to us not only a superior building code for planning a structure to last us a lifetime, but also the blueprints for building our temples ourselves. No one else can do the work for us. All we need do is treat our physical bodies as if the Lord were coming within that day to visit with us in our dwelling place and then remember to extend the invitation to Him.

The times in which we live are especially challenging for this optimal building process. Often it is not easy to achieve the proper balance in our diet, or to find pure, alive foods. But in these times of extra stress, the additional work we invest in a proper nutritional intake will make us more creative and serviceable builders of a new age.

Bonnie Jenks received her B.A. in English from the University of California at Santa Barbara, and a master's degree in library science, along with elementary and secondary teaching credentials, from the University of California, Berkeley. She is currently an elementary school library media specialist in Concord, California. She has also taught cooking and nutrition in elementary and high schools.

Bonnie has been involved in A.R.E. work in various capacities, including Council secretary, coordinator of the summer Asilomar Conference, and a speaker for the San Francisco Bay Area Team. Her special interests from the Cayce readings are diet and health, marriage and family, and the Bible. Presently she is working on a book dealing with pre-natal and early childhood nutrition.

C

Gardening for Times of Change

An Interview with Craig Siska

Thurston: Craig, I started gardening a couple of years ago and I have to admit that when I started out it had something to do with being afraid of changing times and food shortages. But I have a sense there is a deeper reason for that in home gardening. What are your thoughts about that?

Siska: There are a couple of reasons which quickly come to mind. It's better for your body to ingest food grown locally because you're manifesting under the same environmental conditions that food is. Thoreau made a statement, that if you grow tomatoes in rural Massachusetts and ship them into Boston, they are no longer tomatoes. Or, consider the simple economics of it. For example, 24 million pounds of broccoli were grown and shipped from California to New York in 1979. The state of New York is amply capable of supplying broccoli to all the people in the state. So what the people are paying for in New York is cellophane bags, Styrofoam packaging and trucking. They are paying top dollar in the supermarket for what we may be stretching the term to call "food." Even if a person is not willing to consider metaphysical ideas like vibrations of food, local production of what we eat makes good economic sense.

Thurston: How did our society get so hooked on foods being shipped in from far places?

Siska: The only reason that this kind of thing has become economically feasible is because this present civilization is built on cheap fossil fuel—oil. For many years it added only a relatively small amount to the cost of the food if it was shipped a long distance. But now that the price of fossil fuels has risen so high, I think it's naturally going to shift us back into a more sane way of looking at food. The rising expenses of transportation are going to create an economic climate which forces us to start having a personal relationship once again with the food we eat. When you grow your own food, you have a relationship with that food. When you buy your seed from a reputable seed house, and you take that seed in your hand and grow it, you've become a co-creator.

Thurston: The first problem I had in starting my garden was soil fertility. It didn't seem like my backyard clay had much. I even considered trying a new approach I had read about—hydroponics, growing plants in sand or gravel if fed enough nutrients. What does soil fertility really encompass?

Siska: When soil is available to us, I am not in favor of hydroponics. It's an offshoot of agribusiness and big chemical companies. I've never seen plants in nature growing in this fashion. That tells you the answer right there. When we get into the idea of fertility, there is really no such thing as 5-10-5 plant food. Fertility encompasses the atmosphere, the soil, the water, and the animals (like worms and microorganisms). You're not feeding the plant. That's the biggest myth that has come about in the last 50 years. You don't feed the plant. You create an atmosphere.

Let's say we live in an urban area. We go to the supermarket and we buy a 50-pound bag of cow manure. What are we doing? Are we putting something in the soil to feed the plant? No. We are creating soil! We are creating gases. We are creating humus in the soil. The effect extends even up above the soil, into the air which surrounds that part of the plant growing above the surface. We are fertilizing that whole area. We're allowing forces to work in the soil that otherwise would not have come into play.

Thurston: You are saying that the cow manure we work into the soil releases certain forces to go to work with the plants and creates greater fertility. Are these forces metaphysical forces or are they hard-core and measurable scientifically?

Siska: Both. Science can only go so far. I could study one species of butterfly for the rest of my life but I could never *make* it. I

216

could take it all apart and put it in little pigeonholes; I could tell you all about it, but I can't tell you what a butterfly *is*. And that's where reason and intellect stop and something else begins.

Thurston: I'd like to go back to this question of whether or not we *feed* the plant in the sense of spoon-feeding vitamins into a baby's mouth. I certainly have always operated on that assumption, and I think most people who have read about gardening feel that there is a specific chemistry involved in growing a plant. It involves putting a certain amount of particular chemicals (whether organic or synthetic) into the soil so that the plant can gobble them up just like we gobble up our lunch. And you're saying that that's not the whole picture?

Siska: That's not the whole picture and, in fact, that's not the picture at all.

Thurston: How did the wrong picture come into being? Where did we develop these assumptions which you think are the wrong ones?

Siska: I think it came about 100 or 150 years ago. It started with the development of chemistry. We went down the wrong track when we started to get into mineral medicine. Here's an example. We say the word "sulphur." Wonderful, we know all about it; we can chemically break it down, we can find it under a microscope, we know all about it. But let's take another look at how sulphur is created. Sulphur which accumulates as miniscule dust on the cone of a pine is totally different from sulphur that aggregates in a mustard seed, which is again totally different from sulphur that is mined to make matches. Totally different processes are involved. The word "sulphur" ultimately is not an adequate or especially meaningful one.

Thurston: So, how is the nitrogen in my compost totally different from the nitrogen in fertilizer purchased at the hardware store?

Siska: It's made in the test-tube, or it's extracted from an *in*organic source. Here we must get into the metaphysics of fertility. Below the earth you have the rocks, the inert minerals. That's depth—literally and symbolically it is the darkness. Fertilizers produced primarily from this inorganic source will carry with them the vibrations and essence of that darkness. On the other hand, you might use an organic method to collect your nitrogen. For example, you might grow a cover crop, a green

217

manure, or grow legumes such as peas. The bacteria on the nodules of the roots "fix" the nitrogen in the soil. Those plants take the nitrogen *out of the air*—out of the *light*, literally and symbolically—and put it into the soil as fertility. There are certainly some similarities between the two. But they are coming from two totally different areas and the areas that they come from are under totally different cosmic laws or cosmic conditions.

Thurston: Are we killing the soil, then, to put petroleum-based fertilizers into the soil?

Siska: Exactly. You are destroying the life in the soil. We think we know what we're doing, but do we? This relates to your question about how we "feed" the plant. If you took a plant and turned it upside down and you put the roots in the air and the leaves in the soil, you'd have the right way of looking at the plant, and I'll tell you why. The majority of nutrients can be taken by the plant out of the atmosphere around it. I have already mentioned how legumes pull nitrogen out of the air and put it into the soil. Different plants work different ways.

Let's look at another example: the dahlia, a beautiful plant, an exquisite flower. It has great, luxurious growth on the top, growing to four or five feet high. If you dug the plant up you'd find small roots, a little tuber with little strap roots. Where is that plant *actually living?* It's living in the atmosphere. Ninety-five percent of that plant is living out of the atmosphere and not in the soil. So, if I throw some nitrogen or some 5-10-5 fertilizer into the soil, I'm not doing much of anything.

Here's the essential principle: You don't feed plants, the soil feeds the plant. The plant feeds the soil, the animal feeds the soil, the soil feeds the plant and it all works together.

Thurston: Do weeds sap the soil's fertility? The grass on my lawn seems to do better after I use a dandelion killer.

Siska: The minute we see a dandelion or something else we don't like, we call it a pest and we run to a shop and buy a powder and kill it. What we're doing in our society is destroying what we think is *opposition.* But in reality opposition breeds strength. The plant in the soil can be strengthened by having to deal with the noxious or the opposition. When it can do that, it is a truly strong plant. However, our tendency is to try to remove all oppositions. We think we are making plants stronger by not making them have to work to survive. But it may often work exactly contrary to that.

Thurston: Would you say that it's a human vanity to think we know what nature ought to look like?

Siska: Definitely. But more often we don't know what we are doing. For example, the soil is the skin of the earth. But go to Illinois, which is part of the breadbasket of the country. You will see in the spring that the soil is all plowed up. The soil is open. What is that farmer losing when he leaves the soil open that long? All the gases which are an integral part of the soil's *natural* fertility. He's losing all the soil's capacity to receive and contain the forces of the invisible world. It's gone. So what does he have to do? He has to go into hock thousands of dollars to put something back in. Hundreds of farmers a week in this country are going out of business. Millions of tons of top soil are being lost every year.

Thurston: When I put the cow manure and nitrogen on the soil, instead of putting a 10-10-10 petroleum-based chemical fertilizer, what is that cow manure *doing? How* is it creating an environment in which my broccoli plants are going to grow? You used the words "creating an environment." Could you tell me a little bit about how to create that environment?

Siska: I can try. If anybody comes to you and tells you they know *everything* about gardening, show them the door. Let's look at how the cow manure was made. Ideally, you should have growing in your field herbs and grasses that the cow would go to naturally. When a cow is birthing, the natural instinct of a cow right after the birth is to get rid of the afterbirth by going to mentha palugium, pennyroyal, and eating that to cleanse out the system. So what is the cow doing? She's not "thinking," in the sense we usually mean it. She thinks with the diaphragm. So she's *led* to different grasses. And she's also led away from grasses she knows are not good for her. She will not eat grass that grows lusciously in her own manure but will eat what grows from under the manure that the horse left or the rabbit left, and they're all different qualities. So she's ingesting these grasses and, remember, the cow has an intricate digestion system. She deposits her compost and grass grows on that.

But now man enters the scene and says, oh, fertility, look at that grass growing. So we take that to a different part of our farm or garden, a small plot, and we put that in with our natural soil. And let's say that we're starting out with horrible soil: clay and rock. We take our kitchen scraps out of the kitchen, our orange peels, coffee grounds, and we put those together. In four to six months in the compost pile, what do we have mixing with the manure? We have death. And all composting is very simply "death into life into death into life" or "acid into sweet into acid into sweet," and it keeps going. It's an infinite motion, but it's always in motion. So when we put that cow manure in the bed, it's creating a living soil. The forests do it all the time. Nature has to empty and totally renew itself. The phoenix is a great example: the ancient occultist coming out of the fire into new life. That's what a compost pile is. The earthworms and the compost pile are the greatest alchemists on the face of the earth and they probably always will be. They change it. The *life* that cow manure or compost gives to the soil, that life which is beyond all the chemical analysis you want to do is *retrievable* by the plant. This is not what is going on when you dump some chemicals on it, when you use a chemically produced fertilizer from the hardware store.

Thurston: Life isn't just chemical?

Siska: Right. I might say, "Oh, my grass is green and all the weeds are gone. Wonderful!" But, no. I've hooked my plants on heroin, that's what I've done. In the *short term* it looks wonderful, but it won't work. The vitality is not in that plant.

Thurston: So the grass that looks very green is actually going through a slow death process. Is it because it's lost the necessity and the ability to discriminate?

Siska: Yes, exactly. Plants have to discriminate, to be able to deal strongly with opposition.

Thurston: I'd be curious about your dream or your vision of the ideal approach of our culture to food production that can conceivably happen 10 years from now. If you were directing the course of history, particularly on the issue of humankind's relationship to food, what would your ideal society be like?

Siska: If I were running it, I think you would find a lot less dependency on high technology. You would see things going back to very simplistic techniques. But highly *sophisticated* craft. There would be a rediscovery of the true meaning of a spade and a fork and a pair of pruning shears and a watering can. It would be a rebirth. I think it's going to happen. And even if it doesn't, it is what *I'm* going to do.

Thurston: Are we going to have everybody gardening? Or is that realistic?

Siska: No, I don't think so. But I think a higher percentage of people have to be engaged in that than are now. We have 95% of our people living in cities and another 5% supporting them with food. What you're going to see is probably what Schumacher described in his book *Small Is Beautiful.* I agree with him that we are going to see many people farming on a smaller scale.

Thurston: What's your response to the idea of having a higher-technology approach to food production? For example, perhaps through recombinant DNA we could produce plants that are 10 times as productive as they are now? Or with better technology we could harvest under the oceans. Do you feel that that's just extended thinking based on bankrupt assumptions?

Siska: Partly, yes. The green revolution which you are familiar with failed for a key reason. It was dependent on fossil fuel or petroleum products for both machines and fertilizer needed to grow these highly manipulated seeds called hybrids. The word *hubris* (in Greek *hybris*) means the defiance of the will of heaven. That's where we get the word hybrid. Now if we're going to project this hy-tech into the future and say that's going to solve the problem of feeding the millions of the world, *how* are we going to do it? We have a big problem with these hybrid seeds which high technology has already given us. The seeds are so highly developed in a laboratory situation or a greenhouse situation that they are dependent on chemicals (fertilizers and pesticides). To make a pointed analogy to a human infant, they're on respirators. Then when you throw them out into the natural environment, they're vulnerable. They have lost their genetic base and the strength it provided.

Thurston: Can we feed 6½ billion people in the year 2000 using the approach Alan Chadwick was talking about?

Siska: Yes, probably twice that many, because we can get four times the yield off roughly one quarter of the land. But that is really *not* the issue at all—quantity. It is *quality!* A fourth of a loaf of bread grown by what you would term "biodynamic" techniques would do much more for the being of a person than three or four loaves of white bread jammed with additives and blocking his insides up. See? Quality is the point.

This depends, of course, on the type of crop you're growing. It also supposes a willingness on the part of people to get more involved in the production of what they eat. It will mean labor intensive methods, rather than energy intensive ones. But is that really a step backwards for "progress"? One way of understanding progress is as "greater efficiency." The human being is the most "efficient machine" on earth.

Thurston: It's a major change in life style. We're not used to going in the direction of labor intensive economy. We want to have it easy.

Siska: But is life easy now? Take a look at it. Look what modern life—with all its energy intensive conveniences—has done for human health and well-being! I'm not suggesting that we go back into the 12th century. We know a lot more. I'm not criticizing science either. We've learned many important things about our physical environment and about ourselves. But now it's time to marry these insights with *simple,* common sense techniques. We need holistic designs *appropriate* to each unique circumstance on the earth.

Craig Siska is a professional horticulturist and former apprentice to the world-renowned developer of the French intensive/biodynamic method, Alan Chadwick. Craig spent two years studying and working with Mr. Chadwick in northern Virginia. He earned his bachelor's degree in geography and environmental planning from Roosevelt University in Chicago.

Craig's professional interests and experience include biodynamic gardening, tree crop agriculture, herb culture and natural medicines, astrological relationships in the plant kingdom, alternative energy and community planning. He is an accomplished lecturer, workshop leader and consultant. He can be contacted c/o Mark Thurston's office at A.R.E. in Virginia Beach, Va.

Index

Readings Directory

THE WORK OF EDGAR CAYCE TODAY

The Association for Research and Enlightenment, Inc. (A.R.E.®), is a membership organization founded by Edgar Cayce in 1931.

- 14,256 Cayce readings, the largest body of documented psychic information anywhere in the world, are housed in the A.R.E. Library/Conference Center in Virginia Beach, Virginia. These readings have been indexed under 10,000 different topics and are open to the public.

- An attractive package of membership benefits is available for modest yearly dues. Benefits include: a journal and newsletter; lessons for home study; a lending library through the mail, which offers collections of the actual readings as well as one of the world's best parapsychological book collections, names of doctors or health care professionals in your area.

- As an organization on the leading edge in exciting new fields, A.R.E. presents a selection of publications and seminars by prominent authorities in the fields covered, exploring such areas as parapsychology, dreams, meditation, world religions, holistic health, reincarnation and life after death, and personal growth.

- The unique path to personal growth outlined in the Cayce readings is developed through a worldwide program of study groups. These informal groups meet weekly in private homes.

- A.R.E. maintains a visitors' center where a bookstore, exhibits, classes, a movie, and audiovisual presentations introduce inquirers to concepts from the Cayce readings.

- A.R.E. conducts research into the helpfulness of both the medical and nonmedical readings, often giving members the opportunity to participate in the studies.

For more information and a color brochure, write or phone:

A.R.E., Dept. C., P.O. Box 595
Virginia Beach, VA 23451, (804) 428-3588